D1472322

BOARDS AT WORK

BOARDS AT WORK

How Corporate Boards Create Competitive Advantage

Ram Charan

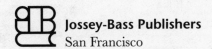

Jossey-Bass Publishers
San Francisco

Copyright © 1998 by Jossey-Bass Inc., Publishers, 350 Sansome Street, San Francisco, California 94104.

All rights reserved. No part of this publication may be reproduced, stored in a retrieval system, or transmitted, in any form or by any means, electronic, mechanical, photocopying, recording, or otherwise, without the prior written permission of the publisher.

Substantial discounts on bulk quantities of Jossey-Bass books are available to corporations, professional associations, and other organizations. For details and discount information, contact the special sales department at Jossey-Bass Inc., Publishers (415) 433-1740; Fax (800) 605-2665.

For sales outside the United States, please contact your local Simon & Schuster International Office.

www.josseybass.com

Manufactured in the United States of America on Lyons Falls Turin Book. This paper is acid-free and 100 percent totally chlorine-free.

Library of Congress Cataloging-in-Publication Data

Charan, Ram.
  Boards at work: how corporate boards create competitive advantage /
  Ram Charan. — 1st ed.
      p. cm. — (The Jossey-Bass business & management series)
    Includes index.
    ISBN 0–7879–1060–0 (acid-free paper)
    1. Competition. 2. Directors of corporations. I. Title.
  II. Series.
  HD41.C47 1998
  658.4'22—dc21   97-45422

FIRST EDITION
HB Printing   10 9 8 7 6 5 4 3 2 1

THE JOSSEY-BASS
BUSINESS & MANAGEMENT SERIES

Dedicated to the hearts and souls of the joint family
of twelve siblings and cousins living under one roof for fifty years,
whose personal sacrifices made my formal education possible.

CONTENTS

PART THREE: BEGINNING AND CONTINUING CHANGE 211

WHAT YOU SHOULD KNOW ABOUT CORPORATE BOARDS

The corporate board is no longer just a legal formality. It is a competitive necessity. Today's chief executives face a bewildering mosaic of fast change, uncertainty, and stiff competition in a world of unprecedented opportunity for growth. Many are wrestling with fundamental and profound questions about how to reposition their businesses. The best and brightest do not always have the answers. But no wonder. Industries consolidate, converge, and diverge at mach speed (witness telecommunications, health care, entertainment), and powerhouses arise from the dust (think Microsoft). The most basic assumptions can become obsolete overnight.

All this where the margin for error is razor thin. Even a short series of bad decisions or a missed opportunity can decimate the stock price and threaten the survival of the company. Bausch & Lomb suffered a $1 billion loss in market value and a permanent decline in its core contact lens business under CEO Daniel E. Gill when the company missed Johnson & Johnson's drive into disposable lenses. Apple Computer, under three CEOs in five years, failed to regain its footing in the software-driven computer industry. In June 1997, many observers wondered whether Apple would survive.

Enter the corporate board. Some boards are going beyond the role of watchdog to provide the counsel and coaching every CEO needs. These boards *influence* decisions. Management *makes* decisions—with the benefit of the directors' independent perspectives, insights, and judgment. What better way for a board to serve shareholders than to save the CEO and top management from serious oversights and faulty assumptions or to help them spot promising new opportunities?

Consider the board's contribution in the following situations:

The NYNEX board encouraged CEO Ivan Seidenberg to "think big." Seidenberg ultimately forged an ambitious merger with Bell Atlantic, which positioned the new company as a leading player in the fast-changing telecommunications industry.

Citicorp Director Roger Smith told Chairman-CEO John S. Reed that he believed the bank was accepting lower level audits than it should. Reed hastened to improve the audit function, which now operates to a much higher standard. Reed says, "We probably wouldn't have seen it from the inside. Smith raised the bar."

As the board of TRW was about to approve a major new venture that would require a substantial investment over time, one director said, "I want to be sure that somebody is prepared to turn this off if it's not wise to proceed." That comment sent a clear signal about accountability for results.

In 1995, the KeraVision board urged CEO Tom Loarie to take the California-based development stage company public. Loarie did not think the company was ready, but the board believed market conditions were right. Loarie says, "We did it, and I've never looked back. It was the right decision."

Earlier this decade, the boards of GM, Westinghouse, IBM, and Digital Equipment Corporation, under extreme societal pressure, set a new standard for corporate governance by revolting against long-time CEOs who had failed to perform. Other tradition-bound corporate boards felt a surge of power and took similar actions against their own nonperforming CEOs. Now a new standard for corporate governance is emerging. The issue is not just nonperformance but underperformance. How can companies unlock the intellectual power of the board to help a good CEO perform better?

The boards in this book have found the key. They have broken the norms and protocols that have kept directors passive and distant for too long. They leverage directors' *collective* knowledge and judgment through open, candid discussions. Although they do not create strategy, they clearly understand it. They have discussed it, have contributed to it, and are aware of its inherent risks. In subtle but distinct ways, they influence the most important decisions the CEO has to make—without infringing on the CEO's right to make them.

In short, these boards work. In the process, directors and managers broaden each other's perspectives, benefit from each other's judgments, and learn together. What emerges quite naturally from such situations is the best business thinking available anywhere. This is the incredible resource available to CEOs and directors. This is the untapped potential to strengthen our corporations. This is the competitive power of the board.

Although only a small handful of companies have tapped the board's intellectual power, the trend is likely to grow. Pressure from the capital markets is real. Some security analysts and institutional investors are already considering the strength of the board as a factor that drives company performance. The environment for competitive performance in the capital markets will only increase the demands on corporations. At the same time, away from the public eye, some CEOs are coming to see the value of a strong, effective board, and directors are discovering the benefits of shared learning through active participation in the company's value-creating processes. The movement has begun.

This Book Is for You

This book speaks directly to those who have the potential to change how the board works. It is written for *directors* who feel frustrated and powerless on the board even though they are confident and successful elsewhere. No one talks about the real issues even when the company is going in the wrong direction or missing opportunities. How can a director break the ice without triggering a coup? It is also written for directors who take pride in their board work and want to make their board the best in the country. What are others doing that they are not?

It is written for *chairmen, CEOs, and presidents* who are doing well but want to get more from the board. How can they get directors more involved? It is also for CEOs who wonder how much support they really have from the board. How can they find out what directors really think? It is for CEOs who are wrestling with their own discomfort with the trend toward more active boards. Does openness mean loss of control?

It is written for members of the *top management team* who interact with the board and for *business unit managers,* all of whom may aspire to be CEOs and directors. The senior managers may attend board meetings sitting quietly in the back of the room. Some may occasionally make presentations to the board. Are they giving directors what they want? How can they derive value from the board's experience and expertise? What will they do when they are on a board? Business unit managers who aspire further must now broaden their perspective and accelerate their personal growth. How do board members engage in dialogue and share knowledge?

It is written for *students of management,* in the United States and elsewhere, whether or not they are in formal academic programs. How do our corporations really work? How are they changing? What can other nations, including the United Kingdom and even Japan, where giants like Sony have recently moved toward more Western-style boards, learn from the United States? And what can nonprofits learn from the corporate world?

This book is also written for other audiences who will participate in or be affected by change at the board level, including:

- *Shareholders and others who have been frustrated or fascinated by the goings on at the very top of the organization.* Do directors really earn their fees? Is anyone looking out for individual shareholders?
- *Institutional investors, fund managers, and security analysts* who must assess whether the CEO is alert to opportunities and whether the board will

have any influence on the CEO. When the stock price is not performing well and the board supports the CEO, is the board rationalizing or weathering a rough transition?

- *Corporate secretaries,* who recognize the need for boards to change but do not know what specific practices to recommend.
- *Legal counsel,* who must understand the changing nature of director responsibility and liability.

This Book Is Grounded in Reality

This book reflects current practices, but it is based on many years of first-hand observation of corporate boards. My first exposure to corporate boards was in Australia in the early 1960s, where, as a young assistant engineer, I was allowed to observe board meetings of a four thousand–person company. Soon after, I continued my study of corporate boards in the doctoral program at Harvard Business School. In later years, as my executive teaching and consulting career evolved and I myself joined the boards of Fisher & Porter and Austin Industries, among others, I developed close relationships with many CEOs and directors of large corporations. I became a kind of personal coach to senior executives at NYNEX, Citicorp, Du Pont, CSX, Royal Bank of Canada, Conrail, GE, and many other well-known corporations, many of whom also served on numerous boards. They in turn brought me in contact with their peers.

Those relationships allowed me to observe a puzzling phenomenon: Most directors were brilliant, confident individuals, yet when they served as outside directors, they did not act on their business judgment. They seemed to believe that if they expressed an unpopular opinion or asked an impertinent question, they could get a reputation for being a troublemaker.

Then about five years ago, as the boards of GM, Digital Equipment Corporation, American Express, and Westinghouse were making news, I began to see some exciting changes on some of the boards I knew well. These boards were not making headlines, but they were making a difference. They were breaking the taboos—opening up the information flows, exchanging ideas candidly, and discussing the issues that were key to the business. Directors were intellectually engaged.

I then began to seek out other boards that were working well, and along the way, had some extraordinary opportunities to observe and participate in the deliberations of more than two dozen boards that were trying to transform their practices. I had the chance to counsel many directors, boards, and chairmen on a number of tough decisions, including decisions to remove a CEO and to select CEOs and board members. On numerous occasions, I was the only outsider to attend a board meeting or sit in on an executive session during which highly sensitive board matters were discussed.

I have counseled directors who were concerned about the CEO's performance and even more concerned that other directors seemed to look the other way. I have helped boards design processes for reviewing themselves and the CEO. I have helped CEOs create a more open exchange of information—and deal with the consequences. I have facilitated board retreats at many companies, including Bank of America, Conrail, Canadian Pacific, NYNEX, AMP, Royal Bank of Canada, Avenor (the Canadian forest products company), KeraVision (a Silicon Valley medical technology company), Orion Capital, and MMI.

I have seen the positive results: board meetings where directors expected a dull recitation and suddenly found themselves engaged in an exciting exchange of ideas, board members who suddenly changed the fate of a company by putting an important issue on the table, senior managers who listened to the board and suddenly saw things from a new perspective.

This Book Goes into the Inner Sanctum

This book is a compilation and deep description of the very best board practices I have seen. It is based on firsthand observation of, extensive interviews with, and consulting to more than a hundred CEOs, directors, and senior executives at U.S. companies, including Dun & Bradstreet, NYNEX, Warner-Lambert, and Citicorp, and a few Canadian ones, including the Royal Bank of Canada and Avenor. The companies are in a wide range of industries, from telecommunications to natural resources and banking. They vary in size from a Silicon Valley Phase II start-up with no revenues (KeraVision) to a $170 billion giant. Some of the boards are very large—as many as twenty-two directors—and others are much smaller. None of these boards does everything right, but each is exemplary in some way.

These boards have given me unprecedented access to their inner workings, which has allowed me to gather the data unfiltered and in real time. I did not piece together events from secondhand accounts after the fact. Rather, I observed the events as they unfolded. Most of these boards are sharing their experiences for the first time. All have allowed me to describe their practices, problems, and discoveries and have approved the release of the examples and cases in this book. Their trust has been essential to the research and writing of this book.

Part One explores the board's potential impact on business success. Chapter One demonstrates the specific ways a board can contribute and the importance of moving beyond one-to-one relationships between individual directors and the CEO. The power of the board lies in its *collective wisdom,* which is released only when the board functions as a *collective body.* Chapter Two explores the common foundation among boards that function well. A description of the board of the former Dun & Bradstreet gives readers a clear sense of what good board dynamics look like.

Part Two (Chapters Three through Eight) describe specific practices, or operating mechanisms, that have proven to have a positive effect on board dynamics. Each chapter is followed by a detailed case of a real company. All cases have been cross-checked for accuracy. Some have been disguised because of the sensitivity of the subject matter.

Chapter Three tells how to keep board structure from interfering with board dynamics. It deals with controversial issues like appointing a lead director or separating the roles of CEO and chairman and explores how an executive committee affects the board's power structure. It tells which issues should go to committee and which to the full board and shows the power of using board retreats to make breakthroughs in strategy and board dynamics. Finally, it describes how one board changed its board dynamics by redesigning its committees.

Chapter Four tells how to find new directors who have the time, motivation, and experience to contribute and how to get them informed and involved quickly. The case of KeraVision, the Silicon Valley medical technology company, shows how to tailor the nominating criteria and process to the company's needs at a specific point in time.

Chapter Five sorts through the board's information needs and prescribes ways to ensure the right kind of learning. In it, one company shares its guidelines for making presentations disciplined and focused. Other chairmen and directors describe mechanisms they use to create depth of understanding, context, and continuity. This chapter includes a detailed case of how NYNEX built a total picture of the company's strategy.

Chapter Six explores the relationship between the board and shareholders. It tells when to listen to investors and when not to. And it describes how and why Warner-Lambert treats shareholders like customers.

Chapter Seven presents processes and instruments boards are using to ensure that the company has the right CEO all the time. It shows how to play the role of coach without compromising rigorous oversight and how to capitalize on directors' instincts in evaluating the CEO's total leadership. It details a feedback process that addresses whether a CEO who has been successful in the past is really prepared to take the company forward.

Chapter Eight describes how boards can make succession planning a routine part of their work. It tells how to ensure that the organization is developing future leaders and explores how and when to choose the next CEO. It also makes the case for ensuring that the outgoing CEO's exit is complete. It explains GE's world-renowned leadership development system and tells how another company put its slow-moving succession planning process in high gear.

Part Three focuses on how CEOs and directors can create and sustain change. Chapter Nine addresses the psychological barriers that preserve the status quo and tells how to get the change process rolling. One CEO and one outside director tell how they initiated change on their boards—the CEO, because he had to, the director, because he thought he should.

Chapter Ten looks at how a board can institutionalize its efforts to improve by applying the principles of continuous improvement. It includes board self-improvement and peer review instruments and sensible options for designing a review process that builds trust. It explains when peer review can make a board world class—and when it can backfire and cause board dynamics to regress.

The concluding chapter, "This Is the Day to Put Your Board to Work," pulls the ideas together into an argument and plan for action.

This Book Has a Unique Perspective

This book takes the position that in this day and age of frequent radical change and rich opportunities, the board can and should be used for competitive advantage. Boards must get to work. Anything less should be considered a failure of the CEO and of each and every board member.

Boards add value through open, trusting dialogue—among directors and between directors and the management team (including the CEO, of course). The content of that dialogue must be significant to the success of the business. When the dialogue is focused on issues of strategy, organizational capability, and performance against objectives, when the best minds are allowed to absorb information, ask questions, and probe the assumptions, when every person in the room speaks with candor and listens with respect, the excitement builds and the energy flows. The intellectual output is superb.

Efforts to put the board to work must be guided by the realities of how directors interact with each other, the so-called board dynamics.

Whether to appoint a lead director, whether to have an executive committee, whether to have six meetings a year or twelve—all will affect the board dynamics, and therefore the quality of the dialogue, for better or worse. Will the flow of information encourage or squelch critical thinking? Will the committee appointments create balance or power plays? Will the schedules, agendas, and seating arrangements enhance or impede the board's ability to make collective judgments and take collective action?

This perspective differs from that of most writings about and recommendations for board transformation. Even GM's Guidelines for Corporate Governance, which the Council of Institutional Investors and Calpers (the activist California Public Employees' Retirement System) have held up as a model, focus on structural fixes, like appointing a lead director or outside director as chairman. Too often, these well-intended recommendations do not effect change below the surface. While structural changes can influence how the board works, they should not be the board's driving force. Real change comes from choosing practices that help the board do what it really must: focus on the right issues, ask the tough questions, probe the assumptions, broaden the perspective, and learn together—and in the process, give the company a competitive edge.

It is time for CEOs and directors to take the lead. As they do, CEOs will find a great ally in leading their organizations, directors will find intellectual challenge, excitement, and personal growth, and we will all see renewed energy and competitive strength among our corporations.

HELPERS ON THE JOURNEY

I am deeply grateful to the many people who have helped me in my lifelong goal of writing a book about corporate boards. The journey began in October 1959 in Sydney, Australia, and continues in February 1998 even as the book goes to press.

This book reflects the wisdom of many business leaders who shared their insight and experience through personal conversations and interviews. I am deeply indebted to each of them for their time and trust. At a time when corporate boards continue to come under fire for lackluster performance, it is truly a privilege to have been permitted to have the trust of so many CEOs and directors who are doing an outstanding job. I wish to extend my deepest thanks to the following business leaders:

William W. Adams, retired chairman and president, Armstrong World Industries

B. Charles Ames of Clayton Dubilier & Rice

B. Frederick Becker, chairman and CEO, MMI Companies, Inc.

W. Marston Becker, chairman and CEO, Orion Capital Corporation

J. G. Breen, chairman and CEO, Sherwin Williams Company

James L. Broadhead, chairman and CEO, FPL Group

Richard H. Brown, CEO, Cable & Wireless, plc

Daniel T. Carroll, professional director

Philip J. Carroll, president and CEO, Shell Oil Company

John C. Cleghorn, chairman and CEO, Royal Bank of Canada

William J. Conaty, senior vice president, human resources, General Electric Company

David A. Coulter, chairman, president, and CEO, BankAmerica Corporation

Martin A. Coyle, retired executive vice president, general counsel & secretary, TRW

Charles Crocker, chairman, president and CEO, BEI Electronics

George A. Davidson, Jr., chairman and CEO, Consolidated Natural Gas Company

Lodewijk J. R. de Vink, president and COO, Warner-Lambert

Samuel L. Eichenfield, chairman and CEO, The FINOVA Group

William C. Ferguson, retired chairman and CEO, NYNEX

Robert E. Gallagher, chairman, Arthur J. Gallagher and Company

Melvin R. Goodes, chairman and CEO, Warner-Lambert

Joseph T. Gorman, chairman and CEO, TRW

Gerald Grinstein, retired chairman and CEO, Burlington Northern

James A. Hagen, retired chairman and CEO, Consolidated Rail Corporation

Michael W. Hall of Venture Law Group

Robert C. Hanna, retired president and CEO, Imperial Holly Corporation

Robert P. Hauptfuhrer, retired chairman and CEO, Oryx Energy Corporation

Charles O. Holliday, Jr., CEO designate, Du Pont

Milton T. Honea, retired chairman, CEO, and president, NorAm Energy

Edgar G. Hotard, president, Praxair

William J. Hudson, CEO, AMP, Inc.

Lois D. Juliber, executive vice president, chief of operations developed markets, Colgate-Palmolive

Emmanuel A. Kampouris, chairman, president, and CEO, American Standard

Howard V. Knicely, executive vice president, human resources and communications, TRW

John A. Krol, chairman and CEO, Du Pont

Jane E. Lawson, senior vice president and secretary, Royal Bank of Canada

David M. LeVan, president and CEO, Consolidated Rail Corporation

H. William Lichtenberger, chairman and CEO, Praxair

Thomas M. Loarie, chairman, CEO, and president, KeraVision

Charles E. Long, executive vice president and corporate secretary, Citicorp

Alex J. Mandl, chairman and CEO, Teligent

James E. Marley, chairman, AMP, Inc.

Chris R. Matthews, chairman and CEO, the Hay Group

Gail J. McGovern, executive vice president consumer markets division, AT&T

John F. McGovern, executive vice president finance and CFO, Georgia Pacific

R. Clayton McWhorter, retired chairman, Health Trust

Jerome J. Meyer, chairman and CEO, Tektronix, Inc.

Rolf A. Meyer, chairman, Ciba Specialty Company

William L. Mobraaten, retired CEO, Bell of Pennsylvania

Douglas E. Olesen, president and CEO, Battelle Memorial Institute

James E. Perella, chairman, president, and CEO, Ingersoll-Rand

John S. Reed, chairman and CEO, Citicorp

Richard M. Rosenberg, retired chairman, BankAmerica Corporation

Alan Rosskamm, president, Fabri-Centers of America

Frederic V. Salerno, senior executive vice president and chief financial officer, Bell Atlantic Corporation

Ivan G. Seidenberg, vice chairman, president, and chief operating officer, Bell Atlantic Corporation

John W. Snow, chairman and CEO, CSX Corporation

William T. Solomon, chairman, president, and CEO, Austin Industries

John M. Trani, chairman and CEO, Stanley Works

Marshall C. Turner of Turner Venture Associates

James C. Walz, vice president, quality, Royal Bank of Canada

Morrison DeS. Webb, director and executive vice president external affairs and corporate communications, Bell Atlantic Corporation

Robert E. Weissman, chairman and CEO, Cognizant

Bruce B. Wilson, retired senior vice president law, Consolidated Rail Corporation

Edgar S. Woolard, Jr., retired chairman and CEO, Du Pont

I am also grateful to the more than three hundred directors not named here who allowed me to observe them at work and from whom I learned so much. I have deep admiration for their intellect, dedication, and special talent of asking the right questions.

I owe much gratitude to Bruce A. McCandless, former CEO of Honolulu Gas Company, who gave me my first job in America and took me under his wing. He helped spark my interest in corporate boards by allowing me, at the young age of twenty-four, to sit in on board meetings and observe board deliberations first hand.

I also wish to thank John F. Welch, Jr., chairman and CEO of GE, for all that I have learned from him and for setting this book in motion. When General Motors first issued its governance guidelines, I wrote a paper arguing against separating the roles of CEO and chairman and sent it unsolicited to Jack, whom I had known for many years. Jack immediately sent the paper to his board. From that, it was clear to me that governance issues were top-of-mind for CEOs and directors, and I put my research and writing into high gear.

Professor Noel M. Tichy, a long-time colleague with whom I worked at Ford, Shell, Bankers Trust, and other companies, had for years encouraged me to put my ideas in writing. I appreciate his persistence. Patti Tichy was equally encouraging. Geoffrey Colvin of Fortune magazine gave me both encouragement and useful feedback on the book in its early stages.

Professors Hugo E. R. Uyterhoeven, Kenneth R. Andrews, C. Roland Christensen, and Thomas R. Piper of Harvard Business School and Professor E. Kirby Warren of Columbia University have taught me a great deal about business, corporate governance, and the fine art of case teaching. I am fortunate to have learned from the best. Some of these teachers, along with Michael Brimm of INSEAD, Joseph B. Fuller of Monitor and Company, John D. Borgia of Seagram's, Hellene Runtagh of Universal Studios, and Leonard I. Hill, Jr., and Gary D. D'Lamatar, both of AMP, took the time to read and comment on a draft of this book.

Susim M. Datta of Peerless General Financial and Investment in Mumbai, India, Ashok S. Ganguly of Unilever House Blackfriars, London, and Vinay Bharat-Ram of DCM Limited in New Delhi, India, shared with me their thoughts on corporate governance over the years.

John Joyce, my good friend and business partner, read many versions and played many roles in developing this book. He has been a great resource throughout the project. Through John, I met Phil Lawler, who gave valuable editorial input, as did Catherine Flynn, Robert Buday, and Charles Burck, all independent writers and editors.

Carol Davis and Becky Thayer did a masterful job orchestrating meetings and interviews and handling the many details such a project inevitably entails. Karen Baron produced consistently accurate transcripts on short notice.

Cedric Crocker, my editor at Jossey-Bass, made suggestions that were right on the mark. Cedric, Cheryl Greenway, Nathalie Mainland Smith, Judith Hibbard, and others at Jossey-Bass made extraordinary efforts to get the final draft quickly into the hands of readers. They were a pleasure to work with.

My special appreciation to Geraldine Willigan, who worked closely with me over several years to gather the data, organize the ideas, and capture them in writing. Geri learned the ins and outs of the topic, became passionate about it, and worked tenaciously to present the information and insights crisply and clearly. I am grateful to her and to her family, Jim and Robbie LiaBraaten, who supported her involvement.

My hope is that the combined efforts of the people mentioned here will lay the foundation for further reality-based research and spur positive change to improve the practice of business.

Dallas, Texas   Ram Charan
January 1998

ABOUT RAM CHARAN

Ram Charan, a Dallas-based independent advisor to CEOs and directors of numerous companies around the world, is well known for his keen insights into hard-nosed business problems. He focuses on corporate governance, global strategy design and implementation, selection of CEOs and directors, succession planning, and issues involving corporate transformation. His clients include GE, Du Pont, Bell Atlantic, Citicorp, Ford, TRW, Warner-Lambert, Unilever, Ciba Specialty, Royal Bank of Canada, CSX, and AMP. His relationships with these companies are long-standing. He has consulted to some for as long as twenty-five years.

Mr. Charan has worked behind the scenes to help many boards redesign their governance processes. He has facilitated board retreats for such companies as Bank of America, Conrail, Canadian Pacific, NYNEX, AMP, Avenor, Royal Bank of Canada, and KeraVision. He is a director of Austin Industries.

Mr. Charan is also a long-time contributor to several university and in-house executive programs. He is a recipient of GE's prestigious Bell-ringer Award and of a best teacher award at Northwestern University's

Kellogg Graduate School of Management. He was named by *Business Week* as the second-best teacher in in-house executive programs nationwide. He has appeared at several Fortune CEO Forums, is a highly recognized Y.P.O. resource, and has been on the faculty of the Harvard Business School and Northwestern University Graduate School of Management.

Mr. Charan's articles have appeared in publications including the *Harvard Business Review, Fortune, Directorship,* and *The Corporate Board.* He has DBA and MBA degrees (MBA with high distinction) from Harvard Business School, where he was a Baker Scholar.

PART ONE

THE BOARD'S
UNTAPPED POTENTIAL

CHAPTER ONE

THE BOARD AS COMPETITIVE WEAPON

Welcome to the era of the high-performing board. At a small but growing number of companies, the corporate board, once a sleeping giant, is waking up and flexing its intellectual muscle. At these companies, the CEO is discovering new ways to tap the board's vast storehouse of experience and business wisdom, and the directors are finding new ways to contribute to the success of the corporation. The board not only protects shareholder value but actually helps create it.

Everyone knows about boards that don't work. At GM, IBM, West-inghouse, Kmart, Digital Equipment Corporation, and other corporate giants, the board seemed to stand idle as billions of dollars in market value went down the drain. The public failure of those boards triggered widespread cynicism about whether corporate boards would ever be more than rubber stamps.

But some boards do work. They listen, probe, debate, and become engaged in the company's most pressing issues. Directors share their expertise and wisdom as a matter of course. As they do, management and the board learn together, a collective wisdom emerges, and managerial judgment improves. The on-site coaching and counseling expand the mental capacity of the CEO and the top management team and give the company a competitive edge out there in the marketplace.

Boards that work demonstrate a compelling reality: Boards can be a competitive advantage to the corporation. In today's complex environment in which shareholders will tolerate nothing short of optimal performance, this reality cannot be ignored. Investors are already recognizing the connection between board effectiveness and market value.

Boards *can* work. Chairmen, CEOs, directors, shareholders—anyone who has a stake in the success of the company—must see to it that they do.

The Quest for Good Governance

Empowered shareholders, conscientious directors, and enlightened CEOs are putting corporate governance on the agenda, each for their own reasons. Institutional investors, still reeling from the frustration they felt in the 1980s and early 1990s when boards stood idle as market values languished, have forced the issue. To the U.S. economy, businesses floundering under poor leadership represented a national competitiveness problem. To investors, they represented undervalued and depreciating assets—whether a brand name, a division, or an entire company—over which they seemed to have little control.

After years of pension fund growth and helped by various shareholder organizations and changes in SEC regulations, shareholders found their voice. In the early 1990s, they began to speak out regularly at annual meetings, in letters, through proxies, in the courtroom, and to the press. CEOs never knew when their annual meeting, once a quiet, docile event, would erupt into confrontation and debate of the core economic issues of the business.

Calpers (California Public Employees' Retirement System), the activist pension fund, has led the charge, targeting underperforming companies in its portfolio and recommending adoption of board practices aimed to make boards more effective. Calpers has, for instance, been a leading advocate of appointing a "lead director" or outside director as board chairman. Although their specific recommendations may miss the mark (as demonstrated in Chapter Three, a lead director or outside chairman actually does more harm than good), Calpers and other activists have focused national attention on the obligations and roles of corporate boards.

Some directors, particularly newer, younger ones, are putting better governance on their board's agenda. Many are a new breed recruited for their business expertise rather than their ties to management. Some are successful CEOs themselves and are not inclined to protect chief executives who defend the status quo in the face of discontinuous change. Denied a socially acceptable forum to ask questions and express candid opinions because of boardroom norms, some directors are seeking radical change in board practices.

A growing cadre of CEOs also is putting better governance on the agenda. Many recognize the wealth of knowledge that directors possess. Also, the abrupt removal of once celebrated CEOs at GM and other Blue Chip companies in the early 1990s is fresh in memory. Many CEOs realize that the empowered shareholder is here to stay and that boardroom coups are not the only—or the best—expression of good governance.

In their quest for better governance, shareholders, directors, and CEOs have arrived at a common realization: The true potential of the board lies in its ability to help management prevent problems, seize opportunities, and make the corporation perform better than it otherwise would. Rarely is a CEO so ineffective that the board must ask him or her to step down, but no CEO is perfect. The board's wisdom and judgment is a valuable managerial resource for any CEO.

The standards for good governance are rising. The search is on for boards that govern more actively and in ways that add value to the corporation. Boards are expected to play a broader role than that of watchdog and to make an ongoing contribution to the business. The quest has begun to release the competitive power of the board and to put the board to work.

The New Frontier

More often than not, boards believe they have the right CEO. For the majority of boards, the relevant question is: How can we make a good CEO perform better? Improving managerial judgment is the new frontier for boards.

Away from the headlines, some boards—like those of NYNEX and Citicorp—are exploring this new territory. These boards try to help the CEO be more effective by serving as a coach, a counselor, and a sounding board. They are not quiet and passive when times are good. They work all the time, even when they have full faith in the CEO, his or her team, and the company's strategic direction. They believe that in a fast-changing world, a CEO has never fully arrived. Even the best CEOs must learn and grow.

This form of engagement is not the kind of interference or micromanaging that CEOs fear. It is constructive, positive, and value-adding. Such involvement can keep established companies alert and flexible. For start-up companies, it is critical to survival.

This new territory is rich with value-creating opportunities. The board is, after all, the best opportunity a CEO has to catch the blind spots and faulty reasoning. What contingency has management overlooked? (Should IBM have geared its investment commitments to the aggressive sales goal of $180 billion in the mid 1980s?) What competitive threats are you seeing but not believing? (Why did Microsoft outwit Apple?) What perspective has management failed to consider? (Should Detroit have considered itself cost competitive with Japan because the yen was at 80?)

The board is the best source of creative thinking about new opportunities for growth. It is, as John Trani, chairman and CEO of Stanley Works and former president and chief executive of GE's Medical Systems, says, "the only body that has the stature and ability to tell the emperor—in a nice way—that he has no clothes."

Alex Mandl, CEO of Teligent (formerly Associated Communications), director of Warner-Lambert, and former president of AT&T, notes: "If board members are really smart and have a lot of experience in different industry environments, the board's participation in strategy will be very useful. If the board is truly global and has lots of contacts, it can help by making introductions to the right people, the right governmental bodies, and so on. Last, the board can keep some tension around the issue of whether the right senior team is in place by asking questions about whether the top people are truly the best available."

Ed Hotard, president of Praxair, the $5 billion producer of industrial gases, and a director of Dexter and other boards, says, "Boards today must have an active role in helping the CEO shape strategy and review implementation plans and progress. The board should understand not only the overall strategy but also how it is enabled by the supporting strategies around technology, compensation, education and human resource skill development, and information technology, and by putting key people in critical implementation positions."

John S. Reed, chairman and CEO of Citicorp, looks at it from the other side: "The danger is when a CEO ignores the board and the competencies it might have because he or she is scared the board will interfere."

How Boards Help Companies Compete

The contributions of some boards are quite visible—when, for instance, a board removes an ineffective CEO, hires an especially good one, or indicates that the company must change course. But outsiders may not recognize the many other ways a board can help a corporation be more competitive.

Identifying Major Discontinuities

Today's business environment is in constant flux. No industry is immune from radical restructuring and external discontinuities. Threats can arise from anywhere. Huge opportunities may lie unnoticed. Nontraditional competitors can suddenly reinvent a distribution system, forge innovative alliances, or use technology in a completely new way. Strategic moves by a competitor can suddenly redefine the boundaries of an entire industry. Credit card companies did not always think they were in the information business, but they do now. Banks did not always think they were consumer marketing companies. They do now. The November 1997 merger of MCI and WorldCom seemed to come from nowhere and sent shockwaves through the telecommunications industry.

Too often management is blindsided by these discontinuities. Most companies view the world from the inside out. That is, they tend to assess their own capabilities first, compare themselves to their traditional peers within traditional industry boundaries, and convince themselves that incremental improvement along the usual measures is the best way to move forward.

Boards can do management an invaluable service by viewing the broader business landscape and helping management recognize major opportunities and discontinuities that will affect the business. As Ed Hotard says, "Boards can add value by encouraging out-of-the-box thinking." John Trani says, "When it comes to an environmental shift, boards can be especially helpful in identifying blind spots where the CEO's experience base is just not in that area."

It is neither their mandate nor their interest to create strategy, but boards can help management assess the need, direction, and speed of change. Does the company need a breakthrough in thinking to sustain it for the next five years? Can it stay on its current trajectory or should it create a new one? Lodewijk de Vink, president of Warner-Lambert and director of Bell Atlantic, comments, "Board involvement is essential when it comes to issues that determine the fate of the company, things like mergers and de-mergers, which can revolutionize or destroy a corporation."

When NYNEX faced technological upheaval and the convergence of players in the telecommunications industry, board members understood that incremental change could be deadly and that radical change was never painless. NYNEX, once a stable monopoly, had to contend with alliances forming almost weekly among companies from a range of industries, including software, defense, entertainment, wireless communications, and cable TV. Some of the directors had steered their own companies through major industry restructurings and encouraged CEO Ivan Seidenberg to think big. Realizing that lingering problems could hold the company back, one director said, "If we have to write off $12 billion for technological change, we will."

The board's comments and encouragement gave Seidenberg the conviction to shed outdated premises and reconceptualize the business to change direction fast. He went on to forge the 1997 merger with Bell Atlantic.

When quantum change is necessary, the board can provide relevant business expertise to help management navigate the uncharted waters. The NYNEX board not only supported the Bell Atlantic merger but also gave the CEO ideas for how to negotiate the finances and the governance structure. Similarly, when Chairman-CEO Robert Weissman led the breakup of the former Dun & Bradstreet, the large information-based company, into several separate entities, his board provided a steady hand throughout the process.

Smaller, fast-growing companies have built-in discontinuities. As every entrepreneur and venture capitalist knows, start-ups move through stages of growth, each with its own characteristics and challenges. Boards can help such companies transition through the phases by providing the expertise and perspectives needed at the time. As KeraVision, the Silicon Valley venture capital–funded medical technology company, prepared to bring its product to market and shift from an R&D company to a consumer-oriented company, it recruited directors familiar with consumer marketing and global financial networks. At the same time, the boards of some large corporations are looking for directors who are CEOs of high-growth companies precisely for their experience in dealing with fast change (for more on recruiting directors, see Chapter Four). They have seen companies such as Dell Computer create unusually large market value unusually fast.

Recognizing the Externals

Boards can provide fresh perspectives on issues that fall short of whole-sale transformation. They can assess whether the company leadership is at least considering a balance of interests and can offer alternative views of the economic, cultural, or industry context. They can help identify missed opportunities or overlooked constituencies, and they can contribute to corporate strategy.

One company was considering abandoning some of its facilities. When an outside director asked how the communities were likely to react, the senior managers conceded that they had not carefully considered that. They agreed to do some further research before making definite decisions. Later, when the decisions were made, the company worked closely with the communities to minimize the negative impact.

When the board and management of Conrail discussed company strategy at an annual retreat, one director raised an issue: "I'm curious about some of your assumptions. You're showing us the averages in GDP growth and other economic changes, but the Federal Reserve could push us into recession in year one. What's Plan B in case the Fed raises rates again?" That simple question helped management prepare for an unforeseen contingency.

In 1995–1996, TRW had trouble with one of its airbag manufacturing facilities, which created some negative community and public relations. Management and the board engaged in a lengthy discussion of what the company was doing to avoid similar problems in the future. One director asked Howard Knicely, head of human resources, at a public policy meeting whether a comprehensive program had been developed to work with the governor of that state and with members of Congress to help them understand the issues around airbags and airbag safety. Knicely notes, "As a result, we gave the board an extensive review of the program and they made several helpful suggestions."

A board can point out when the CEO is missing an important external constituency. One board noticed that the CEO was not doing a good job of building relations with Washington, a part of the job he disliked. To compensate for the CEO's weakness in that area, the board suggested that he hire a vice chairman to focus on government affairs— a remedy that helped the company keep abreast of changing regulations.

Marshall Turner, a venture capitalist who has served on twenty-two boards, describes the board's value in helping start-up company management stay focused on the outside world: "Founders often start their company with a clear idea of the company's competitive environment, but then they spend months or even years with their heads buried in product development. When they are ready to emerge with a product, the market has often shifted or new competitors have emerged. and they wish they had designed the product slightly differently. Directors can help management track the outside world throughout the development cycle."

Assessing the Internals

Boards can make a major contribution by providing another perspective on the company's internal realities, such as people. The board's greater objectivity allows it to spot unnecessary energy drains and other managerial blind spots that may simply be too close to home for the CEO to see.

The General Motors board was instrumental in getting GM to focus on its weakness in marketing. The GM board had tolerated many years of disappointing performance and was keenly aware of the company's deficiencies in the fundamentals of marketing—brand identification, brand coordination, segmentation, and the like. When Jack Smith became CEO, the board wanted to help the company, through the new CEO. As it happened, the board created a new role for one of its outside directors, John Smale, a longtime board member and former chairman of Procter & Gamble.

The board made a structural change, naming Smale the first outside chairman of the board since Pierre du Pont, but even more significant than the structural innovation and formal title was the innovation in function. Aware of the company's uncoordinated, unfocused marketing, Smale worked in partnership with Jack Smith—a role any director can play, with or without the chairman title. Smale and Smith met often to work on sharpening GM's brand image. The result? Major changes in marketing at GM, including creation of a marketing function, an organizational structure that hinges on brand managers (similar to the structure at many consumer goods companies), and selection of a new marketing chief. The genetic code of marketing had been implanted—a value added that will be a legacy of the GM board. Smale is no longer outside chairman; CEO Jack Smith has assumed that title as well.

Another board helped the CEO see that a direct report was not up to snuff. The stock price of this struggling manufacturing company had fallen from $56 to $34. Under great pressure to perform, the CEO laid out his plans to the board. Months passed with no dramatic improvement, and the board became concerned that the company was simply not cutting costs aggressively enough. In particular, they became convinced that one of the critical people, a long-time friend of the CEO, was not prepared to do what was necessary.

When the directors raised their concern at an executive session, the CEO defended his subordinate. At subsequent meetings, the board raised the issue again. When the CEO finally got the message and did some checking, he concluded that the person was in fact holding the company back. A personnel change allowed the company to move faster, and the stock price began to improve.

John Reed says his board often helps him on the people front. "Board members are very astute about the social dynamics of the company. On occasion, they have told me that they don't think a certain person has the energy or vision to play the role I have him in. That has forced me to take another look and to make organizational adjustments."

As start-up companies move through the development stage to commercialization, their limited resources can make them appear risky to potential new hires. An experienced, reputable board not only can validate the venture and make it easier to attract high caliber people but also can help coach senior people as their responsibilities grow.

Setting Goals

Boards can have a tremendous influence on the business by helping management set appropriate goals and ensuring that the company is using the right measures—focusing on creating and sustaining market value, for instance, instead of revenues. Although financial indicators are not all that matter, they are the centerpiece of any scorecard. Here the board can help provide objectivity by keeping in mind the requirements of the external capital markets.

In January 1995, in the face of rising costs, flat earnings, and coming deregulation, management of Consolidated Natural Gas (CNG) presented a four-year plan that promised to turn the company around within that time frame. The board knew shareholders would not wait. "The board said we were thinking too much like a regulated company," CEO George Davidson says. "They enhanced our sense of urgency and timing."

CNG's four-year plan included a lot of front-end reengineering to improve information systems, get people to buy in, and overcome resistance to change. Most of the staff reductions and write-offs were at the back end. The board suggested that management go ahead and make the cuts and then find ways to manage with fewer people.

Davidson continues, "It wasn't a textbook solution, but it was practical, and I embraced the concept immediately. We went back and put together an accelerated plan with lots of confidence that the board would support aggressive write-offs and write-downs and other tough actions we would have to take to restructure and downsize. We got everything into one year, which set us up for significantly improved performance the following year."

Instead of downsizing some 10 percent over four years, CNG made a 14 percent reduction in positions, took a significant write-down on the value of the exploration and production assets, and wrote off some other assets to clean up the balance sheet—all in one year. The following year, earnings improved more than 40 percent on a normalized basis, largely because of actions taken the prior year, and the stock price rose accordingly.

George Davidson says of that experience, "Some CEOs might have looked at the board's input as criticism, but I didn't. The constructive tension between the board and management clearly creates shareholder value. Without the board's input, we would have taken a more moderate approach."

Sometimes the board can help management pull back from unrealistically aggressive goals. One technology company had ambitious plans to expand globally, an effort that would require rapid recruitment and training of people. Some board members were familiar with the problems of recruiting and assimilating people in Southeast Asia and questioned whether the company could really implement its strategy given the personnel constraints. The CEO and the senior human resources executive gave serious thought to the issue. Ultimately, the CEO realized that the company had to slow its growth to allow the recruitment of talent to keep pace.

Traditional performance measures do not always meet new business requirements. The board can impose on management the measures it feels best reflect the proper priorities—for example, top line growth, expansion of margins, asset utilization, return on invested capital, deployment of capital, price-earnings (P/E) ratio, or shareholder value. When NYNEX moved out of a regulatory environment, the board created new performance goals that reflected the new competitive demands. Managers' bonuses were scaled back if the company did not outperform its peers, even if the company ran well above the rest of the Dow Jones Industrials.

Managing Tensions

Boards can help top management strike a balance between conflicting pulls: long-term versus short-term performance, internal versus external demands, and a CEO's personal tendencies. Directors' years of business experience make them particularly good at sifting through the hard and soft data to discern whether nonperformance in the short-term is due to management's inability to execute or is driven by external change. They can be very supportive of a short-term hit if they believe it is necessary, as they were at NYNEX. Equally important, they can detect when the nonperformance comes from lousy strategy (lack of strategy or one that is obsolete) or poor execution.

When, for instance, Monsanto CEO Robert Shapiro chose to emphasize the life sciences (agriculture and pharmaceuticals), it was a "bet the company" choice of strategic direction. He acquired a relatively small company for what many observers thought was an exorbitant price. The board supported Shapiro's move, however controversial in the short term, because it understood the long-term implications. Shapiro had a clear vision, and the acquisition was an important building block. By standing behind the CEO rather than reflexively responding to short-term pressure, the Monsanto board added value.

Because many directors have been around a long time and have had vast experience, boards can be a sobering influence on an exuberant CEO. On the other hand, if they wind up with a conservative CEO, they can start pushing for stretch. One board cautioned the new CEO to be less aggressive financially in describing the company's game plan to security analysts, while the board of another large U.S. company went the other way, helping the CEO see a more aggressive path to grow and reposition the company. At the second company, in discussing various options for repositioning this company in Europe, the CEO and senior managers had quickly dismissed the idea of pursuing an acquisition, maybe because no one in the top team had ever lived through an acquisition in any capacity. Instead, they were exploring swaps of businesses with a large European competitor.

When the CEO discussed with the board the plan to swap businesses, two board members spoke up. Both were CEOs of large global companies. Each had grown a company from zero base to one of the world's largest in its field. Between the two of them, they had made more than twenty acquisitions. They wondered why the company was not going for "the whole enchilada." The directors' questions prompted a lively discussion, through which the benefits of acquiring the whole European company became obvious. The CEO and his team suddenly became very excited about the idea at which they had initially balked. The board had widened their horizon and given them courage. At the writing of this book, the discussions were continuing.

The Power of Collective Wisdom

A board can help a good CEO perform better—but only if it can gel as a group and exercise its collective judgment. The biggest problem with corporate boards is not *who* is on the board but *what* transpires there.

Corporate boards are designed to have collective power; that is, by design, no individual board member—not even the chairperson—has power over any other member. Corporate executives can unilaterally promote or demote their subordinates or make decisions, but no one director can disenfranchise a fellow board member or take significant action on her own. Every member of the board must seek approval and support from her peers. Only the group can make decisions, hire and fire a CEO, ratify company actions, and otherwise act.

Collective judgment cannot emerge, however, unless the individuals have coalesced into a group. Directors must have a chance to build relationships with each other, to get to know each others' opinions and personalities, to develop trust, and to gain comfort in freely expressing their own ideas through candid, open interactions. Only then will each director contribute candidly, only then can directors find consensus, and only then can they act in unison.

Merely assembling a dozen individuals around a table does not accomplish the same thing. Indeed, when the social relationships do not develop, directors who are strong and aggressive in their individual vocations are rendered collectively powerless. CEOs can then dominate their boards just as fiercely or subtly as they dominate their organizations.

What looks from the outside like intentional passivity or poor judgment on the part of the board often is the board's inability to make any kind of collective judgment at all. How is it that the illustrious board of Morrison Knudsen allowed CEO William Agee to drag the company to the brink of financial ruin? Did the instincts of investment guru Peter Lynch, top head-hunter Gerry Roche, and seasoned business leader Peter Uebberoth, who revolutionized the Olympics, really fail? More likely, these individuals did not gel as a group and thus failed to have the kind of open discussions that would allow their individual judgments to come together. The directors of scores of nonperfoming companies must have seen what every outsider could see. Chances are they had no socially acceptable forum to test out their perceptions.

The power vacuum created by directors' inability to connect with each other is precisely why so many CEOs have been able to veer off track without challenge from their boards. Some CEOs can sense this. They work hard to develop relationships with individual directors but undermine any efforts for board members to build strong relationships among themselves.

While these CEOs may boast about the good relations they have with their board, they tend to think in terms of individual directors. They may feel threatened by the board as a collective body. As former Conrail Vice President and General Counsel Bruce Wilson notes, "Even if the CEO has trust with each individual director, as a collective body, it may be different. Something happens when individuals get together to meet as an august body. Some CEOs worry about that."

The real value of a board lies in its collective wisdom. When the board gets information that is unfiltered and truthful and the ambiance of the boardroom fosters critical thinking, directors' individual judgments usually converge quickly, especially in the "soft" area of judgments on people. That collective judgment, having been probed and tested by a group of seasoned business people, is superior to the judgment of any one or two individuals. That wisdom is a valuable intellectual resource.

The boards described in this book are blazing the trail to better governance by fostering the kind of active involvement that brings individual thoughts and instincts together. They function well as collective bodies and are a resource to management. They meet their legal and regulatory requirements, but they are driven by the higher purpose of making the company perform at its best. These boards work.

Key Points

- In today's tough environment, companies must use every available resource to its fullest. The board's wisdom and experience must not lie dormant. It is incumbent on every CEO to use the board to competitive advantage. It is incumbent on every director to participate and contribute.

- Boards that are truly engaged in the company's most pressing issues help management in numerous ways. They identify blind spots and overlooked opportunities, offer multiple perspectives and insights into the external environment, and provide an objective view of the industry landscape and alternative views on people. In general, they provide the reality-checking every CEO needs.

- The real value of the board lies in its *collective* wisdom and perspective. The best learning comes from the candid exchange of ideas on issues that are critical to the business. One-on-one relationships between the CEO and individual directors do not accomplish the same thing. Boards must learn to function as a group.

DOES YOUR BOARD REALLY WORK?
The Effectiveness Test

Directors and CEOs might feel that their board is functioning well because board members read the material they are sent, attend board meetings, listen attentively, and are basically conscientious and well-meaning. But many boards that appear to be dutiful are not optimizing their potential to add value to the corporation. The following set of questions can provide a quick assessment of whether the board is working.

1. Do board members individually and collectively understand the changing external picture of the industry?
2. Are board members individually and collectively clear about the company's strategic direction? Does the board have a process for shaping and approving the strategy?
3. Is a process in place for frequently reviewing the CEO and giving him or her unmistakably clear feedback?
4. Is the board comfortable with the notion that the company has the right CEO? If not, is the board actively dealing with the issue?
5. Is the board fully conversant in the processes for succession planning and leadership development?
6. Is reality put on the table?
7. Does the board have a robust process for self-evaluation and improvement?
8. Is the board evergreen in its composition and relevant to the company's needs (that is, having global diversity, age balance, balance in perspective and experiences)?

CHAPTER TWO

WHAT GOOD BOARDS DO

Boards that work are set apart not by different laws and philosophies of corporate governance but by their attitude and expectations and the positive working relationships among the directors and between management and the board. Hidden agendas and personal ambitions do not get in the way of issues that are mission-critical to the business. Defensiveness and power plays are minimal. Deliberations are informal and open, yet the dialogue is characterized by an incisiveness rarely seen in other collective bodies. Conclusions reflect the thinking of the whole group, not of any one individual. Issues of form, like whether or not the roles of chairman and CEO should be separate, take a back seat to issues of substance.

Many directors and CEOs, let alone critics of corporate boards, cannot imagine how effective, efficient, and exciting board deliberations can be. They have not attended board meetings that are dynamic and intellectually stimulating and that directors love to attend. They have not participated in the kind of deep discussion of corporate strategy, management development, and succession that generates new insights and breakthrough thinking. They have not had the chance to ask their most incisive questions without concern that the question will be perceived as accusatory. Nor have they felt the energy build as group members challenge and build on each other's comments to push the envelope of thinking and the boundaries of perspective. They have not seen CEO-directors become energized by the learning they will take back to their own companies.

Boards that work well experience all these things. Because they do, the board is not a do-nothing formality but a vibrant participant in the corporation's value-creation process.

Familiar Taboos

The typical board is locked into a pattern that seems unbreakable. For them, board meetings are tightly scheduled, well-rehearsed presentations that leave little time for questions or reactions. The directors sit politely at the table, sometimes in order of seniority. Serious questions are considered bad form at best, and any discussion of issues outside the boardroom is viewed as an open threat to the CEO. The presentations seldom give directors the information they really want or need. One chairman-CEO describes board meetings under his predecessor's leadership: "Discussions focused on programs, progress, and long-term objectives. Everything was stiff and carefully scripted. Meetings were like kabuki dances." At several Fortune 100 companies, the chairmen used to have their senior managers read their presentations from scripts that were timed to the minute.

When important topics are presented, the lack of informal, candid discussion means that directors have no opportunity to test out their reactions. Even when they are uncomfortable with management's decisions or are concerned about the company's performance, they tend not to speak out. No one wants to be singled out as an annoying questioner or as a director who initiates boardroom resistance to management's plans.

One chairman-CEO of a multibillion dollar company described his predecessor's relationship with the board: "He was one who would effectively say, 'Here's my plan. I need you to approve it. If you don't, that's the same as a no-confidence vote.' His approach had a very chilling effect on the board environment." A CEO and director of several boards says, "If directors feel that the CEO is uncomfortable with open dialogue, they don't do it."

The board of GM during Roger Smith's tenure shows how ineffective some boards have been. In their book *Comeback: The Fall and Rise of the American Automobile Industry* (Simon & Schuster, 1994), Paul Ingrassia and Joseph B. White paint a vivid picture of the GM board under Roger Smith. Nonexecutive members of the board sat on one side of the table while inside directors (those on the management team) sat on the other. Inside directors got information their counterparts across the table were not allowed to see. The typical GM board meeting consisted of well-rehearsed presentations by management during which the presenter would flip through dozens of slides in a darkened room, reading aloud every word. Roger Smith would not tolerate any deviation. According to Ingrassia and White, when Roger Smith heard that attorney Ira Millstein was talking to directors outside board meetings, he stormed into Millstein's office and berated him for meddling.

Sometimes boards experience a "tyranny of the minority," whereby a small coalition of powerful directors dominates board discussions and decisions. Other directors keep their opinions to themselves for fear of offending their board colleagues. The CEO inadvertently reinforces the pattern through body language or by failing to solicit input from those who are not speaking up.

The taboos against candor and open discussion are so powerful that it takes a certain amount of heroism for boards to break them. Communication and coalition-building take place behind the scenes as directors try to save the day in the eleventh hour. This was the case at GM, where a small coalition of outside directors had to make careful, incremental moves. Decisions were made piecemeal, information was leaked, messages were sent by intermediaries, and a lot of guesswork was left in the domain of the press—all of which sapped the energy of the corporation and tarnished its image.

At American Express in 1992, long-time director Rawleigh Warner made a thorough list of Chairman and CEO James D. Robinson III's shortcomings and shared it with a few board colleagues. The "balance sheet" on Robinson showed an accumulation of some fifteen items Warner thought Robinson had mishandled. Warner had to create his own mechanism for expressing his long-standing dissatisfaction to his peers.[1]

Snapshots of a Board That Works

No board is perfect, but an inside look at the board of the former Dun & Bradstreet (D&B) (before it was split into three separate companies, Cognizant, Dun & Bradstreet, and A. C. Nielsen) shows that constructive working relationships, open communication, and the like are not just theoretical ideals. Outsiders may not know all that has gone on between management and the board at this company, but those on the inside know that the board understood the business and made a clear and distinct contribution to it.

When in 1994 Robert Weissman took over as CEO and chairman of the former D&B, he knew that the industry was undergoing cataclysmic change and that radical action was the only way the company could succeed. He also knew that the directors would not support aggressive action unless they understood the urgency and the strategic logic.

Before Weissman set out to change the company, he changed the relationship between management and the board. Over a period of 18 months, Weissman and his management team presented information designed to create a clear picture of the external environment and the effects on the company. Those efforts paved the way for Weissman and the board to reach a common understanding of various strategic options. Ultimately, the board supported Weissman's efforts to make a $5 billion acquisition—almost equal in size to the former D&B—and when

[1]American Express (A), Harvard Business School, Case Number N9–494–093, rev. June 23, 1994.

the acquisition did not materialize, to move decisively in the opposite direction, breaking the organization into three independent companies.

Open Information, Open Dialogue

When Weissman became CEO of the former D&B, the $6 billion multi-unit information services company had a great reputation, steady earnings, and a pre-tax margin of nearly 20 percent. One of Weissman's first challenges was to help the board see that the status quo was riskier than radical change.

Early in his tenure, Weissman planned a two-day board meeting, during which management educated the board about the changing competitive landscape. In a series of presentations, management showed that while the former D&B had long made money from information, raw or processed, information was fast becoming a commodity. Other companies were finding their way into more lucrative parts of the value chain by using sophisticated computer systems and decision science to process information. Value was migrating from existing product markets to customers' internal decision making, and profits were being squeezed. Smaller companies were being swallowed by two of the former D&B's large competitors, and some of D&B's businesses were no longer near-monopolies.

Then management presented a few slides showing why business as usual would not meet the company's current goals. As one of the profit-generating businesses (a near-monopoly) shifted to a more competitive environment, for instance, price would decline, and the former D&B's share would erode. A viable competitor could achieve more than 20 percent share and force prices down by more than 30 percent. Cost reductions and layoffs could not make up the difference. The result? Earnings would swing down drastically

As directors listened attentively, they learned that other D&B businesses had different but equally serious problems. It was the first time the board had been given a quantification of these competitive forces and economic realities. Board presentations under Weissman's predecessors typically had given tabular earnings projections for the various businesses along with a summary of those growth projections and a wrap-around statement that basically said "That's why the future is okay." The traditional arm's length relationship between the CEO and the board had kept discussions of strategic challenges and risks at a superficial level.

Now the board was getting a visceral sense of the danger. Part way through the session, one director, who had been on the boards of several high profile companies, approached Weissman and said privately, "I think I finally understand why your predecessor decided to retire early." Weissman recalls, "That's when I knew we were getting somewhere."

The board did not have a tradition of dealing with what one director called "the high, hard ones," but the presentations had gotten the directors to start thinking. When Weissman occasionally stopped to ask the board for input, directors were at first reluctant to speak up. Weissman kept asking specific questions and the dialogue opened up.

The next day, every director volunteered a question or comment he or she had thought about overnight. One director asked about the implications of the gap between appropriate reinvestment levels and expected earnings growth. Another director described some lessons learned as he had dealt with some similar situations in his own business. Soon it was clear that management and the board had a shared understanding of the external realities and threats. Structural change was imminent; the need for strategic repositioning was urgent.

When the CEO laid out the set of strategic options and management's proposed plan of action, he looked directly at his nine outside directors and asked, "What are we missing? How do you feel about what we are proposing to do?" The solicitation was sincere, and directors gave their honest reactions. As certain points were reinforced, the excitement level grew. The board concurred that while the core business was threatened, a major move now would position D&B for growth in the new environment. When the CEO asked whether the glass was half full or half empty, a board member responded: "If you don't know anything about the business, it's half empty. But knowing what the business drivers are makes me comfortable that it's half full. We can win."

Before the meeting broke, the senior-most director thanked the CEO for letting the board into the company: "You've exposed us to the structural change in the industry, and you've presented options that make sense. We see the urgency, and we'll help you with it."

Informed Trust

Less than a year into his tenure as CEO, Weissman identified an acquisition candidate that he thought was a perfect fit. The acquisition would give the company the technology, expertise, and market presence it needed to expand its core business. The acquisition was so big that a friend had advised Weissman not to tackle it so soon in his tenure, but Weissman believed the board would support the move. He had already created the context for weighing various strategic options so the board would quickly see the business rationale. Indeed, the board had discussed at length the advantages of a fast growth strategy. Over time, the board had come to see that while growth through acquisition was not the only viable path, it seemed to be the most attractive.

Weissman discussed the acquisition with the full board, focusing on the philosophy and premises behind it as well as the numbers. He stressed the risks and the strategic options. After lengthy discussion over a series of meetings, the board agreed that management should explore the acquisition.

Weissman kept the board continually informed as he set out to negotiate the deal. "You're dealing with an external world here," Weissman explains. "The variables are not all under the control of the company, and they change. The board has to understand that these variables exist and be kept up to date as things happen or don't happen." Some two to three hours of every board meeting were spent discussing changes in the market forces and cost dynamics. Between meetings, Weissman kept the dialogue going through telephone calls and informal notes.

One of the variables that was beyond the former D&B's control was the other company's willingness to be acquired or merged. The company clearly had other plans, and the two parties could not come to terms. For a variety of reasons, a hostile takeover was not possible. Nor were there any other acquisition candidates that made as much sense for the company.

With the offer rejected, Weissman had to revert quickly to "Plan B"— a complete reversal of the agreed-upon growth strategy. Weissman believed the next best plan was to split the company into three separate entities.

While some boards might have taken the CEO's reversal as a sign of indecisiveness, this board knew better. The directors understood that some of the alternatives were sequential, and they had already analyzed the implications. While other CEOs might have feared the loss of credibility, Weissman did not: "We had been through all that with the board, and we were partners." Plan B was an alternative that had been part of the board's discussion for some time. Weissman presented the details of the second plan in less than two hours; the board asked questions for about fifteen minutes. Approval of the breakup soon followed.

Coach and Fiduciary

In the months before the breakup was complete, the board's workload increased dramatically. Management teams had to be reconstructed, compensation systems had to be redesigned, and the board itself had to be reconfigured. As the spin-off unfolded, numerous adjustments and SEC filings had to be made, and many important details had to be ironed out. Weissman describes it as an incessant grind.

Part way through the process, Weissman noticed a change in his relationship with the board. "The board had been supportive at every step, providing all kinds of help and counsel," Weissman says. "Then all of a sudden, there was a problem."

The spin-off triggered some legal changes having to do with bonus payments that were originally part of an anti-takeover provision. There were $100 million of bonus payments to make at the close. Management structured the payments so that most of the bonuses would actually be earned by then.

The board had reviewed the bonus plan in rough form two months earlier, consulted with outside advisors, and agreed to the concept. Seemingly out of the blue, one of the directors lashed out at Weissman about the bonus payments. He was looking at it from the point of view of a shareholder, who might be alarmed by the high number.

Weissman was at first confused by the change in tone, but he soon realized that the board's shift from coach to fiduciary-at-risk was natural. "It was the kind of board a CEO sees twenty-four hours after an unfriendly tender has been made. At one point I said to a director, 'It seems you really have only two questions—Is this fair to shareholders? and, Am I personally covered?' The director replied 'That's absolutely right, but the order is reversed.'"

Weissman and his management accepted the board's changed role, responded to it constructively, and the process went forward smoothly. Interestingly, the board later congratulated management for how well it had handled the bonus situation.

The divestiture was completed in 1996 and the market reacted favorably. Weissman says, "This board didn't take the easy way out. We provided the information and opened the dialogue, and they made the effort to learn and advise. And they never forgot about shareholders. That's what good governance is all about."

The Common Foundation

The board of the former Dun & Bradstreet does not behave like most other boards. That behavior stems from a set of attitudes, expectations, and relationships that are common to other boards that work.

Good Boards Expect to Add Value

Good boards accept as a given the notion of the "value-adding board." They expect to do more than their traditional roles of overseeing management and ensuring fiduciary responsibility. They expect to add value by contributing to the CEO's judgment and wisdom, acting as a resource to the CEO, and at the same time ensuring that the corporation has the right CEO and sound strategic direction at all times.

They realize that it is not enough for a board to vote up or down on a CEO. Even a brilliant CEO can have a weak management team or a strategy that is off-base. These boards want to help the CEO improve the substance of business strategy and the quality of managerial leadership throughout the organization. They are eager to get involved, evaluate, and contribute their expertise. They take the notion of the value-adding board from theory to reality.

Bill Adams, retired chairman of Armstrong World Industries and former director of Bell Atlantic, emphasizes the importance of this mindset: "The attitude with which one approaches the job of being a director is crucial. An ideal director does not come in as a policeman or even an objective critic but with a positive, optimistic view that the company will succeed—that the company has either the ability to succeed or the will to change. A director should also have a sense of collegiality. I know I would never subordinate my principles to a board I serve on, but I would forgo my wishes for the sake of the team."

These CEOs Want the Help

Many of the CEOs in this book have undergone a kind of awakening. Convinced that a more active board is inevitable, they want to ensure that the board's involvement is constructive and focused. Others have become true advocates who see the board as a source of wisdom and counsel they are eager to tap. They recognize the board's input as food for thought rather than dictation, the board's tough, incisive questions as a useful reminder, and the board's judgments as a valuable opinion.

Sam Eichenfield, CEO of The FINOVA Group, Inc., captures this point:

An effective board to me is one that is available to me and other members of the management team when we have questions that their expertise could assist in. Also, when we contemplate certain kinds of strategic activities, I want them to be available for consultation. We recently went through some strategic cost take-outs that involved evaluating positions and downsizing an organization. I called a couple of people on the board whom I knew had gone through that. I wanted to know what worked well for them and what didn't. I also value the questions the board asks. We're in the finance business, but our board members are from manufacturing, insurance, academia. Very often their questions will open our eyes to a different way of looking at things.

Lodewijk de Vink, president of Warner-Lambert and director of Bell Atlantic, sees the board's involvement in strategic issues as natural and necessary. He says, "A CEO shouldn't make those determinations without the board's understanding and involvement."

"Help" does not necessarily mean being on the CEO's side. It can mean healthy disagreement. As Milt Honea, former CEO and chairman of NorAm Energy Corp., a large Houston-based natural gas and energy company, says, "It's helpful to have a board that can help protect you from your own mistakes." Citicorp Chairman-CEO John Reed expresses a similar view, "A good board will stop you from doing dumb things."

Power Is Not the Issue

Stories of ousted CEOs often have been reported in terms of power. Such dramatic one-time events seem to represent an historical and, some say, permanent shift in power away from the CEO and to the board. But the effective boards in this book have broken the power continuum. That is, they do not see power as a continuum with the CEO at one end and the board at the other, which implies an ongoing contest between the two sides. They believe that both the CEO and the board should be exerting influence and having input in creating shareholder value.

When power is the focus, boards tend to push to the extremes of being either passive or dictatorial. An "old time" board's careful politeness signals its acquiescence to the unquestioned, unchallenged power of the CEO. Clandestine meetings of outside directors without the CEO—the kind that preceded the coups at GM, American Express, CBS, and others—represent the board's attempt to usurp power. Neither of these patterns is desirable in the long run.

Bill Adams says, "I don't buy this whole idea that independence means resistance, that there has to be tension between the CEO and the board. If the CEO and the board have a working understanding, then the tension should be between where the company is and where it ought to be. Bringing that tension out early improves the working contract."

They Avoid the "Never Again" Trap

The chronic nonperformance that preceded the boardroom coups of the early 1990s has caused some boards to adopt a defensive stance against the CEO. The appointment of a "lead director" or separating the roles of CEO and chairman makes a statement that the board—not the CEO—has the ultimate power. The message seems to be, "Never again will this do-nothing board let the CEO take such strong, but wrong, actions."

The boards in this book are not focused on preventing chronic nonperformance. Their focus is on making lasting change in the way the board functions and unlocking the board's full potential to contribute. This focus paves the way for directors to balance the contradictory pulls on the board:

- To be involved without micro-managing,
- challenging but also supportive,
- patient but not complacent.

CEOs are learning to manage some tensions of their own:

- To share information without feeling vulnerable,
- seek advice without appearing weak,
- solicit input without appearing to relinquish control over operational decisions.

Finding the balance means shifting roles to fit the situation (consider the D&B board's shift from coach to fiduciary) and finding the middle ground in everyday board deliberations.

Sam Eichenfield of The FINOVA Group summarizes how he and his board achieve participation without micro-managing: "When I'm facing a major decision, I always say to the board, 'I've been thinking of doing this.' Their answer is always, 'We'll give you our opinions, but it's your decision.'"

Accountability Goes Both Ways

Abandoning the power issue does not mean there should be no checks and balances. Today's boards at work seem to practice "mutual accountability." That is, the CEO is (in theory, has always been) accountable to the board, and the board is accountable to shareholders (a reality shareholder activists are quick to voice). But as boards and CEOs endeavor to work together and it becomes clear that boards can contribute and add value, a new kind of accountability emerges: that of the board to the CEO. In short, CEOs and boards are accountable to each other.

The board's accountability to the CEO is not the kind that says: If you don't go along with me, I'll ostracize you socially and damage your reputation. In this increasingly complex business environment, a CEO needs a strong, well-functioning board to serve as a sounding board, a source of counsel, and a check on his or her own judgments about how to move forward. The board's value-added is becoming a requirement. CEOs know whether or not they are getting it, and they have the right to demand it.

CEOs should make their expectations for directors and the board explicit. If they do not feel they are getting the best out of the board, they should not only say so but also suggest practices that help draw the board out.

The Ability to Have Productive Dialogue

Boards that work well have constructive, critical dialogue among board members and senior management. Such open dialogue is the single best indication of board effectiveness. Lodewijk de Vink expands on this point: "If you have meetings where strategic issues are being discussed in an open fashion, where the options management has considered are being brought to the board and the board is well informed enough to make constructive comments, where debate is taking place in the board-room and not just management making a presentation, if management comes to the board and asks for advice because it values the experiences of those who have been CEOs or have gone through a restructuring in their industry—all of that defines a good board."

Charles Crocker, president and CEO of BEI Electronics and director of numerous large and small company boards, was asked what makes a board effective. His answer reinforces the point: "Board effectiveness depends on dialogue."

The Royal Bank of Canada acknowledges the importance of dialogue in its second governing principle: "Subject to the business need for strong geographical, professional and industry sector representation, the size of the Board must be kept to a sufficiently low number to facilitate open and effective dialogue and the full participation and contribution of each Director."

Understanding the importance of open dialogue is key to making boards work. George Davidson, CEO of Pittsburgh-based Consolidated Natural Gas, says, "If you want to get real constructive dialogue and focused insight, you have to make it a safe field of play. Everyone should feel they can ask a tough question or make a negative comment. When you have true candor, you can get into situations that might make a few people feel uncomfortable, but that's a reasonable price to pay for getting the input."

Some CEOs fear such openness, but few have reason for concern. To be sure, open discussions among the full board and the CEO may take unexpected turns, but that is where the real learning takes place. As board members add information, react to each other's comments, and offer different views, the discussion deepens and broadens. New insights arise, and creative solutions can emerge. The CEO and the senior management team clearly benefit.

Some chief executives claim they have tapped the power of the board because they talk with directors individually to seek their advice, but good board dynamics transcend one-to-one relationships between the CEO and individual directors—and so must the dialogue. Although individual directors may have a lot to offer, the real power of the board comes from the overused word *synergy*, from the exciting exchange of opinions and information among a group of intelligent business peers.

Additional benefits come when the inclusiveness extends to managers below the level of the CEO. Boards at work increasingly invite their managers to formal and informal board gatherings. The board gets a good sense of the company's managerial depth and operational capabilities, and management learns what the board really wants. As Tom Loarie, chairman and CEO of KeraVision, remarked, "When the company officers hear what the board thinks, it makes my job a heck of a lot easier. I don't have to tell them what to do or why they should do it." At a KeraVision board retreat, Darlene Crockett-Billig, one of Loarie's direct reports, told the board how she benefited from the interaction: "The questions you directors ask push me to expand my thinking beyond the normal envelope. It is a continual learning process."

Any change in board practice must improve the character of the discussions and the quality of the interactions among directors and managers. The atmosphere in and around the boardroom must allow each member to talk freely, to react candidly, and to learn from others. It takes time to discuss important matters and develop opinions about the strategic direction of the company. Meeting schedules and agendas must reflect this reality. The board must get its priorities straight and spend the bulk of its time engaged in dialogue about where the company is going and what it must do to get there.

The practices, or operating mechanisms, described in the following chapters are not intended to be applied universally. Indeed, Walter V. Shipley, chairman of Chase Manhattan and member of the Business Roundtable, was right to insist, "The substance of corporate governance and how it works is more important than the form or structure of it."[2] Each board should debate and discuss the recommendations and choose those it finds most appropriate. All the operating mechanisms described here have passed the fundamental test of facilitating open, critical dialogue and making a positive impact on board dynamics. These practices help boards work.

Key Points

- Boards that work have broken boardroom norms and protocols. They engage in an exciting exchange of ideas on the topics that matter most to the business, including the strategic direction of the company and its pipeline of leaders. Directors ask incisive questions, constructively challenge management's assumptions, and express honest opinions. Management shares information freely.

- Directors of boards that work expect to add value, and CEOs welcome the input. They are accountable to each other and in pursuit of the same goal—namely, to make the company perform better.

- Dialogue is a revealing indicator of board effectiveness. To achieve better governance, adopt practices that will improve the character of the dialogue.

[2]John A. Byrne, "Governance: CEOs Catch Up with Shareholder Activist," *Business Week*, September 22, 1997.

DOES YOUR BOARD REALLY TALK?
The Dialogue Test

The following questions help the board assess the quality of the dialogue in and outside the boardroom. To add value, the board must engage in courageous, productive dialogue that draws out varied and new perspectives and allows for shared learning.

1. Do all directors feel free to speak their mind on key points without having to suppress their true feelings?
2. Are all board discussions characterized by intellectual honesty, both in board and committee meetings and outside the boardroom?
3. Does the CEO feel comfortable discussing bad news, anticipated bad news, and uncertainties?
4. Does dialogue take place among directors as well as between directors and the CEO?
5. Is the ambiance of the boardroom conducive to critical thinking, incisive questioning, and learning from one another?

PART TWO

PUTTING THE BOARD TO WORK

CHAPTER THREE

GETTING STRUCTURE OUT OF THE WAY

Shareholders that are frustrated with passive boards often press for structural solutions. Appoint a "lead director" or make an outside director board chairman, the logic goes, to ensure that the CEO is subordinate to the board. Require outside directors to meet periodically without the CEO. Limit the number of boards a director can serve on to ensure adequate time and attention. These suggestions are clearly aimed at making boards function better, but some have the opposite effect. Overemphasis on specific mechanisms can distract a board from the real issue, namely, how directors behave and interact—again, the board dynamics.

Boards should choose only those committee structures and leadership designations that clear the path for an open exchange of information and ideas among all directors and between the directors and the CEO. The goal should be to avoid any mechanisms that inadvertently create pockets of power and to select those that streamline communication and enhance the ability to work together.

In this light, replacing the executive committee with a governance committee may be the right thing; appointing a lead director is probably not. The size of the board should be determined with the need for dialogue in mind. Meetings should be designed for balanced participation and depth of understanding. Meetings without the CEO are okay but should not substitute for direct communication with the CEO.

Boards that function well have a minimal number of committees, each with a very clear mandate and each in a role that supports, not replaces, the work of the full board. The important issues are aired and discussed by all directors, each of whom feels his or her input is valued and important. These boards tend to resist the notion of a "lead director" or outside chairman not because the CEO has a stranglehold on the board but because the roles are extraneous and, worse, potentially destructive to the board dynamics.

Meetings are fewer, longer, and structured to encourage deep discussion. The growing use of two- to three-day off-site meetings (commonly called board retreats but more accurately described as breakthrough sessions) allow the board to become totally immersed in company strategy. Conrail, AMP, NYNEX, Royal Bank of Canada, Bank of America, Avenor (the Canadian paper company), the former Dun & Bradstreet, and KeraVision (the California medical technology company) are among the boards that have found these breakthrough sessions essential to their ability to add value to the business.

The catch phrases for this chapter, then, are "less is more" and "function, not form."

Is the Board Too Big for Dialogue?

Most of the boards in this book have about eight outside directors and one or two inside directors. This is in keeping with a nationwide trend toward smaller boards. The median size of large-company boards dropped from fourteen in 1972 to twelve in 1989, and many experts since have advocated for even fewer members. (Royal Bank of Canada, with twenty-two members, is the exception. Its size, typical of large Canadian financial institutions, is based on the historical need for regional representation, weighed against the advantages of a smaller board. This board has been revisiting the issue of its size as part of its corporate governance process. Its current goal for board size is eighteen to twenty-one.)

Although the precise number of directors may vary, the rationale for having a relatively small board is consistent. The CEOs and directors of boards that work almost invariably talked about the impact of board size on the dialogue or board dynamics. To truly work, the board must be able to engage in substantive dialogue. Managing the dialogue to ensure balanced participation among sixteen or more people is a Herculean task for any individual. As John Cleghorn, chairman and CEO of Royal Bank of Canada, points out, outside of board meetings, simply keeping in touch with the other directors on a large board can be difficult.

Battelle Memorial Institute CEO Douglas Olesen's comments are typical: "Our board has six members. Because our board is small, the directors quite often get into discussions among themselves. And this board rarely comes out with split votes. They decide either yes or no, so the group discusses things until they get to a point of resolution. I think the board size is a factor in terms of board dynamics."

He continues: "I've never chaired a board of four or of sixteen, but being a manager and understanding what it's like to have meetings, or committees, I am very comfortable with six to eight. It allows for everybody to have dialogue at a meeting on any issue without consuming a great deal of time. With sixteen you get too many different agendas and uneven participation."

Bill Adams, former chairman of Armstrong, says: "The big-company boards I've been on have too many people. Boards need to be close-in teams—large enough to represent a diversity of views so the team doesn't get locked into something solely out of the past experience of one or two people but small enough for everyone to be involved."

He believes boards can function very effectively with just six outside directors and one inside director. "Beyond that, you're not adding any new perspectives, and the larger number diminishes the board's ability to have long, intensive discussions either across the top or drilling down into the issues. If you take a board of, say, twelve directors, you usually have about six who are pulling the weight anyway."

Three Committees Will Do

A major shift is underway regarding the use of committees. It used to be that any substantive issues were handled by the executive committee or its equivalent, and the full board handled procedural issues only—an arrangement many directors found intellectually unsatisfying. Committee membership was used to control power and cement relationships. Today, however, the important decisions are going to the full board.

This is clearly a positive trend. Boards should strictly limit the number of committees and their sphere of influence. Too many committees can be a scheduling nightmare, especially if the board membership is small. Also, over-use of committees can create unwanted communication filters and layers of power. Most important, committees that are too powerful end up doing the real work of the board. Boards that work well tend to bring the most critical issues to the full board and use committees to do background work or specialized tasks.

Until the early 1990s, it was common for boards to deal with any substantive issues through committees, usually hand-picked by the CEO. Meetings of the full board were procedural, and for all practical purposes, perfunctory. Major acquisitions would go to the finance committee, succession issues would go to the compensation or nominating committee, or all major issues would go to executive committee (often referred to in the press as "the powerful executive committee"). Private relationships and the old boys' network thrived.

The pattern of committees as the center of power has long been the modus operandi of most U.S. boards, but times have changed. The old pattern is unnecessary and should be broken. Where it persists, committee membership becomes a perquisite, granted by virtue of seniority on the board or a special relationship with the CEO. The inevitable result is a two-tier power structure in which some board members broker power behind the scene while others feel disenfranchised.

Ivan Seidenberg, CEO of NYNEX and director of Allied Signal, describes how misuse of a committee can interfere with the board dynamics: "Very rarely do we take key issues and drive them through the committees. Let's say you have the finance committee look into a merger or acquisition. Unless you inform the whole board, you end up with the old two-tier problem. You get the financial experts and the other directors. It makes the others uncomfortable because they're really not involved in the development of strategy."

Decisions that relate to the CEO, to the total strategy of the company, and to the total governance of the board itself must be the preserve of every director. Jerry Meyer, chairman and CEO of Tektronix, the Oregon-based maker of electronic devices, says, "We do not want a committee to deal with strategy. Strategy has to be understood by each director. That means the board as a whole has to spend the time." The availability of directors' time is seldom a problem. As Jim Hagen, former chairman and CEO of Conrail, says, "When boards are wrestling with the real issues, directors willingly spend the time."

When the compensation committee at a large manufacturer tried to take control of CEO succession, one outside director took the initiative to bring control back to the full board. With the incumbent CEO's retirement imminent, the compensation committee members had discussed succession and agreed to make the president the CEO. They brought their "recommendation" to the full board, expecting instant approval.

Several directors had reservations about the choice, and one director spoke up. He sat on the board of another big company that had a state-of-the-art succession planning process. He was not convinced that the company president, who had previously been CFO and had no operating experience, was the best person to take the company forward, the committee's conclusion notwithstanding. He suggested that the committee expand the search for a CEO outside the company. It did, and it ultimately found an excellent outside candidate, whom the board enthusiastically approved. In doing so, the board added tremendous value.

Consider the important role compensation committees have played in recent years doing in-depth studies and bringing their recommendations to the full board. Many have spent countless hours unraveling the complexities of the company's compensation system and trying to adhere to tougher SEC requirements. At many companies, their work has been outstanding. But the best boards do not abdicate their say about compensation to the committee. They realize that while the committee can bring background information and recommendations to the full board, every director must understand the issues well enough to make an informed decision. With contracts for new hires and severance pay drawing public scrutiny, the full board, not just a committee, must be involved.

Bringing the important issues to the full board imposes discipline on the board—to be selective about the issues it addresses and to keep board membership small enough for everyone to participate. Eight to ten directors cannot staff more than three or four committees. Sam Eichenfield, CEO of The FINOVA Group, says:

One of the advantages of having a small board is that it doesn't allow for a lot of committees. We have three: audit, human resources, and executive. Obviously, the audit committee meets on its own and does a lot of the work that an audit committee should do, which is meeting with outside auditors, our inside internal auditor, and reporting to me and the board. The human resources committee does a lot of work on its own, meeting with our compensation consultants, meeting with our HR people, meeting with me, and then reporting to the board. People on that committee probably find themselves spending half their time on committee work and half on board work. Because we're a financial institution, we have an executive committee to approve certain size loans.

Most boards need only three or four committees. Audit and management development (or compensation) committees are mandatory, and a governance committee is a good idea to handle director nominations and ensure that the board functions well. Beyond that, boards should create a fourth committee only when the business requires it—an environmental or public responsibility committee for a chemical company, for instance, or a safety committee for a railroad. Special topics can be handled by ad hoc committees formed to address the subject and be disbanded thereafter. Ad hoc committees are a useful way to tap a specific set of talents with a specific mission for a specific period. A proliferation of committees beyond the basics may be a signal that the board's energy is not focused and is being dissipated by unnecessary issues and details.

Redefining the role of an existing committee also can create opportunities to add value. At Bell Atlantic, for instance, the audit committee performs the usual function of ensuring that the company's controls are working, but it also acts as an internal consultant on best practices. It identifies organizational practices that could be improved and quantifies the savings that result. In the most recent year, the savings were far in excess of $50 million.

Boards that work well do not use committee membership or chairmanship as a signal of prestige. They understand the importance of assimilating new directors quickly and use committee memberships and chairmanships to speed the process. They put new board members on important committees right away, and they rotate committee chairs and members every two to three years to avoid concentrations of power. Jim Hagen also notes another benefit of frequent rotation: "The process has important implications for helping directors develop a depth and breadth of understanding. Committee service requires more frequent interaction, telephone follow-ups and the like with certain managers, so committee members develop deeper knowledge of the team and how the CEO's leadership is working."

Who Needs an Executive Committee?

The use of the executive committee to reinforce special relationships with the CEO and to award special privileges or prestige is out of date. In this day and age of telecommunications, executive committees are rarely needed and often do more harm than good. More than any other committee, the executive committee tends to lead to or reinforce a two-tier power structure that is a major drag on board dynamics.

A two-tier structure is not only bad for board dynamics but also risky from the perspective of director liability. Bob Hanna, director of NorAm, the natural gas company, says: "As a shareholder representative, I don't have any confusion at all about my responsibilities and to whom they accrue. I believe that if the shareholders have deemed it appropriate to elect thirteen members of the board, then they have the right to assume that thirteen members are going to contribute to it. And if they were chosen in the first place to give some diversity of opinions and a broader representation to the shareholders, then creating two classes of directors intentionally and categorically destroys the faith shareholders have put in the board."

Most boards that work have eliminated the executive committee altogether. NorAm is among them. CEO Milt Honea does not miss it: "I haven't had anything come up where I've felt the need for an executive committee. But when we had one, I think we had some hurt feelings by some of the board members who were excluded."

The trend is clear. When Ed Woolard became chairman of Du Pont, he eliminated the "powerful executive committee" that had been established by the three Du Pont brothers one hundred years before. GE had an executive committee in the 1970s. Not anymore.

Some boards have retained an executive committee for a very specific purpose. The FINOVA Group, like many other financial institutions, uses the executive committee to approve certain loans. NYNEX has an executive committee that has authority to act because of potential national security and disaster recovery issues. And Consolidated Natural Gas has one for emergencies only. At these boards, membership on the committee does not bring the board member any particular status or influence, and the committee's work is confined to those special circumstances. Consolidated Natural Gas CEO George Davidson adds, "Our executive committee has never met."

Sometimes a two-tier power structure evolves quite naturally, when, for instance, one group of directors has more business savvy than the others and participates more, or when the CEO relies on some more than others. One director explains: "There are instances where directors are on the board for reasons other than their business expertise. However conscientious and interested those people may be, they are perhaps limited from making a contribution. Those on the board who are better equipped to consider problems and projects evolve into a de facto executive committee. You might also have a CEO who has a select group of people he has recruited and whose opinions he trusts. Then again, they form an inner circle."

Tiers also can develop for geographic reasons or because of personal relationships with the CEO. Members of internal advisory boards often have unequal status depending on whether they come from inside or outside the company. And remember Bill Adams' comments on board size: A too-big board can lead to two tiers, those who are official board members and those who form the close-in team that carries the weight.

These situations can be prevented or eliminated through more objective nominating processes and more attention to keeping the board dynamics in balance. That is, every director should be recruited for his or her ability to contribute. As Bill Lichtenberger, chairman and CEO of Praxair (the Danbury, Connecticut, industrial gases company) and director of Ingersoll-Rand, says, "Where a wide variation in qualifications exists, it must be corrected over time."

Even if directors are on the board for other reasons, the chairman should draw them in. John Trani, chairman and CEO of Stanley Works, says, "Boards, like basketball teams, tend to have 'go to' people. Meanwhile, the rest of the organization would love to play, but they don't get asked. The more you get the others involved, the better they'll feel, and the more well-rounded the input."

Jack Krol, CEO of Du Pont and director of J.P. Morgan and Mead Corporation, says that the Mead board functions well in part because of the CEO-chairman's inclusiveness. "Steve Mason, the CEO, doesn't openly favor any factions on the board. As far as the optics go, we're all equal. We have some very senior people on the board. They do speak up, but it doesn't feel like they're overwhelming. Steve will listen and then turn to someone else for an opinion, so it doesn't look like a one-on-one conversation between him and the senior member."

Some might argue that a strong executive committee is necessary when the board itself is ineffective. True, committees often become the hotbed of debate when a board is not functioning well. Corporate governance, audit, and personnel and compensation committees (or their equivalents) are logical conduits for the feelings and ideas of all directors. More than one director has observed that the intricate dialogue often takes place at the committee level, where there is a lot of tough questioning and informal back-and-forth, whereas meetings of the full board are mostly formal presentations and perfunctory questions.

Reluctance to bring issues to the full board should be seen as symptomatic of a board that needs to develop its board dynamics. A CEO who sits on several boards describes a situation that is all too typical:

> I'm on one board of a very troubled company. One of the businesses has been struggling for a long time, and several CEOs of that business have taken the fall for it. I came to the conclusion that the chief executive had to take a broader view of the whole business context and come up with some alternative approaches. We couldn't just keep hiring new people.
>
> It turns out that two other directors who were on the compensation committee with me thought the way I did, and we started spending a lot of time in our committee meetings talking about the broader problems. We were acting more like an executive committee because we were the ones who seemed to care the most.

After airing and testing out their opinions, these committee members had to figure out how to bring the issues to the full board. When a board is functioning well and is really engaged, committee members don't have that dilemma. The dialogue is not limited to committee meetings or spontaneous gatherings outside the boardroom. Directors can express their opinions in the course of normal board deliberations. Relying on executive committees to compensate for the problem of an ineffective board is, as Praxair's Bill Lichtenberger says, "like trying to cure cancer with a Band-Aid."

No Lead Director

Boards at work make every director feel that his or her input is important to the dialogue. They try hard to avoid giving any individual special status. For that reason, they tend not to appoint a "lead director" when the roles of CEO and chairman are not split, despite the popularity of GM's 1994 corporate governance guidelines, which advocated the practice. Director Lois Juliber has observed that at Du Pont, different directors take the lead on different issues, depending on their interest and expertise. No one person has the designation of "lead director."

When a lead director exists, a smart CEO would want to confer with that person first before bringing an issue to the board as a whole. This wastes the CEO's time, puts distance between him or her and the other directors, and sacrifices speed, flexibility, and responsiveness. Plus, the lead director is in a position to interpret what each side says to the other and can inadvertently or willfully distort communications. A personal agenda—or even the suspicion of one—can breed distrust and factionalize the board. One multibillion dollar corporation had a lead director (not formally appointed but playing the role) who clashed with the CEO. Some board members sided with him, others with the CEO. The board, which was already having trouble reaching consensus, became almost totally paralyzed.

Some advocates of a lead director argue that the practice allows the CEO to concentrate on running the business rather than spending time communicating personally with the board. This argument fails to acknowledge that without communication, the CEO does not have a meaningful relationship and therefore is unlikely to derive value from the board's independent judgment and perspective.

Even when a "natural leader" appears to emerge, boards that work try to keep the personalities in balance. True, some people can appear to be naturally stronger or smarter than others, but it is highly unlikely that the thinking of any one individual is always more valuable than the collective input of a qualified board.

Sometimes individuals appear to have personal power that is not deserved. Sometimes a director's demeanor—the way he or she asks questions or positions himself or herself—makes the person appear to be more influential than others. Also, a chairman can create the perception that one director is more important than the others by going to the same person for advice every time. Past associations can also make one director's opinions carry more weight—when, for instance, the chairman of a Boeing or a GM sits on the board of a much smaller company.

The chairman and the other board members should draw out every member. One CEO-chairman learned this the hard way: "As chairman, you have to be careful not to drift to one or two powerful directors. There's a dynamic you have to think about. My guard is up because I was stung once. I had a strong director—a self-made man, very bright and articulate—and I found myself calling him for guidance fairly often. One morning I realized that he was taking us on a track that was wrong. So I pulled myself up and stopping relying on him so heavily. Sometimes it takes extra effort to draw out a quiet person. I think of it as being a teacher trying to draw out the bright kid in class who never says anything."

No Outside Director as Chairman

Separating the CEO and chairman roles can be even more detrimental to the board dynamics than appointing a lead director. The problems of communication layers and inefficiency still apply, but there is more. Board chairmanship has inherent implications of power that can lead to personal rivalries with the CEO. Even at GM, where outside director John Smale was named chairman in late 1992, the separation of titles was only temporary. Once Jack Smith felt he could devote the time to chairmanship of the board, John Smale stepped down.

Separating the role of CEO and chairman can create confusion and blur accountability. Outsiders might begin to wonder who is really in charge or whether the CEO is on the way out. Any misperceptions outside can erode the CEO's decision-making power internally as well.

Such role ambiguity flies in the face of good governance. "The board's role is to select the CEO and give him or her their full, unequivocal support," says General Electric Chairman and CEO Jack Welch. "They should closely monitor performance and take timely, appropriate action based on performance. It is important that the organization see a unified leadership of CEO and board, particularly in organizations undergoing significant change."

Many CEOs in the United Kingdom, where a separate chairman is the norm, complain privately of the inordinate amount of time they spend to align the chairman with their strategy. CEOs should be focusing on responding to fast changes in the industry, not on the process of internal lobbying, which creates no value.

Boards do need a mechanism to work independently of the CEO to address issues such as compensation and performance problems—and they have it in the form of board committees. The chairman of the organization and compensation committee, for instance, can, with the board's consent, require almost any information from the CEO and is well positioned to convey feedback from the board.

If the point is to be able to call or conduct meetings of outside directors, a committee chairman can serve that purpose. Board committee chairs are natural choices to head separate, formal meetings of outside directors. Robert Hauptfuhrer, former chairman and CEO of Dallas-based Oryx Energy Company and an experienced director of numerous boards, describes how it works at his company: "Directors meet two or three times a year to discuss any concerns a director may have. That portion of the meeting is chaired by the chair of the Board Policy and Nominating Committee. The chair subsequently reports, as appropriate, the substance of the meetings to the CEO. Chairs and members of committees rotate among the outside directors." Other boards use the "huddle" technique discussed in Chapter Seven to give outside directors the chance to talk without the CEO present.

Other recommendations throughout this book can help ensure the board's independence and prompt execution of its responsibilities. No one person should be assigned the task of raising sensitive issues or asking questions that might be considered impertinent. It is every director's responsibility to be vigilant, probing, and independent.

Are there ever situations for which an outside chairman makes sense? Yes, but they are rare and short-lived. One exceptional situation is when a new CEO needs time to focus on internal matters for a short time. Another is when the new CEO is planning to be in the job only a short while.

At one large industrial company, the board zeroed in on a future CEO who was not quite ready when the incumbent retired. That board appointed an interim CEO and retained the outgoing CEO as chairman to provide a steady hand and keep the succession process moving internally. The unusual arrangement worked because the chemistry between the CEO and chairman was exceptionally good and the chairman, keeping his ego in check, ran just the board, not the whole company.

Even when unusual circumstances call for the appointment of an outside chairman, the arrangement should be temporary, lasting only long enough to resolve the crisis or get through the transition. As soon as possible, the directors and CEO should get back to the core business of creating and maintaining the openness and candor that allows everyone at the table to be fully informed and intellectually engaged.

Segregate Formalities and Substance

The best board meetings are relentlessly focused on the kinds of substantive issues that require people to be in the same room, the ambiance is informal, and participation is balanced and purposeful. The agendas are designed to build the board's knowledge base cumulatively and to help the board focus on the critical issues. The dialogue sparks creativity and allows convergence of judgment.

Boards at work discuss corporate strategy in depth. If a board does not have such discussions, it is not working. Lois Juliber, executive vice president of Colgate-Palmolive and a director of Du Pont, says: "The pinnacle of a good board is one that in two or three hours covers the important issues, has a good dialogue, and maybe even strengthens management's recommendations."

Boards can allow more time for such discussion by holding fewer meetings, of longer duration, and decoupling them from the release of quarterly financial results. One director of the former Dun & Bradstreet captured a common sentiment among boards when he told the new CEO, "Don't send me the fluff. Send me the high, hard ones."

The once-a-month board meeting is falling by the wayside. A growing number of boards are moving to a schedule of six meetings a year of no less than six hours and an annual two- to three-day "retreat." The agenda items leading up to and during the two- to three-day meeting help prepare the board to dig into big issues such as company strategy.

Joseph T. Gorman, chairman and CEO of TRW, says: "I think there's a direct correlation between the number of meetings you have and the overall focus. The more meetings you have, the more tactical the issues that are discussed become. A well-structured, efficient board can handle the strategic issues in four or five meetings a year. At TRW, we have five meetings a year. The length varies for us. Generally, the meeting, together with the committee meetings, lasts a day and a half. We cover a lot of ground in that time, and the board loves it."

Boards miss the point if they reconfigure their calendar but spend the extra time listening to a parade of managers present endless details about the business. The quality and content of dialogue must be managed. Presentations by management can be (and often are) stultifying, or in the words of one director, "mind-numbing." The point of longer meetings is to allow more time for open questioning and intellectual give-and-take on key issues. George Davidson of CNG says, "We've reduced the number of board meetings from ten to eight, but we expanded the time available. The real point is to leave time for open discussion and debate."

Jerry Meyer says, "My experience, serving on other boards, has taught me that you can never underestimate the appetite outside directors have for substantive strategic discussion and board interaction on strategy." Bill Adams reinforces this point: "The reason for longer meetings is that you're trying to build a team that knows each other and has time for the full range of constructive discussion—not just present and react, present and react."

As chairman and CEO of Tektronix, Meyer has redesigned the board calendar. The board now meets six times a year, once at the end of each quarter, once for discussion and approval of an annual plan, and once for discussion and approval of the long-term strategy. Meetings generally last four hours and focus on strategic issues. Meyer says, "I feel that the board can read the financials. We don't need to deal with them as a group, unless something unusual comes up. We try to communicate more about what's happening in operations to deliver the financials and how our actions tie back to the strategy of the company. We attempt to look ahead, with the board giving forecasts and assessing risks and issues.

"In the past," Meyer continues, "we had some board members who would have liked to have spent the entire meeting on the numbers. We occasionally had to remind ourselves as a board that management is there to manage operations and the board's role is to govern, to ensure that management is doing its job and the company has a strategy that makes sense."

Ivan Seidenberg of NYNEX explains a technique he uses to ensure that strategic discussions do not get cut short: "One thing I learned from another director is to say that the meeting will go to 6 P.M. and then finish at 5 P.M. You build in the extra time just in case you need it to discuss something you didn't anticipate. Also, I have an executive session at the end of every meeting, just to check to see if there's anything on anyone's mind. At the last meeting, a couple of items came up in the executive session, which were dealt with right away. Then we sat and gabbed for ten minutes and everyone left."

Anything that is purely informational or pro forma (not expected to require any discussion, such as routine dividend payments, approval of auditors, or other compliance issues) should be sent to board members ahead of time and handled quickly at the beginning or end of the board meeting or, when possible, telephonically. Praxair CEO Bill Lichten-berger said, "In this age of telecommunication and video conferencing, you can pull the whole board together from any place in the world for a telephone conference. I just had one last night!"

Royal Bank of Canada uses a consent agenda to free up meeting time for matters of strategic importance. The consent agenda includes "housekeeping items," such as routine executive appointments or cer-tain smaller capital expenditures that can be explained on paper. Jane Lawson, senior vice president and secretary of Royal Bank of Canada, explains: "The consent agenda is circulated prior to board meetings as part of a comprehensive package of information and executive sum-maries relating to matters to be dealt with at the meeting. Any director who wishes may move any of the matters slated for the consent agenda onto the main agenda for board discussion."

At some boards, items not requiring lengthy discussion are handled by telephone conference. In connection with a routine issue, for exam-ple, one board chairman "attended" a committee meeting by phone while traveling to a remote location. It took all of three minutes. The chairman of another board that used the telephone to handle routine board issues said, "Directors claim they don't like phone meetings, but we save a lot of time that way, and it cuts down on their travel."

A schedule of six board meetings allows ample time for these large, complex corporations to cover all the important business areas. Then management can use "board retreats" to show how the pieces fit together.

Use Board Retreats for Breakthrough Thinking

Two- or three-day off-site meetings, generally called "board retreats" but more appropriately called "breakthrough sessions," are an increas-ingly popular mechanism for giving boards time for open discussion. Designed and conducted properly, a two-day off-site meeting is the sin-gle best mechanism for making breakthroughs of many kinds, from transforming the board dynamics to discovering flaws in the strategy and launching the company onto a whole new trajectory. It also allows for bonding and sensing management depth.

Given an open, informal atmosphere and a foundation of knowledge, directors will use the time to probe company strategy, challenge the underlying assumptions, and stretch management's and each other's thinking. The intellectual exchange gets all but the most complacent directors engaged. As the energy level builds, new ideas and insights begin to emerge and whole new patterns of behavior develop. The intellectual challenge is stimulating, and the learning is collective.

Breakthrough sessions draw the best out of the board. The longer time frame provides what regular board meetings typically lack—depth, continuity, occasion for informal discussion and relationship building, and time to put issues into a broader context and to link them to people and actions. These two- or three-day breakthrough sessions are powerful because they offer something no other meeting or combination of meetings can provide: total immersion. Over the course of the two days, directors and top managers become totally immersed in the most complex issues affecting the business.

Total immersion during Avenor's 1997 retreat (the Canadian paper company) helped the board make several contributions to the strategy, such as the suggestions to go international through alliances and to evaluate options for participating in the industry restructuring. At the former Dun & Bradstreet's board retreat, the board had its first visceral sense of the cataclysmic change that was sweeping the industry. At Consolidated Natural Gas's board retreat, the board convinced management to compress its four-year plan into one year because the investment community would not wait. And at KeraVision's board retreat in 1996, management and the board explored how to retain senior management and adjust board composition as the company prepared to commercialize its new medical technology and enter a new phase in its growth cycle.

Breakthrough sessions also pave the way for more open exchange at regular board meetings. Michael Hall, KeraVision's general counsel, says, "KeraVision's board retreats have helped the board get to know the management team. At the same time, they've helped our management team become more comfortable with the board. Consequently, there's more meaningful dialogue, so we get more from our directors than other companies—not just at the retreats but also during regular board meetings. Board retreats translate into greater productivity and engagement all the time."

Directors sometimes balk at the idea of an off-site meeting because they view it as a boondoggle and an inefficient use of time, but boards that have experienced a successful retreat, or breakthrough session, are quick to institutionalize the practice. At the end of the former D&B's first-ever board retreat, one director remarked: "We've never been as energized as we have been in the past two days. We should do it again." At the end of Conrail's first retreat in 1994, management and the board enthusiastically scheduled another. The second was equally successful. Dave LeVan, president of Conrail in 1994 and now chairman and CEO, says, "You almost have to go through a two-day session to understand the kinds of things that can come out."

Reflecting on the September 1997 two-day board retreat, the third of its kind for Royal Bank of Canada, CEO John Cleghorn concludes: "The directors' insights and convergence on three key points helped expand management's thinking. Directors listened to each other's ideas and moved them forward. Out of such a large group of directors, with Royal Bank officers sitting among them at small tables, came creative new ideas and penetrating questions. The retreat was in totality energizing and exciting and definitely caused the bank to think in different terms. This retreat was markedly more participative and value-adding than the earlier ones. It was a great learning experience for the board and the management team."

Turning a retreat into a breakthrough session requires a highly focused agenda and an informal, relaxed ambiance. A CFO who attended his company's first board retreat noted, "Directors could feel that it wasn't rushed." Jack Krol of Du Pont made a similar comment about Mead's two-and-a-half-day meetings: "You can discuss things in a relaxed way, without the time pressure."

While good breakthrough sessions allow time for people to socialize and build relationships, which enhance the openness of the dialogue, the expectation and sense of purpose must be sharply focused on company strategy or other important top-level issues, like succession planning. As Conrail Chairman and CEO Dave LeVan says, "The whole thing has to be business based. That's why we don't provide for golf or other activities. It is strictly a working session. And we set that expectation up front."

Jack Krol says, "The retreat gives you a chance to do things together, whether it's in the meeting room or on a boat ride or sitting on the porch. The constant contact helps you become more comfortable with each other and makes people more willing to speak out."

Krol is quick to add, however, that relationship-building is secondary to the main focus: "You have to make sure that the better part of the session is spent working on the business. If it begins to feel like a vacation, then you've lost the value of it."

Efforts to build a base of understanding for directors should begin long before the breakthrough session itself. Meetings leading up to the session should lay the foundation. Ideally, they should give the board a full picture of the industry, the competition, and the company's own strategic positioning. At Conrail, for instance, an hour or two of every meeting throughout the year is spent laying out one or more parts of the business. These meetings are the building blocks on which the full, two-day discussion of corporate strategy is based. (See Chapter Five for more on informing the board.)

Creating the right ambiance requires careful attention to the many small things that enhance dialogue or cast an icy chill on board deliberations, such as the seating arrangement. Seat twelve directors at a long, elliptical table in order of seniority with no invitation to speak and the discussion is likely to be stiff and guarded. Seat them in small groups or in an open circle, and the ideas will begin to flow. Bank of America, at its board retreats, arranges directors in groups of three around coffee tables. Conrail sat two directors at a small table with one or two managers and arranged the small tables in a semicircle.

Seating people at small tables allows for a technique for developing the dialogue: the discussion leader can ask directors and managers to discuss issues among themselves for a few minutes before bringing their ideas to the full group. This process tends to draw out directors who are more reluctant to speak out and keeps participation balanced.

Because the real value comes from insights and ideas that emerge spontaneously from open dialogue, the person who conducts the retreat should be skilled at drawing people out, keeping participation balanced, and keeping the discussion moving. Although the board chairman can lead the breakthrough session, a third party often is in a better position to set the tone when the board has not had this kind of meeting before and does not regularly engage in open dialogue. The very fact of having an outsider as a facilitator sends a signal that the meeting will not be business-as-usual. The facilitator's skill in getting people involved creates new patterns of participation and contribution that carry over into regular board meetings.

Good facilitators not only can help sort through and record the key points and reactions but also can encourage the directors to push back on each other's thinking with comments such as, "What would be the pro's and con's of doing it that way?" or "Can you expand on Joe's point?" Their objectivity makes it possible to redirect the discussion without appearing to be manipulative (a risk when the board chairman leads the meeting).

A good breakthrough session typically begins with summary presentations by senior management of topics that have been discussed throughout the year. After each, the group should have a chance to react and ask questions, and the key points should be recorded on flip charts that remain in view throughout the two-day session.

As the session progresses from one topic—or piece of the strategy—to another and directors become more comfortable asking questions and speaking out, the discussion tends to deepen. The directors and managers get more and more engaged, and the energy level builds. This is the phenomenon to which everyone who has attended a successful breakthrough session can attest. Even the most skeptical or most reticent directors are drawn in. The social barriers crumble, the discussion spills over into dinner and breakfast the next morning, and the creative sparks begin to fly.

By the time the group comes together the second day, it is ready to pull together the issues and concerns that are spelled out on flip charts across the front of the meeting room. A few key questions during the last few hours can break new ground and bring closure to the whole session:

- What is your comfort or discomfort with the strategy?
- How do you feel about the assumptions about the external environment?
- What are your feelings about the ability of this team to execute the proposed strategy?
- What is your view of the company's management talent?
- What questions are we not asking that we should be asking? What are the "untalkables"?

Conrail's Two-Day Breakthroughs

The Conrail board has held two two-day meetings, one in 1994 to discuss the company's first strategic plan and one in 1996, during which the board explored the option to merge with CSX. Directors and management concur that the off-site meetings allowed the board to wrestle with and resolve issues that were directly linked to the company's future.

Former Conrail Chairman Jim Hagen describes Conrail's first off-site retreat in 1994: "We accomplished a tremendous amount of work in those two days. We had an executive session the first evening to discuss Dave LeVan's appointment as president, and from then on, there was only one topic up for discussion: the company's strategic plan. Our entire yearlong agenda had been designed to cover all the major pieces. At the off-site session, we wanted to show how the pieces came together and get the board's reaction."

After quick overviews of 1994 performance and the strategic planning process, the heads of Conrail's four service groups made fifteen-minute presentations updating the board on developments in their areas. After lunch, the transportation, mechanical, and engineering departments made their presentations. Each was followed by an invitation for the board to comment and ask questions. Hagen and his team answered whatever questions they could and made notes of issues they would continue to work on. No one became defensive or hostile.

When the board reconvened Friday morning and focused on Conrail's future, the discussion really deepened. One director pointed to the assumptions underlying the financial analysis: "You're showing us the averages in GDP growth and other economic changes, but the Federal Reserve could push us into recession in year one. What's Plan B in case the Fed raises rates again?" A few directors asked questions about safety, and soon the board and management were discussing the company's core values.

By the end of the day, the board's contribution was clear. Challenging some of the economic assumptions spurred management to do a sensitivity analysis, and management ultimately came back with a better plan. Contingency planning has since become a regular part of Conrail's planning process. The board's emphasis on safety caused, in Dave LeVan's words, "a post-retreat quantum shift in the intensity of managing safety." Top management got more company officers involved and made a hard-dollar investment in safety, which each division could spend at their discretion without having to justify it in ROI terms. The board also questioned the high capital investment per sales dollar characteristic of the industry, suggested more focus on cash flow, and asked that customer satisfaction be tracked monthly and reported to the board.

The board's feedback was captured in a five-page document, which the CEO used as a guide for follow-up actions. It was clear, succinct, and very constructive. Management implemented all of the board's suggestions.

Would these contributions to Conrail have emerged through the course of regular board meetings? Hagen thinks not. And he emphasizes that the two-day session kick started the board dynamics, paving the way for the board's ongoing contribution.

In a letter to directors following the retreat, Hagen said: "What made the meeting so special and exciting for me was the informality and total candor which somehow does not seem attainable in the set place of the usual Board meeting. The dialogue helped management focus on the critical issues. . . . In short, I believe that this meeting demonstrated that the working together of Conrail's Board and management has risen to a new level."

The 1994 retreat was so successful that Conrail scheduled another for September 1996. It, too, was a significant event for the company and the board. By then, Dave LeVan had become chairman and CEO, and coincidentally, an industry consolidation was underway and Conrail was considering a merger with CSX Corp. LeVan explains: "The industry was restructuring, and we had some significant decisions to make. We used the long time frame of the meeting to analyze what was driving the consolidation from the customer perspective and how we could achieve our greatest value, by remaining independent or seeking a strategic alternative.

"We spent our time exploring the options," LeVan continues, "occasionally stopping to remind ourselves that while the outside world might view us critically in the short term, we wanted to reach the conclusion that we believed was right. We considered a variety of perspectives, which Pennsylvania law provides for, such as the short- and long-term and the impact on all constituencies, not just shareholders."

LeVan contends that the two-day format was absolutely essential to the board's ability to find consensus. The depth of the discussion informed subsequent decisions about the ensuing industry consolidation. "If you had taken a poll on Day One, you would have found that every director had his or her own view of which option was best," he says. "At times, the debate became very heated, in the right sense of the word. But by the end of the two days, we had a very clear consensus.

"You couldn't have taken this issue in bits and pieces," LeVan adds. "You had to roll up your sleeves and work it all the way through. It required a full two days to do it."

Cracking the Code of Inclusion at "Wynnet, Inc."

This board found a way to break the two-tier power structure that kept some directors silent and passive.[1]

In the early 1990s, Wynnet, Inc., had the kind of board that drives investors crazy. The large utility company had it all: high debt, poor op-

---

[1]This case describes a real situation. Names and some details have been disguised.

erating results, overall financial performance far below the industry average, a plummeting stock price—and a board that seemed determined to look the other way.

When the existing chairman and CEO left the company to pursue other opportunities, the board recruited Mark Smith, an outsider, to replace him. The new CEO believed directors should be involved in the business issues at hand and accountable to shareholders for company performance. Every director, he believed, should participate in board discussions, "otherwise it's like boxing with one hand."

The Wynnet board, however, was used to board meetings that were devoid of substance. Influence was exerted behind the scenes by a handful of outside directors on the executive committee who had a special relationship with the CEO. The CEO would get the committee members on the phone and make a decision. The rest of the board would find out about it a month later at the regular board meeting.

Smith recalls his surprise when he discussed with the board a multi-million-dollar contract one of his predecessors had given senior employees. "This contract was very expensive, very difficult to live with, and very difficult to get out of. I was shocked to learn that many board members had never seen any part of it. We all had to undergo a lot of criticism for it."

Smith was determined to fix the board dynamics, which meant overcoming a major obstacle: the insidious two-tier power structure cemented by Wynnet's committee structure. The board had two distinct groups, or tiers, of directors—those who were on the executive committee and those who were not. Even when the full board met, only the directors in the first tier spoke up. Other directors had gotten the signal that their opinions were not important. Those who were in the first tier never stopped to think about the imbalance; those in the second tier had no voice to raise the issue.

Changing a board's power structure is a difficult and sensitive task. Wynnet was able to do it when several factors converged: a progressive CEO, intense external pressure, and the conscience and insight of a powerful director.

Those Who Mattered, Those Who Didn't

When Smith became chairman and CEO, he did not know how much board support he really had. Did the one-time chairman, who was still on the board, harbor resentment toward him? "I tiptoed around very carefully at the first board meetings," he said, "but I did have a structure in mind. I explained my ideas for turning the business around, and I periodically stopped to invite comments. We had interesting discussions and made lots of decisions. It was pretty obvious that we were really going to get something done, and people seemed to like it."

Though some board members were fully engaged, about half the board seemed uninterested in and unprepared to discuss the business issues. Many directors had been recruited for reasons other than their business expertise, such as their political connections. When Smith asked some of the quiet individuals a question, they often had useful things to say. He just couldn't seem to jar them out of their complacency.

A turning point came in 1995, when Smith and several board members attended a workshop on corporate governance at a prominent business school. Smith was skeptical about the directors' motivation in attending the session. "I didn't know whether they were going because they were truly interested in change or because it sounded like an interesting thing to do."

The workshop reinforced Smith's own beliefs about how a board should function and created an ally in Hal Murdock, chairman of Wynnet's executive committee. Murdock had never given much thought to the impact of an executive committee on the rest of the board, probably because he had been on the executive committee of almost every board he had served on. At the workshop, he had a revelation that gave him and the CEO a common focal point for transforming the Wynnet board.

Murdock recalls: "Someone said that the best way to fracture a board was to have an executive committee. That kind of shocked me. I knew there were matters that had been discussed with our executive committee that were not discussed with the full board and information that had not been available to the full board, but I didn't realize that those practices, generally speaking, create two classes—those who are important and those who are not. That came over me like a cold shower and offended me quite substantially."

Murdock asked several members of the Wynnet board who were not members of the executive committee if they felt unimportant and disenfranchised. Indeed they did. Murdock had not sensed it. "People had maintained their own counsel and never said anything about it," Murdock said. "And quite frankly, I had no inkling that this was the case. That just sealed it for me. I believe in equality and democracy, so it didn't take me long to decide that I would suggest that we not have an executive committee. In any case, I would not be on it if there were one."

Smith returned from the workshop to draft a set of guidelines on corporate governance, which the board subsequently discussed, revised, and adopted (GM's set of governance guidelines had been widely publicized over the previous year). The guidelines laid out a new committee structure, one designed to keep the board dynamics in balance.

Rethinking What Committees Do

Wynnet's new committee structure consisted of five committees: audit, compensation and benefits, investment, environmental, and governance. The nominating and executive committees were dissolved. On Murdock's strong recommendation, the guidelines specified that all non-employee directors would be members of the newly created governance committee.

The governance committee would do everything the executive committee did and more—review the CEO annually, review major acquisitions, function as a nominating committee, and review the board's own performance once a year. The compensation and benefits committee would comprise outside directors only and recommend executive compensation. The fact that all the compensation committee members were also on the governance committee created linkage between discussions of performance and pay for the CEO and senior officers.

Executive committee members had no problem letting go of their special status, nor did Smith have any qualms about losing the executive committee. "Each time we needed a telephone call to approve something like a major acquisition, it was just as easy to get the whole board, and the group clearly preferred that. Getting a quorum would not be a problem either. We'd have to have six members of our governance committee to have a quorum. We felt we could do that in emergencies. A quorum of the executive committee would have been four—a small difference."

Making the governance committee responsible for board nominations solved another problem. The board's nominating committee was chaired by an outside director with long tenure and high status who was comfortable with the status quo. As several board members prepared to retire and new candidates were discussed, he did not see any need to change the criteria. Whereas Smith and some others wanted to attract a new breed of director to fill agreed-on gaps in the board's knowledge and experience, the nominating committee chairman wanted to tap the same old networks.

"We just couldn't seem to convince him that we wanted somebody different," Smith said, "and working around him was a little tricky. Changing the committee structure gave us a fresh start with board composition as well. The governance committee could create a new set of criteria for new members."

The compensation and benefits committee, on the other hand, had been a model of good governance. Smith explains: "Our predecessors had very complex, very generous formulas for perks and benefits and salary, which we had just put an end to when the new SEC constraints came along. The compensation committee spent countless hours working on the new formula for compensation. They didn't just show up and let the staff member and his outside advisors do all the work. The committee said, 'Tell us what you've got,' and then they'd study the details and debate them."

Smith credits much of the committee's diligence to the committee chairman's leadership. "He didn't dominate the group, nor did he sit back and abdicate," Smith says. "He always made sure he got the data from staff in advance and spent two or three days going over it, so he was even better prepared to lead a discussion. That was the best committee we had."

Around that time, one of the activist pension funds noted that Wynnet had failed to perform and criticized the company's governance practices. Outsiders didn't know that the new committee structure and governance guidelines were being finalized or that the board dynamics had already begun to change. Before the new committees had actually met, Smith could sense "a higher degree of comfort and participation" among board members. "The board members who were strong continued to be so. Those who used to just come to the meetings and leave became more active and involved. And even those whose skills and backgrounds didn't meet the new requirements starting speaking up more."

An Accidental Hierarchy

The Wynnet board obliterated one kind of hierarchy but inadvertently created another. When Hal Murdock became chairman of the newly created governance committee, he was given the title "lead director." The position gave Murdock a certain amount of power he was not seeking and stirred resentment among some board members. It also caused the CEO to question whether he had gone too far in empowering the board.

Murdock explains how he got the title: "When we created the governance committee, we needed someone to coordinate, or lead, the activities of the outside directors. That's how I became the lead director. I don't really know what it means, and I don't think our shareholders really do either. I guess that's the fellow on the dog sled team that runs first and doesn't get quite so much mud in his eye."

Smith remembers a few occasions when the designation seemed to create some ambiguity about Murdock's role. At times, Murdock himself seemed a bit unsure about his role. He sometimes acted more forceful than usual in board meetings and at one point appeared on the verge of crossing the line with corporate staff. Alert to the need to keep governance apart from operations, Smith responded quickly. He describes what happened:

"Through all the changes, Hal was doing a lot of extra work and was frequently in the office. One time when Hal was there and I wasn't, he asked some people on our management team to prepare some reports to use for a special project. I had two concerns. First, he didn't realize that a lot of that information was already available in other forms, so we didn't need to create new documents. Second, I didn't think it was appropriate for the lead director to assign work to the senior officers without the CEO knowing about it."

Smith addressed the issue. He suggested ways the staff could accommodate Murdock's request without creating a lot of extra work. Then he presented the material to Murdock to see if it was okay. Smith says, "Hal was pleased, the staff was spared the extra work, and the CEO was back in the loop."

Smith also improved his skill at managing the line between exerting leadership over the group and being democratic. "Sometimes the directors would reach an impasse, and they'd look at me and ask me for an answer. I'd try to make a statement that didn't abdicate my responsibility to make a recommendation but also didn't cut off discussion prematurely. As long as the debate continued, the board could eventually reach agreement. Even board members with very strong opinions who you think would never back down ended up agreeing."

The Wynnet board now conducts a self-evaluation once a year. It has recruited four new board members by using new criteria, and it holds an annual board retreat. But Smith contends that the most important breakthrough in their corporate governance has to do with the board dynamics: "We broke the code of inclusion versus exclusion. By educating the whole board about the business and giving everyone a chance to react, we've created the kind of chemistry that allows open debate. That is what makes this board effective."

Key Points

- The full board—not committees—must wrestle with issues such as company strategy and CEO selection. Keep committees to a minimum, make board meetings longer (and fewer) to allow the board to dig in, and use telephone conferences and "consent agendas" to get procedural matters out of the way.

- Executive committees are a relic of the past. They make some board members feel less important and balanced participation harder to achieve.

- "Lead directors" and nonexecutive chairmen send subtle signals about power and importance. They are not needed. Use existing mechanisms to accomplish the same goal, and focus on the real key to good governance: the board dynamics.

- Kick start the board dialogue with a facilitated retreat or "breakthrough session." Breakthrough sessions help people overcome their reluctance to get engaged and increase their desire to contribute. Good board dynamics are set in motion.

CHAPTER FOUR

STACKING THE BOARD WITH TALENT

The power of the board as a competitive weapon depends on the quality and diversity of directors. Without the right composition, the dialogue may never take off, the board's competitive power may never get released. In some cases, directors do not have—perhaps have lost—the intellectual edge that comes from frequent skirmishes in a fast-changing business environment. In a few rare instances, well-planned breakthrough sessions have flopped because none of the board members possessed the intellectual edge and energy to cut through the issues.

The criteria for board service must be designed around the notions of active engagement and balanced participation. Each director should have something important to contribute and should be able to function well in a group of equals. Boards must be on the offensive to attract and recruit the very best directors for the company and the board at that particular point in time. As John Trani, chairman and CEO of Stanley Works, says: "It should be a situation-specific board, not an old-boys'-network-forever board."

The old boys' network is indeed waning. Ask any of the major head-hunting firms. Many boards are taking a hard look at the criteria for board nomination. Some are going to great lengths to achieve diversity in the conventional sense of race, gender, and ethnicity. Some go further to find diversity in perspective, experience base, geography, age, and even personal style. Diversity, however, cannot come at the expense of good board dynamics. Chemistry matters.

Are all the good directors taken? Not at all. When the criteria, not personal relationships, drive the search, new directors—including qualified women and ethnic minorities who are eager to serve on boards that allow them to contribute and learn—turn up in surprising places. Some small entrepreneurial company boards are even having success attracting Fortune 100 CEOs because of the tremendous opportunity for learning. Indeed, the benefit of crossing over between big and small companies is becoming more widely recognized, thus creating exciting opportunities for companies of all types and sizes.

Orientation programs and other simple mechanisms make it easy for new directors to participate right away. Paying attention to the social dynamics associated with being on a board is also helpful for getting the best out of new members.

What to Look For

More than ever, outside directors control the process of nominating new board members. Board nominating committees, whose membership is increasingly restricted to outside directors only, are working with search firms and extending the invitation to new members. The CEO typically meets the candidates to test the chemistry. Any hint of bad chemistry between the CEO and the nominee should take the person out of the running. George Davidson, CEO of Consolidated Natural Gas, says of the directors brought onto his board in the past five years, "They are not people I brought forth. Some of them I not only didn't know but had never even heard of before our process." He adds, "The independence of the process is vitally important."

What drives the search process is just as important as who drives it. As John Reed of Citicorp says, "You can't leave the membership of the board to chance." The search criteria are all important. Getting the criteria right may be the only hope of changing the genetic code of an outdated board and creating or preserving an active, participatory, value-adding board. The board should articulate its needs and expectations for new members and then list the criteria (see "Expectations of Board Members for Value Creation" and "Should This Person Be on Our Board?" at the end of this chapter).

Boards need, first and foremost, people who are keen business people who can cut through complexity. "Good" directors are combat tested. They have demonstrated that they can take into account and incorporate many perspectives at once and that their judgments are sound. They are not intimidated by technology, are on the front lines making decisions in a fast-changing and unforgiving environment, and are willing to dig into difficult issues. They have the guts to ask tough questions. And they are often described by others as incisive. (Incisiveness is a rare quality overall but one that is common among good directors.)

The majority of board members should be actively engaged in their profession, because their information will be current and their mental capacity sharp. As Alex Mandl, chairman and CEO of Teligent (formerly Associated Communications) and director of Warner-Lambert and other boards, says, "There's a crispness that comes with being in the battle." Marshall Turner, a venture capitalist who has served on twenty-two boards, adds another piece of advice. He says that start-ups, especially those with relatively inexperienced CEOs, should be wary of directors who are underemployed former CEOs "because they are rarely supportive of the CEO if trouble hits. They tend to conclude too quickly that they could do a better job."

Global diversity is essential, and boards can find it. Ed Hotard, president of Praxair and director of Dexter, emphasizes this need: "Particularly as U.S. companies expand in Asia, they need to get an Asian on the board. Some boards have benefited from having a European or a Latin American, but few have recruited directors who understand Asia from the Asian perspective." Another CEO who is trying to grow the business in part through global expansion said of his board, "For several years now I've been telling the board that our industry is facing major changes and we have to expand internationally. But because few of them have direct international experience, instead of asking how we're going to be successful globally, how we're going to get good people, and what the critical success factors are, they're sitting back and worrying."

The National Association of Corporate Directors lists certain other "givens," such as integrity, time (no more than three boards for an active CEO), and independence (no conflict of interest or interlocking directorships). Its "Report of the NACD Blue Ribbon Commission on Director Professionalism" elaborates on these points.

Not all criteria should be generic, however. The criteria should help define people who can help with the company's current challenges. Bob Weissman, chairman and CEO of Cognizant and of the former Dun & Bradstreet, says: "Let's assume I am the CEO of Netscape and I'm dealing with the typical mix of business issues—changes in the marketplace, the competitive mix, changes in cost dynamics being driven externally. If I have on my board five experienced, intelligent people, all of whom have spent thirty years working in a slow-moving, regulated industry, they won't be able to help me much. Not that they're incompetent or disinterested. They just won't understand my market, my customers, or the dynamics of a highly fragmented and competitive marketplace simply because they have no experience with it."

KeraVision, the venture capital–funded medical technology company, sought very particular skills in its new directors as the company went through various developmental phases (see the case at the end of this chapter for more detail). AMP, the world's leading manufacturer of electrical connectors, developed a plan to recruit a complementary range of talent as it prepared for the imminent retirements of more than half its directors. CNG's George Davidson says, "The backgrounds of our directors have evolved over the past ten years because the business has evolved. The danger of not opening up the field is that you're not going to get current competencies going ahead in the business mix."

At one large utility company, the CEO inherited a board that was "full of people who were local and politically oriented," who had been recruited in a different era. The CEO explains: "My predecessors believed that to make money in this business, you had to have political influence so regulators would be lenient about rates. When I had to make decisions about our distribution strategy or our compensation strategy, I was on my own. Some of the directors had been in politics all their life. They couldn't help me." This CEO worked closely with the board to redefine the criteria and recruit a new breed of director who could help with business issues.

The CEO of another utility that was facing the need to adjust to structural changes in the industry felt his board's conservatism was a competitive disadvantage. The board had a hard time recognizing important growth opportunities and was sometimes inhibited from getting involved in business issues for fear of legal liability.

In choosing directors, diversity is important. Lodewijk de Vink, president of Warner-Lambert and director of Bell Atlantic, makes this point: "The board is essentially a teaching institute that helps the CEO avoid making major mistakes. Therefore, the board should have members come from various industries. That way, when a problem occurs, the CEO and other directors can draw on that person's experience. Look at Exxon's Larry Rawl, a director of Warner-Lambert and other companies, who was leading Exxon when oil went from $30 a barrel to $18 a barrel and had to restructure his business. What are the implications for pharmaceutical companies like Warner-Lambert when we go from high prices to dramatically lower prices?"

Praxair CEO Bill Lichtenberger had the chance to create a board from scratch when the industrial gases company was spun off from Union Carbide in 1991. Diversity was one of his main objectives: "I wanted a board that was diverse enough so that whatever subject came up—whether it was safety performance or leverage financing or doing business in China—at least one board member's eyes would light up and that person would say, 'Hey, that's an area I understand.' If someone has something to contribute by virtue of experience, chances are they're going to speak up, and the flow starts."

While Lichtenberger wanted diversity, he also wanted good chemistry: "I had to think beyond how the person related to me and consider how he or she would fit in with the rest of the board. I wanted people who were comfortable with each other and were willing to speak their mind and respect each other. Could these people communicate in such a manner as to not put off the other person from adding to the dialogue? Could they bind together for the same goals?"

When Lichtenberger wanted a board member who understood the perspective of the investment community, he shied away from investment bankers because he didn't think the chemistry would work. Instead, he recruited Dale Frey, who at the time was running GE Investments.

Qualitative search criteria, such as personality, the ability to work as part of a team, or attitude and orientation are important and should be made explicit. One CEO describes the benefits of having the right personality mix:

> Our board runs from an individual scientist to active CEOs and a retired CEO and retired vice chairman of a mega-company, all of whom have different personalities. One guy is extremely aggressive and tends to be the one who brings up controversial points and really pushes them. Two other directors came out of regulated industries and are careful and conservative. They tend to look at the whole problem and take a very studied view of things. Then there's another director who tends to be very pragmatic. He always seems to know when it's the right time to sum things up and say, "Here's what we have to do."
>
> If you didn't have someone to poke needles in things, you wouldn't have as many discussions. If you didn't have the conservative types to take a more studied approach, I would worry that you might jump to conclusions. If you didn't have somebody with a penchant to wrap it up and reach a good decision, we'd never have closure. All together, the mix makes for a very effective group.

John Reed describes one of the Citicorp board members as "a natural child who is intensely curious about everything, asks a lot of questions, and causes the discussion to be more substantive than it might otherwise be. His disruptive influence on the board is very welcome."

Ed Hotard of Praxair describes a fellow director of Dexter who is head of chemistry at MIT as "an out-of-the-box business thinker and a significant contributor with creative, innovative thinking and challenges."

Venture capitalist Marshall Turner says to look for people who have participated in group tasks, "because the board is a group task," and for those who are willing to act on behalf of all shareholders, not a particular constituency. Bob Hanna, a director of Houston-based NorAm Energy Corporation, says discussions about corporate governance can help screen out candidates who may become micro-managers later: "With the proper selection of directors and the proper orientation, there's a chance to preclude some of the people who cross the line from observing and understanding to intruding."

Boards can and should go hard on the issue of racial, gender, ethnic, and global diversity but not at the expense of other criteria. With so many qualified women and minorities in business today, boards can find candidates who are African-American or female or have a global perspective and also can contribute to the corporation in a meaningful way. New York–based Catalyst, for instance, has long lists of women qualified to make substantive contributions to a board. CEO John Reed says, "You can't have a European on the board who doesn't bring you anything, just because you have a tradition of having a European. Pretty soon the board dynamics don't work."

Insistence on the criteria can force the board and its headhunting firm to seek candidates from nontraditional sources, generally meaning candidates outside the realm of existing relationships and the ranks of prominent CEOs. When NYNEX needed new board members with consumer marketing experience and international experience, it managed to find a CEO of a financial institution in Puerto Rico, a chief operating officer of a global company with a background in Europe, and an African-American who was president of the National Urban League. When Du Pont needed a woman and consumer marketing experience, they found Lois Juliber, who was running Colgate-Palmolive's North American division. These directors had no previous relationship with the CEO.

Search Unconventional Sources

Conventional wisdom holds that good directors are hard to find, but when boards hit dead ends it is often because they turn to the same old sources. Many boards that work have recruited new members who are not household names but who meet all the important criteria and have successfully passed all the due diligence checking. Sometimes the new recruits have not served on a board before or are on only one other board. What the new recruits may lack in terms of board experience they make up for by bringing a fresh intellectual edge, new ideas, and broad business experience. Consider the following sources.

Other Number Ones and Twos

Many people who run big businesses never appear on lists of CEOs because they do not have the CEO title. They are division managers running a great business inside a corporation, whether for a geographic region or for a business line. These people are often CEOs in their own right, running a profit and loss (P&L) and balance sheet, having to deal with fast change, being externally oriented, and taking the broad view of a general manager—all excellent qualifications for today's boards. Many have had to build a business on the fringe of the main business, which requires a track record of creating networks, often globally.

Jack Welch, early in his career, grew the plastics business at GE, then on the periphery of GE's main businesses. He would have been an excellent director back then. When Warner-Lambert asked Alex Mandl, formerly of AT&T, to join its board, Mandl was not CEO but president of a unit. He met all the qualifications. Similarly, when Du Pont asked Lois Juliber to join its board, she was doing a superb job as president of a $1.7 billion division within Colgate. In 1997, the GM board named a division manager of Pfizer to its board.

Any corporation that has a P&L type organizational structure, such as GE, Allied Signal, or Emerson Electric, is a potential source of directors.

Headhunters, personal networks, or the Conference Board with its organizational charts can help identify this population. Then look for the criteria the board has defined.

Some might argue that the relatively young age of these candidates might make them impatient, less tactful, and more susceptible to political and social pressures. There are people out there who are tougher than nails, however, and the screening process can sort them out. Many have strong values and tremendous confidence in a peer group. Besides, many have experience interacting with the board at their own companies.

If boards are concerned that these younger candidates may not have cultivated the judgment and insight of a good director, they can use their personal networks to check their track records. Reference checking should not focus solely on accomplishments but also include questions about how the person handles himself or herself in a group and whether the person's reputation has been earned by self-achievement or by riding on others' coattails. And of course a board can try to balance young directors with others who are older and more seasoned. The younger directors will bring vibrancy and energy that is more in tune with the daunting challenges of dramatic external change. The more experienced directors will provide the steady hand and wisdom.

When Conrail discovered Gail McGovern at AT&T, she was not even number two, but she was running a $20 billion business. Shortly after McGovern joined the board, Conrail was immersed in issues regarding the industry consolidation and a possible merger with CSX. Conrail Chairman Dave LeVan says of McGovern, "She hit the ground running and made outstanding contributions from the start. She's a very valuable director."

Some boards may also have concerns that if they recruit a director in his or her early forties, they will be stuck with that person forever. Simple solutions to that problem include establishing term limits (recommended by the National Association of Corporate Directors in 1996) and relying on a peer review process to weed out directors who no longer contribute. (Chapter Ten discusses these approaches in more detail.)

Some "number twos" are also potential director material—as long as their perspectives are not functional or otherwise narrow. They must meet the criteria of being able to see the big picture and so on. Some executives who have titles like "executive vice president" have truly helped the CEO build the business and create value. As the CEO of a $25 billion company, the world's largest in the field, said of his company's recruitment efforts, "I'm not stuck on putting only CEOs on the board. I want the number two person who meets the criteria because I'll get more out of that person."

Beware, however, of senior-level people who have lost out to someone else for the CEO position. Individuals whose ambitions have been frustrated sometimes try to wield power on a board. Any attempt to use a board position for personal power is bad for board dynamics.

CEOs should not object to letting a division manager serve on another company's board. There is no better way to broaden the person's horizons and perspectives, making him or her a better leader. Lois Juliber, executive vice president of Colgate-Palmolive and director of Du Pont, says, "The insight I've gotten from serving on the Du Pont board has been invaluable. Serving on the audit and compensation committees, in particular, has exposed me to areas and issues that I would not ordinarily think about or get involved in during my day-to-day responsibilities." The risk of losing the manager through this kind of exposure is no greater than through headhunters. Such experience prepares young talent to be excellent CEOs and directors in the future.

Other "Big" Companies

In measuring the size of a company, look at total market value, not just revenue. What companies create market value? In October 1997, Intel's twelve-month revenues were $25 billion, whereas its market capitalization was $153 billion. Coca-Cola's revenues were $18 billion, its market capitalization $148 billion. Microsoft's revenues were $12 billion, its market capitalization $184 billion. Dell Computer's market value grew from $1.27 billion in 1992 to $36.4 billion in 1997 (based on $100 share price on October 21, 1997, compared to $3.578 on September 30, 1992).[1]

[1]Dow Jones NewsWire and Standard & Poors.

Market value is important because of all it implies. Chances are these market value creators have faced more change, faster change, tougher competition, and dealt with more complexity than a U.S. Steel or an Alcoa. Eckhard Pfeiffer has grown Compaq from a PC-based business to a large, total-solutions global company and more than quadrupled its market value. Pfeiffer's ability to position the company, create value, understand large companies as customers, and run a business with declining margins can be very valuable to a company like GM, whose board he recently joined. Such people have a way of looking beyond how much the company has improved to what portion of opportunity the company is capturing.

Now go back to the point about the "other number ones and twos." Is there someone just below the level of CEO who has helped create the market value? Are there others in the company running a P&L? Do they meet the criteria? The number two person at Intel may be more valuable to the board of GM than the CEO of an old-time company that does tens of billions in sales and creates low market value.

Be sure that any leader of a "small" company has a broad perspective. Directors who cannot see the big picture tend to concentrate their energy on petty issues to the detriment of the business.

Foreign Companies in the United States

Rather than looking overseas for business leaders with a global perspective, consider the leaders who are stationed right here in the United States. Many foreign companies have U.S. divisions led by very capable executives who are likely to assume very senior positions when they return to headquarters. Tapping this resource eliminates the logistical problems of traveling from Asia or Europe.

Commercial Banks

Those outside the banking industry may not realize how much the industry has changed. It used to be that CEOs of banks were on the board because the bank had the company's business. Those days are over. Parts of banking are more like consumer businesses. Executives in consumer banking have the instincts and perspectives of consumer marketers.

Venture Capital Firms

Some people argue that venture capitalists only understand small high-technology businesses, but some venture capitalists have served on the boards of big companies like Apple, Intel, and Tandem by virtue of having funded them early on. Even those who are short on experience with "phase four" companies (large, complex organizations) have an experience base and perspective that can be of great value to the board of any size company.

These people really understand issues of expansion. Partners of Kleiner-Perkins Caufield & Byers, New Enterprise Associates, Brentwood Associates, and Hambrecht & Quist, for example, have funded many ventures, some of which have failed, some succeeded. The best of these venture capitalists (Ben Rosen, chairing Compaq, one of the world's largest and fastest growing computer companies, and John Doerr of Kleiner-Perkins Caufield & Byers) have a special skill in judging which projects are likely to work and which are not. They have learned to ask the right questions, whether on the people side, the market side, or the project side.

Venture capitalists are comfortable with change and industry transformation. Almost all the new businesses they have funded over the years have involved change in the industry status quo, and as the ventures have grown, they have had to reevaluate and reposition themselves continually. The venture capitalists have also had to reevaluate management continually as the businesses passed through developmental phases. These skills can be applied to big companies undergoing major transitions.

Because their reputations and money are on the line and they cannot opt out of the board without putting their investment at risk, venture capitalists also tend to get more involved in operations than the stereotypical big company director. Venture capitalists can therefore help a passive board become more active. They feel comfortable in making constructive suggestions to management. Venture capitalist

Marshall Turner adds, "It's not a problem to teach directors of small companies that their job is to maximize value." Reference checking can weed out those who tend to micro-manage.

The Corporate Giants

Small, high-growth companies may be surprised to learn that leaders of the corporate giants are not all out of reach. Indeed, many CEOs of Fortune 100 companies have begun to entertain the idea of director-ships on small, fast-growing company boards, in large part because of the opportunity for learning. Software and Internet-related companies are especially interesting. The potential financial rewards through stock ownership are attractive, but many big-company executives cite other reasons as their primary incentive. Ed Woolard, chairman of Du Pont, joined the Apple board because he liked the challenge. He clearly made a difference at that company.

Alex Mandl, while still at AT&T, described his interest in serving on the board of a small company: "I'm not looking for the prestige of a big company. I'm interested in smaller, fast-paced, entrepreneurial compa-nies that must reinvent themselves often, because that's where I can learn the most." Another big-company executive said, "If offered a board seat, I would want to know if the business was technology driven, consumer oriented, globalizing, and fast growing. It's okay if it's small."

Mel Goodes, chairman and CEO of Warner-Lambert, and Chad Holliday, director and CEO designate of Du Pont, are among several large-company executives who have joined small-company boards in recent years. Many others are quietly looking.

How to Approach Good Candidates

When boards really work, attracting good people is not a problem. For the "psychic income"—the shared learning and intellectual stimulation, the broadening of their perspectives, and the chance to develop their skill in judging people and zeroing in on critical issues—busy people will-ingly rearrange their schedules and reorder their priorities. Board candidates are increasingly aware of the opportunities a good working board can provide and increasingly wary of boards that are there for show.

Colgate's Lois Juliber says of her experience on the Du Pont board, an active, global board: "For a potential CEO and existing divisional business manager it is a great developmental experience to join a board. It gives the person a totally new orientation and experience. It is a real expansion of personal capacity." Another director said, "When I'm asked to join a board, I want to know whether I would be able to contribute but also whether I will learn something. Will it expand my horizons?" A third director said simply, "I ask myself: Will serving on this board make me more effective in my current job?"

Ed Hotard of Praxair says, "I don't want to go on a board for a social event. I want to be able to really help shape and change things and be with a diverse group of people who will help me learn and grow." Dick Brown, CEO of Cable & Wireless and nonexecutive chairman of Pharmacia-Upjohn, adds: "Rubber-stamp boards are no fun to serve on, and you don't grow as a board member."

Another CEO and director of three boards describes what he looks for when deciding whether to join a board: "One thing that's important is whether I like and trust the CEO. There's one board I joined that I shouldn't have because the guy turned out to be untrustworthy. At that time, I was sort of enamored that somebody would ask me to go on a board. I became much more choosy after that. Now I sit down with the CEO and try to really understand the person. I ask him or her what the three most major pressing business issues are, and I try to judge how candid he or she is. When I did this recently, I got very excited and decided to join that board. I was convinced that the board and the CEO want to hear what I have to say."

Directors willingly make time for exciting boards. Du Pont's Chad Holliday says of Analog Devices, a small-company board he joined in 1997, "I do whatever it takes to get to every meeting, and I find that I go three or four hours early to have some one-on-one with management. It's something I look forward to. When I travel, I visit their offices overseas. That way, I get a feel for the business and the overall climate."

It is becoming common practice for a board representative, presumably the chairman of the nominating committee and not the CEO, to approach the director candidate. In doing so, the person should try to characterize the board as accurately as possible. Is it the kind of board that has exciting discussions? Do board members fully understand the key business issues? Is the board really immersed? Is it trying to change?

Before any commitments are made, however, the candidate should meet all board members and the CEO. Many boards skip this step because of the logistical challenge. But those meetings will confirm for the candidate how the board really functions and can also safeguard against a good-old-boys' network. Jerry Meyer, chairman and CEO of Tektronix and AMP director, says, "Our board prefers not to take up discussion of a director without having the person come in and meet the whole board. When the board abandons that process, you run the risk of creating 'a good old board.'"

The early overtures should allow the board or the candidate to bow out gracefully if the chemistry is not right. One former CEO describes his reason for advocating this practice: "I was asked by a headhunter to consider going on the board of a big Midwestern manufacturing company. It was supposed to be a great fit. I flew out to meet with the CEO, but before I went, I asked the CEO on the phone if we could make it an interview either of us could walk away from if we were not completely comfortable. He liked that idea.

"After our meeting, two things happened: I didn't think it was right, and he didn't think it was right. It wasn't right for me because in talking with the man, I didn't feel I could trust him. He talked about current board members by name, criticizing many of them. Then I learned from the headhunter that the CEO didn't think it was right because he already had three proactive directors and he didn't want another Type A personality sticking his nose into things. Fortunately, the ground rules were clear before we had that initial meeting. Nobody assumed the match would necessarily be successful."

Give New Directors Instant Inclusion

What's the point of recruiting top-notch directors with a wealth of experience, and then putting them on hold for the first several board meetings by allowing senior directors to dominate, providing no window for the new director to contribute? Even in the 1990s, some boards seat directors at the table according to seniority—a constant reminder of who is the new kid on the block. Boards at work go the opposite way. They find quick and easy ways to inform new directors about what is expected of them, how the business and the board operate, and, equally important, they go out of their way to make the newcomer feel welcome to participate.

Some boards have begun to create formal orientation programs. Some boards have also been considering sending their members to an academic program or conference on corporate governance as a way of introducing them to the current thinking about how boards should function. Harvard's workshops on "Making Corporate Boards More Effective," Stanford's Directors' College (out of the law school), and Wharton's Directors' Institute (co-sponsored by Spencer Stuart) are among the special programs for educating directors. Although first-time directors are likely to benefit most from these programs, other directors might like the opportunity to attend. Such workshops can stimulate thinking about how the board can improve.

Directors learn best by asking questions. The board should arrange for new directors to meet one-on-one with key managers so directors can ask whatever questions they have about that area. Initial meetings need only be about an hour long. Directors can ask for more time if they feel they need it. At Florida Power & Light, new directors are given a series of presentations by several senior executives, during which directors are invited to ask questions. Chad Holliday met with each of the vice presidents of Analog Devices for about an hour when he joined that board. The CEO arranged the meetings. Holliday says, "I asked each of the vice presidents about their personal histories and their families, and they ended up telling me a lot about the company. Afterward, I wrote each one a thank you note summarizing the things we talked about, and I sent the CEO a copy of the letters. That way there'd be no misunderstandings."

Some boards allow one-on-one meetings to occur piecemeal as the new director requires, but others prefer that the new person set aside a full day. When asked whether the full-day requirement is reasonable, one director responded, "Joining a board is a job, not an honor, and a well-paid one. Any responsible executive should be willing to make the time." A well-conducted annual strategy retreat is also a quick indoctrination for new directors.

Du Pont CEO Jack Krol describes how J. P. Morgan helped him get oriented: "The first thing they did was have their chief legal counsel, head auditor, and CFO come visit me in Wilmington (because they knew I was busy) and explain the company to me—what it was trying to do, what the issues were, and who was who in the organization. Then each time I went to New York for a board meeting, they spent another couple of hours with me. I'm on the audit committee, so one session was on auditing, which has a different emphasis in a bank than in our company."

Krol found the sessions to be tremendously helpful. "Joining the Mead board was so much like Du Pont that it was déja vu. But banking was a whole new universe—the language was completely different, the mix of people was different, and what's important is different. They spend a lot more time managing risk as well as looking for growth opportunities. Those early sessions allowed me to ask a lot of questions, as simple as what do the acronyms mean, which could be a waste of time at a board meeting."

When it comes to the social aspects, every new director has the same concerns about wanting to fit in and be respected. First impressions count. No one wants to ask a stupid question or express an opinion from left field when he or she first joins the group. Yet the longer a person remains silent, the more pressured the situation feels. The desire for acceptance is human and natural. It does not mean the new director is being co-opted. Indeed, good directors are amiable and harmonious without sacrificing their integrity.

Boards can help directors break the ice by making the behavioral expectations explicit: "We want your opinions right away." Even simple statements and gestures can signal to the new director that there is no holding-out period. One board designates a director to take the new person around and make introductions. Another has an area set aside for breakfast before the board meeting, so the new person has a chance to talk casually with others beforehand. Citicorp gives its new directors a formal description of board responsibilities, and John Reed tells new members that he wants them to talk back at him.

One director says of the board he recently joined, "They did a pretty good job of helping me assimilate, but it would have helped if someone like the head of the nominating committee had said, 'There's no cooling-down period here. We want you to feel free to ask questions your first day.' That one-minute comment would have put even a crusty guy like me more at ease."

Some boards assign new directors to important committees to get them involved. Lois Juliber, for instance, was asked to serve on the audit and compensation committees soon after joining the Du Pont board.

Royal Bank of Canada has an orientation program that provides, among other things, an overview of the whole group as well as of the financial services business environment. CEO John Cleghorn says: "We give directors an opportunity to meet with senior management to discuss Royal Bank Financial Group's business. As well, all receive a Director's Guide, which is part of a Knowledge and Information system that management is establishing. This system will include a Director's Bookshelf, containing written reference material and a computer knowledge base to which all directors will have access."

When it comes to the first board meeting attended by a new director, Royal Bank of Canada always arranges for someone—either a person the director knows or the chair of the corporate governance committee—to take the person around, make introductions, and make sure he or she feels comfortable. Because the board is large, new directors are assigned to a committee right away. The assumption is that breaking into the board dynamics is easier in a smaller group.

Royal Bank also has a continuing education program for directors. As the financial services business has become more complex, all board members have had to understand the basics of portfolio balances, foreign exchange, derivatives, and other areas of importance to the bank. In 1995, Royal Bank started having special education sessions on particular topics. The first was on derivatives. It also invited directors to meet with the company's foreign currency traders.

Building the Board You Need: The Case of KeraVision

How a small company got directors who could help with its evolving business needs.

KeraVision is in many ways a typical Silicon Valley start-up. The company was established in 1986 by three pioneers—an optometrist, a scientist, and an executive from the contact lens industry—and was funded by seed money from two venture capital firms.

The company was built around the invention of the optometrist: a ring implanted in the cornea to correct common vision problems—nearsightedness, farsightedness, and astigmatism. Over nine years, the company raised a total of $80 million and overcame many technical challenges to develop a breakthrough technology that is an alternative to contact lenses, glasses, and newer forms of vision correction surgery. The company launched its product in Europe in late 1996.

While typical in many respects, KeraVision stands out from other venture capital–funded companies in one important way. The composition of its board has evolved ahead of the company's changing needs. Whereas many venture capital company boards are static over time, KeraVision has gone out of its way to find board members whose experiences and perspectives could help the company make the transition from one developmental phase to another. The combination of good board dynamics and good board composition has made the KeraVision board a true resource to the CEO throughout the company's history.

The Need for Money

KeraVision's board was a well-functioning, value-adding board from the start because of a combination of good luck and good sense. When John Petricianni founded the company, he wanted what any founder wants: start-up money and a good board. Yet he knew his choices would be limited. For start-ups, the choice of board members is largely a take-it-or-leave-it proposition: You accept whatever board members the investors choose to represent their interests or you don't get the money.

KeraVision was lucky that the initial efforts to raise money landed two "good" directors on the board—Steven N. Weiss, representing lead investor Montgomery Medical Ventures, and Charles Bauer of the W. R. Grace Venture Fund. A "good" director in Silicon Valley start-up terms is someone who has solid networks that can help the new company access capital later on and someone who knows how to manage the natural tension that exists between founders and other early individual shareholders and professional investors and management. Venture capitalists are always interested in building incremental value as quickly as possible and cashing-out in, say, seven years, while management is trying to build something that will last beyond the initial public offering.

But Petricianni did not leave it at that. He also recruited Charles Crocker, a well-respected investor (his family had been investing in business endeavors since the mid 1800s). Crocker was not a typical venture capitalist. He had vast experience investing his own money in big and small companies in a wide range of industries as well as substantial management experience.

Crocker had only a small financial stake in KeraVision, but Petricianni wanted him on the board as a kind of middleman between the two inside directors and the two venture capitalists. Crocker agreed to serve on the board because he and Petricianni had both been investors in Barnes-Hind and Flow Pharmaceuticals, two extremely successful ophthalmic companies, and so had a longstanding business relationship. Crocker brought to the board his deep understanding of what it takes to create a great business over a long time horizon.

The board chemistry worked. Dialogue was open, discussions were focused, and directors gave Petricianni sound advice without interfering in operations.

When Petricianni was diagnosed with a terminal illness in 1987, the board hired Thomas M. Loarie, formerly an operating executive at American Hospital Supply, as chairman and CEO. Upon Loarie's arrival, the company had only three employees but a strong, well-functioning board. Loarie was by nature open and candid, and the board continued to function well under his leadership.

Loarie was quick to recognize that each board member (and Michael Hall, secretary and general counsel) made an important contribution to the group. When he noticed that Crocker's attendance at board meetings was sporadic because of conflicting demands and the long drive from his San Francisco office to KeraVision's Fremont headquarters, Loarie was concerned that Crocker would soon leave. He set out to get Crocker engaged in the business, and he moved board meetings to San Francisco.

The Need for Credibility

As KeraVision's business challenges changed over the next few years, so did Loarie's wish-list for new directors. As the company continued to grow, it would need capital—but the technology had yet to be developed, and there was no way of knowing whether it would actually work. If it did, the product still had to clear the U.S. Food and Drug Administration (FDA) approval process. Loarie had seen promising companies in other specialized fields killed by boards that panicked when the technology hit a glitch. At the same time, if all went well, the company would probably go public in the next few years.

These challenges translated into several criteria for new directors. Money and experience were, as always, important, but credibility in the capital markets was also on the list. Loarie made it a personal mission to find blue-ribbon investors who would validate KeraVision as a company with a significant new technology and lay the foundation for future growth. "I went out personally trying to find well-respected investors, like 3i Ventures Corp. and Brentwood Associates," Loarie explains, "because they would give future investors a sense of confidence. The risk, of course, is if they turn you down, the word gets out on the Street and you're tainted."

Loarie also wanted people who had general management experience in a medical technology environment and would understand the issues associated with running a business in the face of changing U.S. FDA regulations. He also sought individuals who had a background in medical technology research and development, who would understand that research moves backward as well as forward.

KeraVision's search was successful, landing David W. Chonette of Brentwood Associates and Michael A. Henos of 3i Ventures. Both were well-respected investors. In addition, Chonette had general management experience in medical technology, had come up through the ranks from R&D, and had experience in surgical ophthalmology. Henos had operating experience in medical technology and experience in vision correction, having helped launch soft contact lenses. Chuck Bauer, whose belief in the product concept had helped the company get this far, left the board.

The board's experience with R&D soon came into play when the technology hit an apparent dead end. "We were working on the simple concept of inserting a tiny plastic ring into the periphery of the cornea," Loarie says. "We had a lot of technical problems with the preclinical animal research."

From 1987 to 1989, KeraVision performed preclinical animal research on the rabbit eye to gather safety data in the hopes of gaining FDA approval to begin human clinical research. In using the rabbit eye as its model (the traditional model in eye research), it ran into the problem of "gaping," or spreading of tissue, where the tiny cut in the cornea was made. To further complicate the situation, the rabbit eye heals differently from the human eye.

Despite great effort, KeraVision could not overcome the gaping problem and in 1989 decided to use the human blind eye as the model. Researchers hoped to find evidence of a change in the curvature of the eye to focus light rays properly on the retina to get a clear image. Instead, they found that the inventor's idea of expanding or contracting the diameter of the ring to flatten or steepen the cornea was not viable. KeraVision had no choice but to find another way to make the concept work.

Timelines had lengthened and money was running out. The board, however, did not panic. "Throughout all of this," Loarie says, "the board had a 'bet the company' mentality that withstood the risks. And we just kept going to work every day, solving one problem after another, trying to establish technical feasibility."

The Need for Industry Knowledge

By 1992, the technology was working. The venture capitalists thought it was time to think about an initial public offering. Preparation for this event created opportunities to add to the board. The current directors continued to be helpful, but Loarie was starting to think longer-term. He was eager to enhance KeraVision's credibility in both the surgical ophthalmic industry and the medical technology sector of the public stock market. Given how much the U.S. FDA had changed since Kera-Vision's founding, recent operational experience in the medical technology industry seemed helpful.

Two criteria—name value in the ophthalmic industry and operational experience in medical devices—drove the search. As Loarie says, "I didn't want friends on the board. I wanted people who would add value collectively and assist us in making the transition to both a commercial company and a public company."

This time, the search led to John R. Gilbert and Lawrence A. Lehmkuhl. Gilbert, recently retired at the time, had spent his entire career at Johnson & Johnson, where he had grown a surgical ophthalmology business from $8 million to over $200 million. Due diligence reference checking found that he was the most respected business person in the ophthalmic field. At first Gilbert was not interested in serving on the board, but Loarie convinced him to visit the company. Months later, after performing his own due diligence evaluation of KeraVision, Gilbert agreed to join.

Gilbert added great value from the start. He used his vast network of industry people to answer business questions for KeraVision quickly and reliably. He introduced the company to key ophthalmologists worldwide and helped bring them into the research team. He raised important questions about the ultimate use of the product, forcing KeraVision to a higher standard in meeting customer expectations. His contributions were so significant that Loarie asked him to work half-time on behalf of KeraVision. With the title of vice chairman, Gilbert developed a foundation in Europe that would be used for the commercial launch.

Lehmkuhl, the former chairman, president, and CEO of St. Jude Medical, which makes heart valves, had grown that company from $25 million to $300 million to become the world market share leader in the research, manufacture, and marketing of heart valves. Similarities between St. Jude and KeraVision were striking: both were developing, manufacturing, and marketing implantable medical devices, the most stringently regulated segment in medical technology; both started as single-product companies with a similar financial profile (high margin products, low capital intensity); and both were serving global markets in a surgical specialty. Lehmkuhl also knew "the Street" and was well respected there.

Lehmkuhl made an immediate contribution when he urged Loarie to join the Health Industry Manufacturers Association. Loarie says, "HIMA has been a tremendous asset for me and KeraVision. Through it, I've built a network of valuable industry relationships. Some of our industry's biggest companies have been helpful in providing practical advice. And I've been able to interface at the highest levels of government to increase my knowledge of the agencies that regulate our industry.

I would have missed out on all these growth opportunities had it not been for Larry's urging."

When KeraVision finally did go public in 1995, the venture capitalists tapped their financial networks, introducing Loarie to investment bankers and networks of institutional investors, and Lehmkuhl provided direction on the market analysts. The presence of Gilbert, Lehmkuhl, and Crocker was attractive to prospective "public" investors, who often see venture capital–dominated boards shorten the business development time frame once the company becomes public.

The Need for Marketing and Global Networks

In December 1996, after many long years of developing and testing the technology, KeraVision employees and board members raised their champagne glasses to toast the company's first product shipment. The previous month, the company had received approval from the European Union to affix the CE mark to its product to treat nearsightedness, thus allowing the company to begin commercialization. The month before that, KeraVision had received approval from the U.S. FDA to begin phase III clinical testing, the last testing phase prior to commercialization.

The board anticipated the many challenges management would face as the company began the major transition from an R&D company to an operating company. Discussions of the business at the August 1996 retreat had brought those challenges into sharp focus: management could no longer think of the company solely in terms of a medical technology company, it had to think of the company as a consumer company; management had to adjust from growing a business to running one; and the company would have to address a myriad of specific marketing questions, such as where to launch the product and whether the doctor or the end-consumer made the actual purchase decision.

The upcoming challenges shaped the discussion of board composition on day three of the 1996 retreat. Although the board had become such a tight, well-functioning team that none of the directors really wanted to leave, it was time for three of them to move on. Their investment in KeraVision had paid off, and they had to shift their focus to newer investments. In filling the seats, the board wanted to bring in some new skills.

The board decided its new directors should have global networks (for consumer marketing and global financing purposes), knowledge of the health-care industry, and experience in consumer marketing. Preserving the good board dynamics as membership turned over would be accomplished in two ways: one of the venture capitalists would extend his service a few months longer, and the other two outgoing directors would be invited to participate in board meetings on an ex-officio basis up through the August 1997 board retreat.

Within months, KeraVision found two new directors with the experience it was seeking: Arthur M. Pappas and Kshitij Mohan. Pappas had many years of pharmaceutical experience in North and South America, Europe, and the Pacific Rim. He brought geographical breadth and, through marketing over-the-counter drugs, experience with consumer health products. Mohan, a vice president of a large health-care company, had experience in technical oversight. He was also a former regulator.

Pappas and Mohan began to blend in right away, but the 1997 board retreat, with its built-in time for informal conversation and social interaction and its total immersion in issues of strategy, made their assimilation complete. Over the course of two and a half days of discussion, Pappas and Mohan both came forward with sharp comments and questions from their areas of expertise as well as from their wider range of business experience. A long-time director remarked, "We've always had a sense of camaraderie at the board level. We've now brought on two new people and it feels no different."

Discussions during the 1997 board retreat brought to light the ongoing need to shore up KeraVision in the area of consumer marketing. As the third venture capitalist prepared to leave the board and the company began its transition from an R&D company to a consumer company, the board needed little discussion to determine what kind of director should fill the vacancy: "Consumer marketing" would drive the search for the next new director.

Key Points

- Boards should have a mix of backgrounds, perspectives, and ways of contributing. Set the criteria for new directors, and let the criteria drive the search, but ask "What will this person contribute?" not "What does this person represent?"

- Director talent is available outside the usual sources and the good old boys' network. The opportunity to contribute and grow will attract good people.

- Test for chemistry. Directors cannot add value if the board dynamics are not right.

- Get new directors involved right away by assigning them to important committees and soliciting their opinions. Some boards let new members chair a committee within the first year.

EXPECTATIONS OF BOARD MEMBERS FOR VALUE CREATION

Every board member should do the following:

1. Engage in dialogue on substantive issues to add value.
2. Maintain independent judgment at all times about issues and management.
3. Put forward without hesitation any potential conflict of interest, real or perceived.
4. Take initiative to counsel other directors and the CEO as appropriate, inside and outside the boardroom.
5. Help make board dynamics positive and effective.
6. Be attuned to "soft" information about management, the company, and the board to allow distillation of insight and judgment.
7. Constructively participate in reaching concurrence on strategy and evaluation of top management and ensure appropriate controls in audit and performance, including strategy execution.
8. Use judgment in navigating gray area between active involvement and micromanaging. A passive role is not welcome.

SHOULD THIS PERSON BE ON OUR BOARD?

1. **Perspective:** How will this individual add to the composite perspective of the group of outside directors?

   Does this individual—   Yes   No

   have a track record of success (in the top
   quartile in his or her profession)?   ___   ___

   have an affinity for and expertise in some aspect
   of the external environment?   ___   ___

   have the ability to see the business as a whole?   ___   ___

   focus on the big picture rather than operational details?   ___   ___

   exercise that perspective in his/her full-time work?   ___   ___

   have the ability to cut through complex issues
   and ask incisive questions?   ___   ___

   have the courage to remain independent while
   possessing the compassion to help management
   by counseling, coaching, and giving feedback?   ___   ___

   help create balance between directors who are
   creative and probing and those who are focused
   and pragmatic?   ___   ___

   have a set of experiences that is additive to
   those of other directors?   ___   ___

2. **Board dynamics:** Will this individual enhance the dynamics of interaction among directors in committees and/or in board meetings by constructively challenging management and other directors, stimulating creative thought, contributing incisiveness to discussions, and helping bring closure to debate?

   Is this individual—   Yes   No

   a good collaborator, not someone who prefers
   to fly solo?   ___   ___

   able to exercise independent judgment while
   being collegial?   ___   ___

   aware of the importance of group dynamics?   ___   ___

   a strong presence?   ___   ___

   someone who is willing to participate and
   challenge fellow directors?   ___   ___

   someone who will make this board more effective?   ___   ___

SHOULD THIS PERSON BE ON OUR BOARD? cont'd.

3. **Leadership:** Does this person have a record of leadership in his/her area of activity and have the gut instincts of a CEO?

	Yes	No
Will this individual be willing to serve as a sounding board for the CEO when necessary?	___	___
Will this person support the CEO's and/or the board's efforts to ensure an orderly and well-executed succession planning?	___	___
Is this person truly interested in learning the industry and the business?	___	___
Is this person articulate and cogent?	___	___
Is this person free of conflicts of interest?	___	___
Will this person devote enough time and be accessible?	___	___
Is this person of high integrity and ethical standards?	___	___

CHAPTER FIVE

WHAT THE BOARD SHOULD KNOW

Uninformed boards do too little or too much. Either they defer to management completely, or they refuse to support the CEO in making major strategic shifts, even when such action means survival of the company. Boards must understand the basics of the ever-changing industry dynamics and the business if they are to give management their best advice and if they are to put their own reputations at risk to back the CEO in taking difficult but necessary actions. When mergers, divestitures, consolidations, strategic alliances, and joint ventures make front-page news daily, every company must be prepared to make major changes sometimes on short notice. The board needs to be well informed about the right issues at all times.

Management must hone its skill in making information meaningful and accessible. But opening up the flow of information to the board is psychologically charged. Some CEOs fear that the board will micromanage. Especially when it comes to actions they are proposing but have not yet taken, they fear that the board will second guess their decisions or recommendations or act precipitously.

This fear comes from the inherent tension in the board's role. While the board may want to help the CEO, every chief executive is keenly aware that the board ultimately can fire him or her. Bob Weissman, CEO and chairman of the former Dun & Bradstreet and now of Cognizant, captured this reality: "The board is essentially saying, 'I want to be your helper, mentor, and coach, and I therefore want the discussions to be honest, open, and focused on objectives. But I also am a judge of your performance, which creates an implicit threat over your head.'"

For reasons already discussed, CEOs simply must face this reality and help the board understand and focus on the issues that are critical to the business. The board's contribution is too great to miss. The so-called mushroom effect of keeping the board in the dark is a losing proposition all the way around.

CEOs who do a good job of informing their boards craft the board agenda to build an understanding of the company's strategy piece by piece. They provide an overview of the important issues and trends in the external environment and update it continually. They give directors as much direct contact with managers as they need to get a feel for the company's internal resources. They make sure information flows both ways by being receptive to the board's input and responsive to the board's questions, and they keep discussions on track by channeling the boardroom dialogue and managing the board dynamics to keep discussions focused and balanced.

Boards at work insist on getting the information they need. They invest the time to learn about the key trends in the industry, no matter how fast-changing or complex. They become intellectually engaged in the toughest issues management faces. They are in the game, all the while mindful of the distinction between governing and managing a business.

The Art of Sharing

Most of the CEOs in this book completely redesigned the kinds of information the board receives and the way it is conveyed. Their practices stand in sharp contrast to practices that persist at most other boards, where defensiveness and distance are the norm.

Information blackouts are all too common. Many boards receive only perfunctory information, consisting of historical financial results (usually in aggregate) along with reports on decisions management essentially has already made. One outside director explained why one of the boards he sat on did little more than rubber stamp management's proposed strategy: "Many times we had no critique and no suggestions because we were terribly unacquainted with the strategy. In the space of eighty minutes, we were expected to absorb, react to, and approve a plan that management had spent months putting together."

Other defensive means of informing the board include the "kitchen-sink method" or "happy talk." The CEO inundates the board with detailed reports designed to obscure the important issues and provide a built-in defense ("it was in that report"), or they present only the good news.

John Cleghorn, chairman and CEO of Royal Bank of Canada, describes how different levels of information can affect the board's perception of the Bank's strategic options: "When we first discussed with the board the idea of going into a new business, management had been considering and discussing this opportunity for some time and was very comfortable. But because the idea was new to the board, the directors were concerned with potential risks. We had to provide them with background material as to the issues and then have an informed debate."

Opening up the flow of information takes courage and clarity. When Bob Weissman became CEO of the former Dun & Bradstreet, he was eager to give the board more information, but he did have some concerns, which he dealt with by discussing them with the board up-front. Before he took office, Weissman began asking the directors (many of whom were strong and successful, like the CEOs of McDonald's and Baxter International) how they envisioned the board working. From those discussions, it was clear that they wanted open access to information, and they wanted to talk about only the most critical issues. Weissman took that to mean the issues where there was great uncertainty, risk, or opportunity.

Although the new CEO was eager to discuss those issues with the board, he wanted some clarification. "Those were not the kinds of things where the answers are obvious," Weissman explains, "so I needed to establish some ground rules." Weissman told the board that he wanted directors' input, but he cautioned: "If you start saying, 'This is an important area. We expect you to bring us the answer,' we won't get a good dialogue going. And as a result, I'll start giving you slicker answers—not necessarily better ones, but slicker ones.' I said it to them just that way, and they got the point."

Directors agreed that it was not their job to second-guess management but to help management make the best decision. Comments like, "We have to remember that it's not our job to come up with a better answer than management but to help management explore all the alternatives," gave Weissman the confidence to approach the board in a different way.

What CEOs fail to share openly directors have often been reluctant to ask for, probably because CEOs send a variety of signals to let directors know that their requests are not welcome. Ignoring questions and requests for more information are typical responses. It is legendary that only a few years ago, not only did the GM CFO appear not to have product-line profitability information but also management failed to respond to directors' requests to have such information available.

In another company, when a director raised a question, the chairman-CEO haughtily reminded the board that time was limited and that they "had a lot of ground to cover." Milt Honea, chairman and CEO of Houston-based NorAm and director of several boards, says: "In many of the companies I've known, the chairman would go into a meeting with a clear desire to have the thing get over with in a hurry. The underlying message was, approve what we've got, we don't want it changed."

When Jerry Meyer became chairman and CEO of Tektronix, he inherited a board that had allowed the company to deteriorate without, he contends, finding out why: "The board always tends to shift the blame to management. But they never remember that they didn't ask for the information. When my board recruited me, they kept saying how bad the previous management had been. So I said, 'Excuse me, but how long have you been sitting on this board? What didn't you see?' A company doesn't go from $750 million of idle cash with no debt to being two weeks away from not making payroll without any indicators. If the board wasn't getting briefings down to the nth detail to understand what was going on, they can't blame management alone."

Directors must take responsibility and demand the information they need. They should not only ask about events or facts they do not fully understand but also take the initiative to do some tracking of their own. Subscribe to trade magazines, go to the Internet once in a while, and let the CEO or the sales manager know that you want to visit customers. Some Du Pont directors, for instance, have even been as far as Japan to visit Du Pont customers there.

Determined board members can influence the board agenda. "Consistently asking questions about a particular topic has real impact," says Alex Mandl, CEO of Teligent and director of several boards. "I recall a time when someone asked on a regular basis about quality results. There was ripple effect—all of a sudden people at the management level were asking about consumer reports and quality standards, and it became a sort of side agenda. From there, quality moved up in status to become a more central theme on the agenda."

The Way Around Nit-Picking

Nearly every CEO whose board works well admits to having wondered: What if I'm sharing too much information with these people? But an important lesson has emerged from boards that work: Micro-managing rarely occurs if information is clear and meaningful and if the CEO (who is usually also the chairman) manages the board dynamics.

Providing the right kind of information—that is, relevant to the company's most pressing issues—can help keep the board both focused and energized. Joseph T. Gorman of TRW comments: "The important thing is to focus on where the strategy is going, not necessarily on the day-to-day tactical items. Most companies overdo the emphasis on trivial stuff, which detracts attention from the bigger, more important things—like business mix, new product lines, key people, major budget line items, industry trends, and overall financial structure." As a rule, directors want to focus on the big picture. Director Bill Anders, former CEO-chairman of General Dynamics, advised Doug Olesen, CEO of Battelle Memorial Institute, "Don't bring the minnows, bring the whales."

A sharp focus on the company's most important issues is the single most effective way to keep directors interested. Directors tuned in and immediately began wrestling with the options he had presented. Jerry Meyer of Tektronix says of the strategy sessions he has with his board, "This is where the board really interacts and wants to understand."

Once the information has been laid out, the CEO should exercise his or her skill at keeping the board discussion on track. As former Conrail Chairman and CEO Jim Hagen explains, "If you just lay out the information and leave it lying there, you'll probably get beaten by your own club. But if you say this is our strategy, these are our challenges, this is what we're doing about them, and then you manage the board dynamics, it works well."

The newly appointed chairman and CEO of an information technology company decided to share with the board the details of his operating plan, which his predecessor had closely guarded. In the early months of his tenure, the new CEO found that the more he shared, the more harassing the board became. Three directors in particular started asking nitpicky questions and simply wasted meeting time discussing irrelevant details.

The CEO began to question whether he had made a grave mistake by sharing so much information. After some serious soul searching, he concluded that the problem was not with how he was managing the information flows but with how he was managing the directors' interactions. He truly believed that the board needed to be well informed, particularly since he knew he would need their support in making major strategic moves and investments, but he realized that he had to do a better job of managing the flow of the discussions. At later meetings, he became more aggressive in interrupting directors at times and setting items aside for separate consideration. Discussions became more productive.

Experienced board members often help balance each other. When one of the directors at NorAm drifted into detailed questioning about a procurement contract management had negotiated, another board member said, "Look, that's management, not governance." At another company, a director wanted a copy of a contract that management had negotiated with a foreign business. The CEO-chairman said, "My purpose is simply to advise you on this. We're always open to advice, but I think we have this one under control." Another director reinforced the CEO's message, saying "He's explained it enough. That's not a board issue."

At yet another company, when one director repeatedly raised the subject of how he had handled a compensation problem at his company, another director intervened. "That may be how they did it at your company, and I could tell you how we handled it at my company, but what we're here to talk about is how this CEO is going to do it at this company."

Most directors respect the line. Jack Krol, Du Pont CEO and director of J.P. Morgan and Mead, says: "I don't want to be asking, 'Why did your cost at this mill do what it did this last quarter?' If productivity is well off the mark for the company, directors should be asking, 'What do we need to do to turn that around?'"

When the CEO and the board share the same information base and engage in an open discussion of the issues, agreement usually follows. There are times, however, when the CEO and the board disagree. Boards that work understand that the CEO is ultimately accountable for decisions and must therefore have the right to make the call. To them, the line between management and governance is clear. A wise CEO, however, will assert that right judiciously. Jim Hagen says, "I always had the feeling that if I felt really strongly about an issue, I would have the ability to explain that to my board. But if you play that card every month, then it loses its effectiveness."

Citicorp CEO John Reed says, "I've always made it clear that unless I strongly disagree with the board members, I'm generally going to move in their direction. Obviously, there are some lines at which I'm not willing to bend, but I give them the benefit of the doubt."

Jerry Meyer of Tektronix described how he handles disagreements with a director: "If there is disagreement, my approach is to say 'I hear you and I strongly disagree.' Then I explain my position and decide whether it's a management or governance issue. If it's governance, I defer to the board. If it's something like how much we're paying for print engines in Japan, I say just that—'This is a management issue.'

"Sometimes I will take an issue to a committee to get resolved," Meyer adds, "because it's easier to test how serious the various sides are in a smaller group. But if the CEO doesn't learn to listen when the board feels strongly, the directors will quickly shift the conversation from the issue at hand to the incumbency of the CEO."

Create a Total Picture

Boards that work have open access to a wide range of information about the company and industry. That does not mean that directors have to know everything. In fact, immersing the board in all the numbers and details would essentially be adding another layer of management. If directors think they are supposed to know everything, they may hesitate to ask questions. Instead, boards must focus on the "big picture." They should have a complete mental picture of the company strategy, the context for that strategy, and the organization's capabilities for achieving it.

A board's information needs are similar to but greater than those of a good security analyst. Board members should be informed about

- the external environment—anticipated external discontinuities, anticipated changes in markets, technologies, deregulation, currencies, and the like
- competitive strategies of traditional and nontraditional competitors—joint ventures, industry alliances, industry consolidation, and blurring of industry boundaries

- company strategy—its good points and weak points
- the company's critical people (information not easily available to security analysts)
- resource deployment—including human resources
- execution issues—what do we have to do well to succeed? what problems do we face?
- customer satisfaction
- the business model—how do we make money in this business?— the risks and opportunities.
- what is working well and not working well in operations and the marketplace.

When directors are informed about the key points in each of these areas, they get a sense of the company's overall health, its greatest challenges, and the areas of opportunity and vulnerability. Then they can let their incisive and discerning questions and common sense apply.

Reed of Citicorp says that the framework he uses for working with the board drives the information flow and agenda.

We agree to tell the board what we are seeking to accomplish operationally over the next two years, and we have to provide enough information for the board to see when we begin to deviate. Also, we expect the board to have an independent view of the risk we're taking (risk is important in our industry). We therefore have to provide information that allows the board to sense when the risk profile doesn't look right. As I share the strategy with the board and ask whether it makes sense, I have to contrast it with the strategy of other players in the arena so the directors can make some kind of judgment about it.

If you have a framework, then you know how to put together an agenda that can feed into that. If you don't know what you're trying to do with the board, it's very difficult to figure out what the agenda should be and what you should spend time on.

The information flows between management and the board at NYNEX, Conrail, Tektronix, GE, Du Pont, and Citicorp are exemplary. These CEOs convey information that is meaningful, not just financial, and in a format that makes effective use of board members' time. They present alternative views and plans, and they make the important distinction between fact and opinion. As a result, the board understands what it really takes to make money in that industry.

At these companies, the board receives information from a variety of sources. And they receive it before management takes action or makes a final decision.

Anatomy of the Strategy

It is imperative that the board understands the thinking behind the company's strategy. Many boards sit through hours of presentations about strategy, but unless management takes the time to break it down into its key components, the board will have trouble analyzing it. Of course, many CEOs design strategy discussions to minimize the board's input, but for reasons already discussed, going it alone is risky. For the board to work, management must educate directors about the strategy, the underlying assumptions, and the alternatives it has considered.

The entire agenda should be designed to give the board an integrated view of the strategy. That is, presentations cumulatively should build an understanding of the major trends, issues, and challenges the company faces. Management should be sure the board is presented with more than one view of issues like industry restructuring, competitors' strategies, and company strategy.

Conrail, NYNEX, and Du Pont design the board's year-long agenda to build cumulatively a picture of the company, the industry, and the competition. At Conrail, at every board meeting, one of the top managers spends one to two hours laying out the issues and strategy for his or her part of the business. The presentations are tightly disciplined to cover the key points in less than half an hour; the remaining time is allocated for open discussion.

The discussions of the individual parts of the business culminate in an annual strategy retreat, a meeting lasting two or three days during which management pulls the building blocks or pieces of strategy together.

The September 1994 Conrail board retreat, for instance, included a series of nine presentations that recapped discussions held throughout the year. By the time the retreat came around, the board had developed enough of a knowledge base to see how the four service groups, three production units, human resources management, and management information systems all fit together.

The Business Context

Board members must understand the industry to have confidence in the strategic direction. Managers often fail to deliver this. Tektronix CEO Jerry Meyer says, "Too often it is presumed that all board members understand an industry as well as management does. But if I sit on a board and am not in that industry, I want someone to explain it to me so I can reach conclusions about whether management is on the right track. And I want it in simple terms. I, of course, have an obligation to take the time to learn about the industry."

Security analyst reports (particularly the institutional investment analysis reports) can go a long way in giving the board a sense of the industry dynamics. Management should consider compiling three or four such reports for the board, along with its own commentary. It might also consider using outside experts to analyze the competition, as Burlington Northern has done, or potential restructuring of the industry. One company brings in outside experts to explain important trends in technical issues affecting the company. Royal Bank of Canada uses seminars as one means of providing important background information relating to banking and the financial services industry. A recent one was on derivatives.

When Bob Weissman and his senior management team laid out the industry context for the board of the former D&B, directors were taken aback. Double-digit revenue growth was unlikely in many of the businesses, expense reduction could no longer drive double-digit profit growth, the business model for some key businesses was uncertain, the competitive environment was worsening, and the company had real financial constraints, like dividend policy. One director later said, "I see the vision, the strategy, the options. I see the need to try to be flexible." Another said, "Nobody knows the final outcome, but I know we have a process in place to wrestle with the key issues."

Perception of Outsiders

Because the ultimate test of a business is external, the board must take the time to analyze how the company is viewed from the outside. Is its brand equity growing or eroding? Are customers generally satisfied? The board of one of the largest bank holding companies in America gets information on customer satisfaction unfiltered by management as a way of gauging how the company is doing.

The board also needs to know how stockholders see the business. Analyst reports and directors' personal networks can help the board stay informed on this front. At one company, the investor relations director meets with the board occasionally for an update on how shareholders feel about the company. (For more on this topic, see Chapter Six.)

The Organization's Capabilities

Boards that are active and add value have a good sense of the organization's human as well as financial resources. They regularly interact with managers below the most senior levels to sense the depth of the organization's skills and talent. This sensing helps them raise great questions. Such contact also can help the board identify possible weaknesses in strategy or problems with implementation at the operational level, assess the degree of support for the CEO, and better understand the business. Directors can quickly discern when a CEO is respected down the line.

Sam Eichenfield of The FINOVA Group says: "I allow the board to have access to anybody on my staff they want to contact with whatever questions they might have. I invite it. If they want to talk to my controller or one of my business heads about a particular business question, they ought to feel—and do feel—they have the right to make that telephone call directly. And that's all right with me. Similarly, I expect any of our people to be able to access any director to tap his or her particular expertise."

Conrail shares that philosophy. Conrail's former general counsel Bruce Wilson says, "We're really talking about taking out one big barrier between the board and the people who really operate the company." Once, when Conrail discovered an environmental problem in Boston, it was decided that Wilson should call the directors to answer any questions they had and to give them the answers unfiltered and immediately. Former CEO-chairman Jim Hagen said: "Rather than having me get the facts from Bruce and explain what had happened, why it happened, and what the potential reaction of the EPA and the state authorities was likely to be, it made more sense for Bruce to call these people and tell them the facts."

Bruce Wilson called a few directors who were on the ethics committee to explain. "We have something that's going to develop into a serious problem. I'm going to give a full report on it at the next board meeting, but I want you to have advance preparation here." The heads-up gave the directors a chance to think about the issue before they met to discuss it and saved them the embarrassment of being caught unaware.

Jim Hagen was entirely comfortable with having Bruce Wilson talk to board members, even to deliver bad news, because the focus was on facts, not power. Hagen says, "The point was not who was in charge but to all be informed at the same level at the same time. That's how our board works. It's like, 'We're in this together. If you have a problem, tell us about it and we'll try to help you.'"

In another instance, a director initiated a call to Bruce Wilson to get the background on a legal problem that arose in his hometown. The director had heard through his social networks about the possibility of a lawsuit with a local transit authority. Wilson explained the nature of the dispute and informed the director that he was going there next week to try to work out a deal.

Such contacts work at Conrail because of the high degree of trust among the CEO, the senior managers, and the board. Jim Hagen adds,

"If you don't trust a person who reports directly to you to talk to the board, you probably shouldn't have that person in the job."

The Options

Every company bases its strategy decisions on assumptions about externals often beyond management's control. The board should have a chance to probe those assumptions and to see how the strategy holds up under different scenarios. Management should be sure to provide several different views, not just its own best guess about where the industry is going. When Conrail presented its strategy at its first board retreat, one director asked what would happen if the Federal Reserve raised interest rates. Management subsequently prepared alternative action plans.

Discussing a range of options—variations on what competitors or economic trends might do—helps the company respond quickly. After building the board's working knowledge of the industry, the former D&B's Bob Weissman laid out several alternative strategic directions and explored with the board the implications of each. When the "growth through aggressive acquisition" strategy didn't work, Weissman could immediately revert to Plan B. "Exploring different scenarios is imperative," Weissman says. "That way, when the barbarians are at the gate, you'll know what to do. You will have already thought about it."

The Economic Implications

The board cannot allow management to gloss over the economic implications of its proposed strategy. Here the CFO's role is crucial and sometimes sensitive. The CFO must put a value on the strategy and give an honest opinion as to whether it meets the company's economic goals. Sometimes the CEO's pet strategy falls short, and the CFO has the unpleasant task of making the board aware of that fact. Good CFOs have the confidence and intellectual honesty to speak the truth as they see it, even when it seems to contradict management's plans. They also have the maturity and interpersonal skills to express disagreements in a professional manner and to make sure that they are business driven rather than personality driven.

Georgia-Pacific CFO Jack McGovern says minor disagreements with the CEO go with the territory. "I can't imagine that any two people will agree on everything," he says. "Everyone has their own way of explaining things and their own spin."

If directors feel those differences are not being fully aired (perhaps because the CEO feels threatened), they have at least two options. One is to arrange one-on-one meetings with the CFO in the privacy of an office. Another, better approach is to listen carefully to what operating management wants to do and then simply to turn to the CFO and ask, "Do you think this will accomplish our economic objectives?" "A healthy environment," McGovern says, "is when the CEO can say, 'This is my opinion, but this guy here has a slightly different take on it.'" (See Chapter Eight for a description of how GE CEO Jack Welch invites dissenting opinions on succession candidates.)

Combine Facts with Gut Feelings

Boards that work recognize the importance of "soft" information beyond the quantitative, fact-based data most boards see. They explicitly consider things like how deeply the CEO has analyzed the strategy, whether the strategy is being effectively implemented, and how energized the management team is. Such soft data are critical to the board's ability to make independent judgments about the company's strategic direction, the quality of the CEO's leadership, and the company's management depth. Directors' experience and diversity of experience can add tremendous value in this area when directors see things through a lens different from management's.

Seasoned business people often make comments that acknowledge the importance of this kind of intuitive, soft information in giving them confidence in their instincts. Jerry Meyer, chairman and CEO of Tektronix, has talked about the need for the board to "feel good about the strategy," and Sam Eichenfield, chairman and CEO of The FINOVA Group, has stressed the importance of giving the board "a chance to sense how people really feel inside."

It is often the intangibles that win a board's support despite the presence of bad financial reports or other hard facts. The board of Citicorp in 1991 supported John Reed's plan to turn the bank around despite the continued slump because Reed's interpretations and explanations were convincing. Reed had discussed the bank's problems openly and explained his five-point plan with great specificity. The clarity of his vision and his comfort in fielding the board's toughest questions gave the board confidence in his approach to solving the problems.

Good boards aggressively seek the kind of informal contact that provides the clues they need to make reasoned judgments. Good CEOs encourage directors to meet with managers one-on-one or in small groups. Some boards make off-site visits to customers or plants for additional qualitative input. TRW occasionally holds board meetings near their overseas plants so directors can visit key customers and employees and better understand the local culture and business environment. Conrail directors have made informal visits to the railroad terminals.

Former director Bill Adams recalls a visit he made to Bell Atlantic NYNEX Mobile headquarters that gave him a feel for the internal environment. "I noticed the layout of the offices, and in particular, an open meeting area in the center, where people could gather for coffee and snacks. I could see that informal interaction was part of the everyday routine."

Streamline Meeting Preparation

Boards can insist on getting the information they need, but progressive and confident CEOs take responsibility for keeping the relevant information flowing. They feel comfortable in telling the bad news, present and anticipated, and they encourage open communication inside and outside the boardroom, among the directors and between management and the board. They spend whatever time and effort are needed to make it easy for directors to prepare for board meetings, they design meetings around the open exchange of substantive information, and they stay in touch with the board between meetings.

Pre-board Meeting Materials

Any materials that management sends the board should be designed to make the upcoming meeting efficient and productive. Before each board meeting, the board should receive in writing basically two kinds of information: background information on the substantive issues on the meeting agenda and other kinds of procedural information the board must be aware of for legal or administrative reasons. Every piece of information should be purposeful. One big-company director put it bluntly when he told the new CEO, "Don't send me all that crap because I'm not going to read it anyway."

Providing written information on routine or procedural items is a useful way to preserve meeting time for more interesting subjects. The board must review quarterly financial reports, for instance, but this can be done outside the board meeting. NorAm chairman and CEO Milt Honea sends the financials out in advance to let board members study them. He does not spend any time going over them at the meeting unless someone specifically raises a question about them.

Royal Bank of Canada's "consent agenda," described in Chapter Three, is a useful model for informing the board about routine agenda items. Board members of course have the option of requesting more information. Jane Lawson, senior vice president and corporate secretary of Royal Bank of Canada, says, "We've never had anyone request further information or a full board discussion, in part because we select items we believe will not require it. The process is very efficient."

The FINOVA Group sends directors very extensive packages two weeks before board meetings. CEO Sam Eichenfield explains, "It's wrong to have to spend forty-five minutes educating somebody about agenda items. We take the time to put the package together, they take the time to come to the meeting prepared to vote or ask questions."

Some of the best packages of pre-board meeting materials include a letter from the CEO that gives directors a sense of the overall theme and important issues for the upcoming meeting, like a magazine editor's "Letter from the Editor," and a cover sheet for each attachment that clearly summarizes the four or five key points. The letter is an important vehicle for focusing the board's energy and demonstrating the CEO's business acumen. Such letters should be crisp and to the point (two pages is usually enough). They should be written by the CEO; delegating the letter to a staff person defeats the purpose.

Disciplined Presentations

One-way presentations by management are not inherently bad; in fact, they are generally necessary. But they must be disciplined to be effective. Beginning in 1993, Conrail strictly enforced a rule that presentations consist of no more than ten overhead slides, be no longer than twenty minutes, and allow at least as much time for open discussion. Capable people learn quickly. Now that Conrail managers have developed the habit of making highly disciplined and sharply focused presentations, the company is less rigid about imposing rules.

Conrail managers start each presentation with a clear statement of objectives for the presentation (on the first slide) and end with a clear conclusion (on another slide). They use the following questions as a guide in preparing their presentations:

1. What are the two to three insights the board should get from this presentation?
2. What are the two to three issues on which the presenter will benefit from the board's insight?
3. What are the two to three points about which the presenter believes the board should be fully informed?

The CEO is in the best position to enforce this discipline by reviewing everything with the demanding standards of a director in mind. Imposing the discipline is simply a matter of sending the presentation back to the manager because it is too long or too unfocused (not because the CEO is trying to filter everything through his own point of view). Conrail's outside directors have gone out of their way to praise management for making the presentations useful.

Another aspect of disciplining the presentations has to do with developing good delivery skills. Dimming the lights (not necessary for overhead projectors) and reading from slides will put people to sleep. Making eye contact and talking from the gut will engage them. At Citicorp, all presentations are done with handouts at a round table, where the presenter sits with everyone else. Here again the CEO can be the standard bearer. Chairman-CEO John Reed says, "I've gotten rid of the podiums. I won't allow anyone to talk down to the board." Feedback from the board can reinforce the positive.

Continuity Between Meetings

A lot can happen in the two months or so between board meetings. The idea of sending directors a monthly letter or memorandum between meetings is not new; many CEOs do it. But such communications are increasingly informal and content driven. CEOs are increasingly using the letter format not to recount financial results or for public relations purposes but to say, "Here's what's happening at this point in time and this is how we're dealing with it." Directors tend to view such candor as an open door and are more likely to call the CEO when something bothers them.

Shortly after Jerry Meyer became chairman and CEO of Tektronix, he started sending his board a letter every month. In that letter, he talks not only about the financial statements, which he sends, but also about the significant developments. "I say things like, 'Remember at the board meeting we told you we had real problems in inventory. Well, we took the following actions and things are improving.' I try to steer the board toward the significant items in the financials." He writes the letter in an informal, conversational tone and makes it no more than two pages ("because I don't like to write and they don't like to read more than two pages").

Jerry Meyer compared his letter with reporting he receives from other boards he serves on: "Each company and each CEO is different. I find that I'm better able to sense the general health of the company when the CEO offers his or her views about the period's performance rather than just sending the financials."

Dick Brown, CEO of Cable & Wireless, revamped the letter to the board, which had become data driven and staff written. "I made it my letter, using a fraction of the numbers and plain language to put things in context. The irony is, I simplified it tenfold, and the board thought it was more detailed than anything they had read."

CEOs who fear they will be opening a can of worms should consider the following story of how a CEO benefited from between-meeting communication: "We have some property that we were trying to sell, and I mentioned it in a letter to the board. I explained that I had talked with someone about turning over our property to a real estate investment trust (REIT) and having him manage it. A board member called and said, 'I just want you to know that I couldn't support that. I'm not saying that forming an REIT to eliminate excess property is wrong. But the person you're dealing with is a crook. If you bring it to the board, I will have to vote no and encourage others to do the same.'" The CEO immediately dropped the nefarious contact.

Internal company publications can also be useful in keeping directors informed about the business. Royal Bank of Canada also sends a "Friday mailing" containing news releases, analysts' reports, and clippings of important articles about the bank. The danger lies in giving the board too much information, but when open communication is encouraged, directors are likely to let the CEO know when to cut back.

Sam Eichenfield of The FINOVA Group says he sends six to eight memorandums between quarterly board meetings. "I want the board to know what is going on in the company and not be embarrassed to find themselves reading about the company in the newspaper instead of hearing it from me."

Bring in the Managers

Whether or not they say so, boards generally want to get to know managers below the level of the CEO's direct reports. They want to get their questions answered by the people who are on the line and get a feel for the overall competence of the management team. Some boards are encouraging such contact by inviting managers to board meetings and including them in golf outings, lunch, or dinner before or after. Such access requires that senior managers be secure, self-confident, well-informed, and know how to handle themselves.

When a few members of the Conrail board said that they weren't getting enough exposure to the people who were "really running the business," Jim Hagen, then chairman and CEO, was not at all offended. He had assumed that the board did not want such a large group at board meetings. His immediate response was "Okay, we'll get them here next time."

"Next time" was a board retreat, which the heads of the various business units attended. Hagen says, "Each of the managers really got down into what drives the business, why we are in it, and how to do it better. That gave the managers a real exposure to the board, and they came away with a real respect. At the same time, the board had a good feeling that these people are bright and aggressive."

Conrail has continued the practice ever since. Now the board routinely directs questions at the appropriate individuals and gets answers and information direct and unfiltered. When someone does not know the answer, the person says so without embarrassment. The directors have a good sense of each manager's capabilities and personalities—essential information for succession planning—and great confidence in the company's management depth.

CEO George Davidson explains the benefits of having senior management of Consolidated Natural Gas attend board meetings: "The management team gets a sense of the talent we have on our board and the specific individuals who are supporting us. The flip side of that is our board gets exposed to a number of people in our organization. The directors can see them, talk with them, and test them."

This kind of give and take is a great developmental exercise for managers. They get to observe firsthand how directors' minds work, how they focus on the big picture and cut through complexity to zero-in on the key items, and they learn the skill of asking incisive questions.

Bill Adams, former chairman and president of Armstrong, stresses the importance of letting managers stand or fall on their own, an approach directors tend to prefer. "The temptation is to dive in and help them out. But the best test of a manager is during the dialogue before and after the presentation—if the CEO sits back and lets the person sink or swim. The board learns more about the person, and the person develops the skills to interact with the board."

Informal contact with managers can be arranged by seating directors and managers together for lunch or dinner at tables of three or four. The small number forces intimate dialogue. The Bank of America invites managers to dinner the night before the board meeting. The seating is always designed so directors and managers sit next to each other at small tables. Sam Eichenfield describes the practice at The FINOVA Group: "The day before a board meeting, we start committee meetings at around two o'clock in the afternoon. In the evening, we have some thirty-five people together for dinner. We invariably invite management and expect mixed seating."

Having managers hear the board's concerns and support firsthand can be a developmental tool and a way to align interests. One company's management team attended a board retreat at which the board stressed the need for drastic cost cutting. The CEO commented, "Now they're committed to do the quantum thinking. They understand the need. They're the ones who have to cut the work force drastically. How else do you motivate them to do that?"

The CEO also should be sure to give directors an opportunity to communicate without senior management present. One director noted that having the usual eight or nine managers in the board meeting made it more difficult to talk candidly when he had some doubts about the CEO's performance. To avoid that problem, George Davidson of Consolidated Natural Gas has an executive session (outside directors and the CEO only) at the end of every board meeting. He says, "That way, the board can counsel me a little more directly than they do in the board meeting."

Jerry Meyer reserves the last hour for the board to meet with him alone. "I feel very strongly that the board needs to have private time with the chairman. Unstructured time, if you will. I always make a point of saying that the chairman's agenda is complete, and then I open the meeting to the board to talk about anything they want. If they want to say I'm doing fine, that's okay; if they want to talk about problems, that's okay too. The board has told me that that is the most valuable hour they spend."

Making the Board Industry-Literate at NYNEX

The open exchange of information laid the foundation for NYNEX's ground-breaking merger with Bell Atlantic.

When Ivan Seidenberg became chairman and CEO of NYNEX in 1995, he didn't have a groundbreaking merger with Bell Atlantic on his mind, but he could feel the earth trembling. Technological changes and deregulation were shaking up the telecommunications industry. Unpredictable alliances were emerging almost weekly among entertainment, cable, software, and local and long-distance telephone companies. Proposed mergers and failed attempts (like Bell Atlantic and TCI or US West and Time Warner) were setting off major shock waves. No one knew what the industry would look like even two years out.

In the midst of great uncertainty about technology, deregulation, legislation, and global competition, Seidenberg had to set a course for transforming the business. He wanted the board's help. That meant the board had to learn the basics of an extremely complex business. Directors had to know enough about the externals to discuss various strategic options—but not so much that directors were overwhelmed. Seidenberg and his senior management team had to strike the right balance between inundating board members with endless details and insulating them from the realities of NYNEX's world. In short, Seidenberg had to make the NYNEX board "industry literate."

Until then, the flow of information to the board had been uneven. The board was ready for more. In fact, under Seidenberg, the board had been revisiting all of its practices and preparing a report similar to GM's corporate governance guidelines. The NYNEX report, released late in 1995, explicitly stated the need for the board to have open access to information and people. Even if Seidenberg got cold feet, there was no turning back.

For any chief executive, lifting the wall that keeps management information from the board is a confidence issue. Seidenberg had an intellectual belief that the board should be well informed, but he was keenly aware of the personal risk. He explains: "For me, the most difficult thing in transforming the board was having the confidence to make the information flow more quickly and freely. When you widen the circle of information, who knows what will happen?"

Little did Seidenberg know that facing his own insecurities would allow the company to make corporate history. By leading changes in the structure and content of board meetings and in the communication before and between meetings, and, most important, by demystifying the industry, Seidenberg has been able to tap the experience and wisdom of his illustrious board. The board ultimately helped him craft the biggest strategic move in the company's history—the 1997 merger with Bell Atlantic—and set in motion a wave of mega-mergers.

Every Meeting an Experience

At NYNEX under Seidenberg's leadership, industry literacy was something that was acquired gradually over time, not at a once-a-year meeting. Although some boards were starting to hold annual off-site retreats to discuss corporate strategy (see Chapter Three), NYNEX did not. Having used the retreat format to jump-start the board's new working relationship,

NYNEX made strategy an ongoing discussion. As Seidenberg explains, "I didn't like to think that we did our bonding and strategizing once a year and the rest of the time we did administrative details. We tried to make every meeting an experience."

To allow time for strategy discussions, NYNEX cut the number of board meetings from eleven to eight but lengthened the meeting time from a few hours to half a day. The board covered routine matters— committee reports, dividends, and the like—expediently at the beginning or end of the board meeting or through telephonic board meetings. For quarterly meetings, the board took care of business first— the dividends, quarterly release. In the between-quarterly meetings, routine business was handled at the end. The sequence was varied intentionally, to keep things interesting.

At least an hour of every meeting was reserved for discussing some aspect of company strategy or the drivers behind it. Sometime during each meeting, the CEO gave his personal interpretation of how recent events and industry trends were affecting corporate strategy. By discussing the company's strategy and the assumptions it was based on repeatedly over the course of eight or ten board meetings, everyone developed a common knowledge base that was continually revised in light of technological changes and competitive moves.

At the beginning of the year, Seidenberg planned out a series of strategic topics to be covered during the year, making certain that each major division of NYNEX operations got a strategic discussion. He also encouraged directors to suggest topics. One meeting, for instance, focused on long-distance telephone service, another on Yellow Pages, another on the Internet, and before that, Asia and opportunities for international partnerships. Director requests put the discussion of wireless telephony and NYNEX's combined cable and telephone ventures in the United Kingdom high on the agenda.

Discussions were not necessarily tied to a particular decision. Seidenberg says, "We didn't always wrap our discussion into a transaction. Directors love to have unedited discussions of strategy. Then they can think about it and let their thoughts develop over a series of meetings."

One quality that distinguished NYNEX board presentations from others was management's ability to find the right level of detail and to put the information into context. As Seidenberg says, "Directors don't have to understand how you install fiber in the streets, but they do have to understand how the installation of fiber impacts the economics of the business."

Two or three senior managers typically attended NYNEX board meetings to take part in the strategy discussions. Their preparation was taken very seriously, because, as Seidenberg says, "If you throw something on the table, directors will react. If someone casually remarks that we have some liability with an environmental waste problem and then moves on, the board will say, 'Whoa, time out. Let's talk about that.'" The managers also were prepared to stand on their own in answering the board's questions. That way, board members could "touch and tug and interact."

Several steps ensured that managers did their homework. The presenters met with Seidenberg far in advance when the agenda was still being shaped so they had a sense of how their presentations fit into the whole picture. They met again later to discuss the specific issues and ideas they intended to bring to the board. Then one week before the actual board meeting, they did a dry run—not to make the presentation airtight but to ensure that the focus was razor sharp.

Seidenberg never assumed that board members could keep up with the industry because of the speed of change and technological complexity. He took the time to translate and simplify and bring out the patterns and common threads. When, for instance, management discussed NYNEX's goal of becoming a wholesale provider of core network services and a retail provider of services to the consumer, Seidenberg talked about other major industries that had gone through the same thing. He said, "Look at airlines. You used to make your reservation directly with the airline to buy your ticket, then you started making them through the travel agent, who becomes your retail interface and is buying tickets wholesale. But you can still call the airline if you want to. Wholesale and retail."

Before and Between Meetings

Directors came to board meetings prepared to discuss and debate, largely because of improvements in the communication before and between board meetings. NYNEX had a longstanding practice of sending out a binder of written material before every board meeting, but the content of this pre-board package was changed. Management began to send more material than before but made the information more accessible and interesting.

NYNEX board meetings were on Thursdays. By the previous Thursday night, management sent out a package of advance materials on the key strategic discussions. They also included a selection of newspaper articles to help keep directors current on industry events. The CEO always included an agenda letting directors know the particular topics that would be discussed at the meeting. Directors could thus focus their attention and use their prep time efficiently.

To avoid information overload, NYNEX sent the board summary charts of many of the presentations. Directors could read the key points without having to read a lot of text. "Big companies typically use a lot of charts at their board meetings," Seidenberg explains. "We sent the charts out in advance, and we had a rule that board members had to read them. The only ones we used during meetings were number charts or maps. For the most part, we used the round table format at meetings. The officers tended to remain at the table as they led discussions—not to stand up front near a screen."

Management tried to make it easy for directors to zero-in on the key facts but did not withhold more detailed information. If there was a dividend issue, for example, management sent the full report to the finance committee and a "cc" to the rest of the board, so those members could dig into it if they wanted and come to the meeting ready to ask questions. When a presentation on NYNEX's health care cost containment efforts was on the agenda, the pre-board material provided all the statistics. The "presentation" was a discussion led by the vice president of human resources, who explained his view of future trends and possible public policy debates. All the directors were active in the discussion, because they had done the preparation.

Communication continued between board meetings. Seidenberg explains: "One thing I learned from my predecessor, Bill Ferguson, was to talk to one or two directors every month. There was always something—compensation, or a financial matter—that I wanted to talk to somebody about. I found that the number of unsolicited inputs and questions was greater as a result. Directors also talked to each other and our managers. Sometimes at the monthly board meeting I learned that two directors had called general counsel or a staff person and asked a lot of questions about this or that. It's the sign of a good environment."

Bad news was another thing. "I didn't respond to everything in the newspaper," Seidenberg says, "but if it was something significant, I called and explained. If you wait until the next board meeting, you invariably get into a credibility problem."

Openness Equals Authority

The process that Seidenberg thought might curtail his decision-making authority actually expanded it. "The more I told the board, the more they trusted me. We had far more problems when information was segmented and directors felt they had to interrogate management. We got to the point where if they thought we were holding back on them, they just said so." The annual chairman and CEO evaluation discussions (conducted separately) gave the board a formal opportunity to raise concerns.

Boardroom discussions, grounded in the board's industry literacy, helped Seidenberg reposition NYNEX as a major player in the telecommunications industry. "As it turns out," Seidenberg says, "the board helped us make that major transformation. Managers don't like to admit that they don't have the grander view, but the fact is, there are people out there who constantly give you good ideas. The board helped us understand the need to think bigger than we might have otherwise.

"The more the board learned about the industry, the more they pushed us by asking, 'How are you going to grow earnings 10 percent per annum in the next five years and blow away the competition?' and 'Are you moving fast enough?' They were a driving force behind the decision to merge with Bell Atlantic."

The board's literacy, Seidenberg contends, gave the board the confidence to pursue the merger. "As a board member, you don't go along with such a huge transaction unless you have a lot of confidence that it's the right thing to do. You can see in the proxy the string of meetings we had to discuss that. Every director had been through every aspect of it over the course of fifteen months."

The board's value added went beyond supporting the merger decision. Once NYNEX was into the merger, the directors had great coaching tips. Nearly every board member had experienced some version of it, so the intellectual property was immense. "If you look at the way the Bell Atlantic deal was structured," Seidenberg says, "you can see that we couldn't have made up some of the things in that deal by ourselves."

"There's nothing scientific about this," Seidenberg concludes. "Talking about the strategy and the drivers behind it consistently over time builds a foundation of knowledge. Then you are always prepared to take advantage of the opportunities."

Key Points

- The onus is on the CEO to give the board a clear picture of the business and its external context. Boards that do not get it should insist on it. The quality, quantity, format, and frequency of information must be designed to help directors cut through the tonnage.

- Spend less time on history, more on what lies ahead, less on things that are going well, more on challenges the company is facing.

- Give directors frequent updates on external trends and issues, along with the CEO's best thinking about where the industry is going. Separate fact from assumption, discuss the unknowns, and lay out alternative plans.

- Give directors opportunities to gather "soft" data through frequent contact with people below the CEO's direct reports.

- Boards that formulate strategy or make operational decisions are adding an unnecessary layer of management. Directors must help each other respect the line between governing and managing.

CHAPTER SIX

WORKING FOR AND WITH SHAREHOLDERS

Boards that work recognize the new realities of corporate ownership. They know that institutional investors own more than half the stock of the Fortune 500 and that these shareholders will not tolerate managerial arrogance as performance declines relative to a peer group or the S&P. A good board makes sure top management is being responsive to shareholders by listening to their concerns, communicating the company's plans, and delivering on commitments. It recognizes that credibility is key.

Good boards use their experience and sophistication to differentiate stockholders who are true owners of the company from speculative investors who seek huge short-term gains. They make their own independent assessment of which shareholder concerns are legitimate and help CEOs and CFOs stand up to maverick investors who try to bully them to divest, restructure, or otherwise unlock value for those few investors' own self-interests. When the board fully understands and agrees with the company's plans and believes the CEO is striking the right balance between the short- and long-term interests of the majority of shareholders, it is willing to support the CEO despite pressures and complaints from the outside.

Boards that work are independent of management *and* of individual investors, though they are closely attuned to both. John Reed, CEO and chairman of Citicorp, explains this important role of the board vis-à-vis shareholders: "In the old days, boards felt they were part of the company and owed allegiance to the CEO. Now boards feel that they represent the stockholders and are more sensitive to their concerns. In that sense, the loyalty has changed.

"On the other hand," Reed continues, "a good board doesn't blindly follow what shareholders dictate. A really effective board knows how and when to exercise its own judgment." Reed's conviction comes from experience. Despite intense heat from investors, the Citicorp board backed Reed during an extremely difficult turnaround. The board's independence clearly served shareholders well: Citicorp's market value grew from $4.5 billion to $55 billion in five years. In early September 1997, it stood at $60 billion.

Boards have an important role in determining goals and linking management incentives to the mix of goals appropriate at that time. Because there is always a time lag between an action and its effect on company performance, the board must use its judgment to assess the fundamental reasons for the action.

The board also can help the CEO balance shareholder concerns with those of other constituencies. Shareholder value is important, but it cannot be achieved at the expense of other constituencies that may come back to haunt the business later. The Exxon Valdez oil spill and reports of racial slurs at Texaco are reminders that organizations function in a broader context.

Bring Investor Relations into the Boardroom

Boards at work know what shareholders think of the company all the time. They insist on getting balanced, clear, filter-free information about what shareholders are concerned about. Some analysts understand the operational issues, are well-versed in what competitors are doing, and have good ideas about how to release value. Some analysts even hire consultants to analyze industries and identify where value can be unlocked, especially when the industry is in consolidation. The board must insist that management consider these viewpoints and suggestions and keep directors informed of them as well.

A number of boards that work have discussions of shareholder-related issues several times a year. Many more get written summaries of analyst reports. Some companies go even further to bring investors' concerns to life for the board. At Tektronix, the director of investor relations occasionally attends board meetings to give his impression of how investors are viewing the company. When directors ask questions and make comments, they are communicating directly with the person who is on the phone with shareholders every day. They can sense the mood.

Sam Eichenfield, chairman and CEO of The FINOVA Group, describes what his board does in this area: "We have a practice that is a little unusual. A couple of times a year, we meet with our shareholders, both large and small. I ask the directors to come too, because that way we have a common understanding of the expectations. I also want the major shareholders to understand that our board is an active one, that it understands the company's strategy and is representing their interests in board meetings."

Consolidated Natural Gas periodically invites a top-rated securities analyst to speak to the board. CEO George Davidson says, "I don't want them to tell the board how great we are. I want them to talk about the industry from an analyst's point of view. What does a generic company have to do to compete?"

Unless the board insists that these investor reports be thorough and candid, they might not be. Milt Honea, chairman and CEO of NorAm, explains why: "When I took over as chairman and CEO, the company had not been doing well. People used to write to me as chairman of the board at the business address in the annual report thinking they were getting to the board. But unless I made a special effort, the board members would never know about it. The same with calls to our investor relations group. One time there was an article about us in the *Wall Street Journal* and we got a hundred phone calls in two days. I had our investor relations director summarize those things so we knew what was coming in. Imagine if those complaints were about the CEO. Do you think they'd get to the board?"

One director notes that analysts have been watching who goes on the boards of many medium-size companies. When he was asked to serve on such a board a year ago, a couple of analysts commented, "Now that you're going on the board, maybe we ought to start covering that company again."

How to Disagree with Shareholders

Although good boards listen to shareholders, they do not let shareholders dictate strategy or coerce management into acting precipitously. Shareholders are, after all, a diverse lot—the grandmother who owns ten shares as well as the activist pension fund. Some fund managers are in it to push a merger and make a quick gain, a move that might not be in the best interests of longer-term holders. Some executives tell of instances when a fund manager invited them for a weekend of golf with other CEOs. The fund manager's objective often is to get to know the CEO and make it easier to call him or her later and make suggestions about what to do with the business. The CEO is then in an awkward situation.

Boards that work do not automatically listen to the loudest and most forceful investor. They use their access to information and their unique vantage point to decide for themselves whether the CEO is pursuing the right course of action for shareholders. They then hold their ground, even in the face of criticism from outside, and they help unsuspecting CEOs and CFOs push back at aggressive investors with credible information.

At TRW in the early 1990s, management and the board, which fully backed the CEO's strategy, skillfully turned that company's harshest critics into allies. TRW's earnings were suffering primarily because of the large upfront investments being made in its airbag business and its European rack and pinion steering business. Dale Hansen and Richard Koppes of Calpers (California Public Employees' Retirement System) noted the earnings and asked to meet with the CEO. CEO Joe Gorman obliged. (Calpers later acknowledged that TRW was the first large company that had agreed to meet.) As a follow-up, Calpers asked to meet with several of the outside directors. Again TRW obliged. When CEO Gorman was called away at the last minute, he asked that the meeting occur in his absence.

Calpers came away from that meeting understanding what the board knew—that TRW was making a sensible commitment of resources to promising products. Management was making a sound judgment of which the board was well aware. Later, when *The New York Times* reported that Lens, Inc., had identified TRW as a breakup candidate because of it performance, Calpers stepped in. Before TRW could respond, Calpers, based on its knowledge of TRW, had already convinced Lens to drop TRW as a candidate.

CEO Joe Gorman and Marty Coyle, former executive vice president, general counsel, and secretary, have since become true advocates of an open, cooperative relationship among management, the board, and the investment community. Marty Coyle says, "If we can educate shareholders, bring them in as team players, and do it in a constructive, positive manner, we're going to have a situation where we won't be living from one quarter to the next. We'll have patient shareholders, and we won't have to spend time fighting off uninformed owners when we ought to be dealing with competitive issues."

Marty Coyle compared TRW's approach with that of other companies with which he is familiar: "Many other companies treat shareholders like the enemy. I know of one meeting a company had with its institutional investors where management sat on a platform and made all the investors sit two feet below. It was so poorly orchestrated that the institutions walked out after a few minutes. Nobody was talking about the key issues and trying to find a way to deal with the shareholder base. You've got to build the relationship."

Boards that work consider multiple constituencies, such as the local community, the environment, the regulators, and employees, in making their judgment about the appropriate course of action. The Conrail board is a case in point. In its September 1996 two-day strategy session, the board evaluated a number of strategic options, including a merger with CSX, taking into account the interests of shareholders, employees, and the community. The board authorized the chairman to pursue a merger with CSX, which was bitterly fought by Norfolk Southern, a rival that had had its eye on acquiring Conrail earlier. When the case went to court, the courts sided with the judgment of the Conrail board. The institutional investors took a strong stand to persuade the CSX chairman to match the bid by Norfolk Southern, and eventually a three-way settlement evolved.

In 1991, the board of Citicorp also took a decidedly independent stand in supporting CEO-Chairman John Reed during a difficult turn-around. The bank, which had been outperforming competitors for years, was suddenly facing a credit crisis. Real estate markets were sinking, and investors were alarmed. So were regulators.

The board was well aware of the bank's problems, but the directors had some important information outsiders did not—namely, deep understanding of and agreement with John Reed's plans and confidence that Reed was keeping the board well informed about the bank's progress. Reed describes that turning point in Citicorp's history:

In March of 1991, when I was on a business trip to Spain, one of my directors called me to say that some of the directors were concerned about the bank's situation and didn't know what to do about it. I thanked him for telling me and said I would take responsibility for putting the issue on the table. At the next board meeting, I did.

I laid out what I thought were the three fundamental questions the board members had to consider: (1) Do you believe we have properly assessed the nature of our problem? (2) Do you think our response is adequate? and (3) Do you think we can get it done? Then

I asked each director to speak separately on each subject, starting with the most senior person.

The net of that discussion was that the directors believed we understood the problem and that our plans were good. But could we get the job done? No, they didn't think so. Obviously, that led to questions of why not. I had to put everything on the table, including myself. Was I up to getting the job done?

Board members agreed that Reed's leadership was not the problem, but they had a problem with some key people, the organization, and how it was being run. Reed made commitments to change those things and to keep in close touch with the board about how things were going.

At a subsequent meeting, Reed laid out for the board his analysis of the company's problems and then presented a detailed five-point plan to turn the bank around, including periodic benchmarks. The board liked what it saw. Over the next few years, Reed and the board were deeply engaged in the turnaround, a difficult task of raising new capital and earning their way out of the losses. Reed kept the board updated about the changes monthly. As new problems developed, and many did, the board was fully engaged. There were the usual meetings, many phone calls, and occasional reasons for Reed to visit with the directors.

Those practices cemented the board's support. Even when shareholders complained about the bank's losses and the elimination of the dividend, directors were steadfast in their commitment to Reed because they knew where the company was going. When regulators questioned Reed's ability to pull Citicorp through, the board defended the CEO. They had deep firsthand knowledge of Reed's plans, the progress, and the prospects. They had confidence in John Reed.

The board's confidence paid off. Citicorp is now one of the most successful financial institutions in the world. The P/E, which at its worst had fallen to 6, rose to 15 within a few years. John Reed says, "I think we survived because we had a good board, and I think the stockholders were well served—although I don't think they recognized it at the time."

Take the Company Message to Investors

There is a right way and a wrong way to present the company to investors. The wrong way is to offer bold assurances that the CEO is doing what is necessary. The right way is to present credible information. Boards that work make sure the CEO is building credibility with investors. Frequent, open communication is a must. As Alex Mandl, CEO of Teligent, former president of AT&T, and director of Warner-Lambert, General Instruments, and Dell Computer, says, "Wall Street doesn't like uncertainty. When there's little or no communication, it's a negative."

For some CEOs, the ability to talk to investors is a skill that must be cultivated. CEO Ivan Seidenberg describes NYNEX's learning curve: "Soon after I took over, we ran an annual meeting that was terrible. I got defensive and was arguing with people who I thought were asking ridiculous questions. Although some people said it wasn't all that bad and made excuses for me, I spent the next year mad at myself. At the next annual meeting, I worked hard to explain our business to the analysts, and the tenor was completely different. Our board of directors was convinced that the management team knew how to interact with the public. We were open with the board and with stakeholders."

Warner-Lambert does an excellent job of educating its shareholders. Chairman-CEO Melvin R. Goodes has led an extraordinary effort to cultivate a group of investors who understand the company's strategy and are looking for long-term value. During an industry consolidation when the company was under pressure to merge, the CEO himself visited investors to explain why the company would create more value for them by remaining independent. Through careful explanation of the key points in the company's "Bridges to Prosperity" program, not through flashy but superficial public relations, he preserved the loyalty of a pool of patient investors. Investors have been rewarded beyond their expectations. (For more detail, see the case at the end of this chapter.)

Although some boards interact directly with shareholders (Avon, for instance, has directors attend meetings with shareholders), most do so only in times of crisis. When Control Data was creating Ceridian, the board met with eight of Ceridian's largest investors to explain the major restructuring and to calm investors' nerves. Big events may call for unusual measures, but when boards insist that CEOs build open relationships with investors, such situations seldom arise.

John Trani, chairman and CEO of Stanley Works, invited his board to attend the presentation to a hundred analysts on July 18, 1997. He gave directors a run-through of the presentation beforehand. "The board wanted to be informed about what would be said and made some solid recommendations regarding emphasis," Trani explains. He invited the board for two reasons: first, so directors could hear the questions and answers directly, and second, so analysts would correctly assume that the board was very supportive of the direction of the company and the changes he was making.

If the board gets feedback directly or indirectly that the CEO's relations with investors is somehow inadequate, the board must make that concern known. Alex Mandl suggests: "If the CEO does not discuss shareholder relations, the finance committee might want to make an independent assessment of its own either informally or by hiring a third party to evaluate the company's relations with the investment community."

Of course, communication alone is not enough. Credibility is built by delivering on commitments over time. Mandl says, "If there's an underperformance issue, the CEO should share his or her objectives, time table, and game plans for turning things around. Of course, if those promises or commitments don't materialize, then clearly that won't work either."

Open, informed dialogue between management and investors can eliminate the need for more drastic efforts to align interests, like Chrysler's decision in February 1996 to put a well-respected mutual fund manager on its board. Though Chrysler's move has been widely praised as a win for shareholders, as a general practice, it is risky. Chrysler's choice of a director seems to have been a good one, but other fund managers may lack the kind of balanced perspective and broad experience a board really needs. Appointing board members to represent one particular constituency is seldom good for board dynamics. Conrail's Jim Hagen warns: "Chrysler's solution is interesting. On the surface it looks great for shareholders. But it is uncharted waters."

Make Governance Part of the Message

Investors are beginning to recognize and value the board's potential to contribute to the company's prosperity. Evidence is growing that the presence of a truly independent board can curb stock market fears and raise a company's P/E, much the way the appointment of the right CEO— like Lawrence Bossidy of Allied Signal or John Trani of Stanley Works— does. A 1996 McKinsey study entitled "Putting a Value on Board Governance" found that many investors, particularly those with lower turnover ratios, are willing to pay a premium for good governance.[1]

When Stephen Bollenbach, the successful chairman and CEO of Hilton Hotels, joined the board of Time Warner in 1997, market reaction was perceptibly positive. Investors believed Bollenbach's influence would be felt. Dick Brown, CEO of Cable & Wireless and board chairman of Pharmacia-Upjohn, says, "No matter what people think, the image of the company in the marketplace is tied to what the marketplace thinks of the directors. And it will be more so in the future."

Many CEOs whose boards are truly independent and value-adding believe such market reaction is entirely appropriate. John Reed wishes stockholders would look more closely at board composition and what it can do for the business. In May 1997, two months before the Apple board forced CEO Gil Amelio out, Reed said: "When an Edgar Woolard, chairman of Du Pont and a Citicorp director, joins the board of Apple, he can't necessarily turn the company around—if Apple's in trouble, it's in trouble. But you can be sure there'll be disciplined discussions at the board level. And the directors will do more than come to meetings. Investors should learn to appreciate this subtlety."

[1]Robert F. Felton, Alec Hudnut, and Jennifer van Heeckeren, *McKinsey Quarterly*, 1996, Number 4.

Richard M. Schlefer, an assistant vice president at TIAA-CREF pension fund, is among those who are trying to make the governance-performance connection. A November 1996 *Business Week* article ("The Best and Worst Boards") quotes him as saying, "If a company has a governance structure that doesn't withstand scrutiny, we don't want to wait until there is a problem to get involved."[2] In other words, board effectiveness counts, regardless of current company performance. If a board is not functioning well, the company is at risk.

The converse also might apply. When the board is functioning well, it is unlikely that the company will lag. More likely, the company will be performance oriented all the way down. This possibility increases the importance of making outsiders aware of the company's governance practices.

Business Week and others recently have tried to evaluate board effectiveness. The November 1996 article mentioned above and its 1997 sequel, for instance, list the best and worst boards based on scores in four areas: accountability to shareholders, quality of the directors, independence, and corporate performance. Unfortunately, most measures and surveys of boards fail to get below the surface and still fall short of revealing whether the board is truly functioning as it should.

Boards should encourage management to take the offensive and let investors know that the board really works. To quote the conclusions of the McKinsey study: "Given that many investors do care about board governance, what action can companies take to improve their own practices? A good first step would be for senior executives, investors, and board members to learn how to talk together about substantive governance issues in a productive way. The survey indicates that a much broader consensus exists on board issues between management and investors than has typically been portrayed, and that there are likely to be opportunities for much productive discussion."

CEOs can get the message out through their investor relations professionals and in their own interactions with investors and analysts. One

[2]Reprinted from the November 25, 1996, issue of *Business Week* by special permission. Copyright 1996 by McGraw-Hill Companies.

CEO said: "This morning my investor relations guy mentioned that he had been talking to one of our major shareholders who said his hot button was outside directors. The investor relations person told the investor exactly what we were doing—the way we've reorganized our governance procedures and the way we're proceeding to select new board members." This same CEO was also considering saying something about the governance changes in the proxy.

Tom Loarie, CEO of venture capital–funded KeraVision, which went public in 1996, noticed that few on Wall Street understood the painstaking work the company was doing in transitioning the board. He decided to include the changes in his presentations to investors. He laments that still only a handful have picked up on what the board is doing.

When the new CEO of a $2 billion global manufacturing company met with investors, an institutional investor suggested two candidates for the board. Both were CEOs who had made their names by creating shareholder value. The two people met the CEO's criteria, and the CEO decided to act on the suggestions. In so doing, he took a first step toward building a board that is a competitive advantage in the capital markets. This is not a widespread phenomenon, but it is an emerging trend.

Of course, many security analysts have the kind of access that can give them insight into the board's functioning, even if it is not forthcoming from management. For any outsider, the focus should be on *function, not form*. Analysts can deduce the board's independence and contribution by asking the CEO the following kinds of questions:

1. How is the CEO using the wisdom, judgment, and counsel of the outside directors, individually and collectively? Good buy-side analysts often see the CEO one-on-one. They should use those opportunities to really probe this question. What process does the CEO use?

2. What is the nature of the information the CEO takes to the board, formally and informally? Does he share with the board what he anticipates in the future? If so, what variables is he or she considering—market share, productivity, sales, margins, new technologies? Are the goals appropriate? Is performance evaluated relative to the peer group, the S&P, or a broader group?

3. What outside information does the CEO provide to directors, especially those that may contradict the CEO's judgments (for example, J.D. Power Associates customer satisfaction information, or Jim Harbor productivity reports on the automobile industry)? Do not accept the CEO's remarks that directors have no time. The CEO may not be using directors' time properly.
4. What, if any, instrument is the board using to evaluate the CEO?

The degree of candor in answering these questions will itself give the analyst a strong indication of the climate in and around the boardroom.

Send the Right Signals

Boards cannot downplay the importance of shareholder perception. Shareholders want to know that directors' interests are aligned with their own. The National Association of Corporate Directors, in its 1995 Blue Ribbon Commission Report on Director Compensation, recommended that directors' pay be tied to performance through payment in stock and recommended establishing stock ownership targets for directors. Benefit programs, including pensions, meanwhile, can compromise the board's credibility with shareholders.

It is well known that boards are moving to a combination of cash and stock and are eliminating pensions. NYNEX paid the retainer half in cash, half in stock, and dropped the benefit pension plan. The company did, however, intentionally steer clear of stock options. Seidenberg explains: "The feeling was that one of the key roles of the directors is to approve dividends. Options come with no dividends. So for what it's worth, the more stock directors have in which they could touch dividends more often, the more intellectual linkage we had. Options tend to look a little more short-term than stock does anyway."

Some boards are moving away from cash payments entirely. Many other companies make it optional. Some companies, including Ashland Oil and BankAmerica, require directors to own stock equal to a multiple of the retainer.

As boards invest more time and add value, Ed Hotard of Praxair speculates, public perception of directors' pay might change. "Right now, most people think board members don't earn their fees. But if you consider the time some board members devote and the contribution some boards make, we may have to look at the compensation issue differently."

When it comes to executive compensation, directors must be sensitive not only to the linkage between compensation and shareholder value creation but also to the magnitude of the stock awards and severance packages they are granting. Astronomically high severance packages have been particularly controversial of late. It is the board's responsibility to balance the concerns of multiple constituencies in making these determinations.

Boards can further demonstrate that their interests are aligned with shareholders' by imposing internal performance measures that more accurately reflect the issues shareholders care most about. Money managers pay attention to the predictability and consistency of earnings growth, and always in comparison with a benchmark group. The board should look at the appropriate benchmarks.

At NYNEX, a piece of management's long-term compensation was based strictly on how well the company did against its peers. That measurement system was a big change from the older regulatory driven compensation plan, and investors liked it. Seidenberg explains:

> If the peer group ran at 30 percent shareholder returns for the year and NYNEX ran at 28 percent, management lost. That's what happened in 1995. We ran at a pace well above the average of the rest of the Dow Jones, but we were in the middle of the pack with respect to our peer group of ten companies. As a result, that piece of our bonus was scaled down. We had about as good a year as we could ever have, but compensation-wise, we didn't get the full bonus.
>
> It was a tough standard, because as we reduced the regulated piece of our earnings stream, we made a lot of investments that could impact shareholder value. But the board said it was my problem to maintain steady growth for the shareholder, even during the

transition. The compensation plan didn't reward us if we couldn't do both at the same time. As an incentive, it worked. We had nine straight quarters of earnings expansion.

CEO-Chairman John Reed says that some Citicorp board members occasionally remind him that while company performance is great, stockholders expect even more. In the area of executive compensation, the Citicorp board avoids simplistic solutions. Reed explains, "Recently when we were talking about how many shares of stock senior executives owned, the board warned us not to be over invested. They were concerned that if people had every last nickel invested in the stock, they might become too sensitive to short-term things and lose their perspective. Our board members can see both sides of the issue and are superb at bringing balance. They are truly independent thinkers."

Treating Shareholders Like Customers at Warner-Lambert

Building credibility with investors goes hand in hand with building the business.

In 1994, the pharmaceuticals industry was in motion. Glaxo Holdings merged with Wellcome, Pharmacia with Upjohn, American Home Products with American Cyanamid. Warner-Lambert, with its $8 billion market capitalization, was fair game, and some speculative investors began to buy its stock and press management to sell the company.

Warner-Lambert survived the merger mania intact, however, saving some 12,000 to 15,000 jobs and delivering more value to shareholders than if the company had been sold to the highest bidder. A core group of shareholders believed management's promise of a higher payoff two to three years out and held the stock, keeping it out of play.

Management's credibility with the investment community was well earned. For years company management, under the board's watch, had made extraordinary efforts to keep investors informed about the company and to respond to their concerns. In fact, for nine consecutive years, analysts have rated Warner-Lambert first or second for management accessibility to investors among seventeen pharmaceutical companies. Throughout the industry consolidation, CEO Melvin R. Goodes kept a steady focus on the long-term plan to bring promising new drugs to market, and he "sold" the idea to investors through open communication and candor.

Goodes did not let shareholders determine the company strategy, but he did listen to them, and by listening, was able to discern some legitimate concerns. He took a hard look at Warner-Lambert's assets and operations and took decisive steps to boost reported earnings in the short term. Along the way, he and his team kept the board well informed about shareholder sentiment and their response to it through frequent, direct communication between directors and the head of investor relations.

Shareholders who held Warner-Lambert stock between 1994 and 1997 are glad they did. The company's market value grew from $8 billion to $38 billion, and the stock price rose from $30 to $140 after a two-for-one split.

At a time when relationships among management, shareholders, and the board are often strained, Warner-Lambert's approach to investor relations is a model of how to align interests. Warner-Lambert sets the standard in shareholder relations to which all boards should hold the CEO.

Investors to Die For

At Warner-Lambert, the investor relations department is a powerhouse that is valued as highly as any other functional area. It is staffed by high-powered people who are in frequent communication with all of senior management and the board. It is a function people get promoted into and is seen as a developmental opportunity. Its responsibilities go beyond the usual.

Every year the investment relations department creates a kind of marketing strategy for Warner-Lambert stock. At the core of this strategy is a list Goodes calls "Investors to Die For." These are investors that Warner-Lambert would like to have owning its stock because their investment goals are consistent with those of the company. In the early 1990s, Goodes noticed that consumer goods companies like Wrigley, Gillette, and P&G were selling at roughly twenty times earnings. Warner-Lambert competed against those companies, but its P/E was much lower. Goodes believed that long-term investors could help stabilize the company's market value and boost the P/E to the level of its consumer goods competitors.

In 1993, the investor relations department assembled its first list of long-term investors, defined as investors who are known to turn over less than 30 percent of their portfolio a year. These are investors that keep their stock an average of three years. The list has been updated each year since. Initially, most investors on the list were from the United States, but the company has recently improved its tracking in Europe, where investors tend to hold stock longer. Each year, the company undertakes a one-week trip to Europe to cultivate investors with long-term investment perspectives.

The list of "Investors to Die For" guides the company's investor relations efforts. For those who do not own Warner-Lambert stock, the aim is to inform them about the company to get them interested. For those who do own the stock, the aim is to keep them well informed so they do not sell it off when rumors about the company circulate. Reaching investors before they sell is important. Goodes explains: "There's a lot of politics in these big investment firms. Once the fund managers sell the stock, they're not likely to buy it again."

Those on the list also get access to senior management, up to and including the CEO. As Goodes says, "I'll talk to anybody on the list at any time." Investors who are not on the list do not get management's time, even when they are the biggest, most prominent funds. "Investor relations is no different from any other business function," Goodes says. "We target our efforts." When one large fund requested to meet with the CEO and the investor relations director when they were making a trip to New York, Goodes flatly refused. "They had a bad history with us," he explains. "A while ago, they had a significant position in our company, and they told us they were a long-term investor. But in one quarter, at a time when we were a potential takeover candidate, they sold off over 80 percent of their holdings. We would rather spend our time with investors who meet our criteria."

Every quarter, the investor relations department contacts large investors by phone to discuss earnings and answer questions. Though investor relations fields many questions and calls, Goodes ensures his direct involvement with investors in several ways. For one thing, he sees all the reports that are sent out by the sell-side analysts. For another, he listens in on the monthly phone calls investor relations makes to investors, on tape if he cannot do it live. Most important, he goes out on the road or picks up the phone whenever he hears that the investors on the list are unhappy.

Credibility Through Intellectual Honesty

Warner-Lambert wins over and keeps the most desirable new investors not through slick public relations campaigns but through intellectual honesty. The point is not to buy time but to win loyalty by making the company's value-creating processes and plans available and known to outsiders. That means telling investors the truth about significant events in or around the business. Communication between the investor and management is filter-free and often preemptive. Goodes recalls:

At about 6 o'clock one evening I had heard that a leading investor in Europe, who had held our stock for four years, was thinking of selling. I asked my investor relations people for the guy's home phone number, and at 5 o'clock the next morning East Coast time I tried to reach him. His secretary didn't believe it was me because I called directly and didn't use a secretary or anything. I had to leave a message for the guy to call me back.

Fifteen minutes later, the investor called back and we talked. Of course, he assumed I was in Europe. Why else would I call? I explained that I was home but that we were getting in touch with our most important investors to tell them about some major developments that were going on in our company. I didn't tell him I knew he was going to sell.

Everything I told him was true and accurate. I wasn't making empty promises. I was just giving him the facts. That guy has a lasting impression of us, and he has held us through thick and thin.

When another big stockholder was planning to sell the stock, the investor relations people contacted him to ask why. The investor said that he had already gotten his full ride. The investor relations department explained the value he had yet to receive because of things the company would be doing in the next year or two.

Investors who are not accustomed to getting information directly from the CEO can be skeptical. When Goodes visited one fund manager following a negative and inaccurate story about a deal Warner-Lambert had made, the person questioned why Goodes was out "hawking stock." The CEO explained his philosophy: "I told him that we respect our investors as much as our customers. That's why I want to tell you face-to-face why the story is not valid." The press had in fact gotten it wrong, and through the course of the discussion, the fund manager was convinced that the company did not have a serious problem.

In explaining its plans as openly as possible, management puts its best thinking and judgment on the line. The investment community does not always approve. When controversy erupts, Goodes himself is willing to go toe-to-toe. He remembers a meeting with analysts when one attendee challenged everything he said. Goodes finally said, " 'Look, you have a choice. You can either believe what I say and buy our stock or be sorry you didn't a year from now.' As confrontational as that is, I tried to deliver it in a matter-of-fact way, because I was presenting the facts as I knew them to be."

Goodes continues: "If I had a nickel for every time somebody said I should divest one group or another, I would be a wealthy man. The point is that you have to give shareholders' suggestions reasonable consideration, but you can't let investors run your business."

Another analyst at the same session was convinced. "As a result of my response," Goodes says, "one person there became a real believer. She came up with a buy recommendation when the stock was trading at around $38. Two years later, it was $140. Needless to say, she came out looking great."

Credibility Through Action

Warner-Lambert management walks the fine line between being receptive to shareholders' concerns and adopting knee-jerk solutions in response to market pressures. When some Warner-Lambert stockholders tried to push the company to merge in the early 1990s, Goodes took a hard look at the business.

The CEO had made a point of visiting the labs and talking to the people who were actually involved in research. He was convinced that the drugs in the pipeline were real and commercially viable. With FDA approval probable, the company's long-term investments would soon begin to pay off. Goodes concluded that merging was not the way to maximize long-term value. Sure, investors would reap a short-term gain (and Goodes himself would profit handsomely) if the company were to merge, but if the company stayed intact and commercialized the drugs, investors would stand to gain much more value, and some 12,000 to 15,000 jobs would be saved.

But the reality was that shareholders were demanding short-term earnings as well. Management's "reasonable consideration" of shareholder concerns translated into a transitional plan to bolster short-term earnings while continuing to invest $100 million a year to commercialize the drugs. The transitional plan, called "Bridges to Prosperity," included dozens of ideas for improving reported earnings. Goodes himself marketed the plan internally, speaking to seven thousand people to muster support.

Selling nonstrategic assets was an obvious fix. Determining which assets were strategic was not so obvious and forced management to rethink its assumptions. "We had to ask whether there was interconnectivity between our consumer products business and pharmaceuticals business," Goodes says, "and that gets back to your corporate purpose. After a lot of disagreement and discussion among senior management and the board, we decided that because pharmaceuticals is high risk, it was good to have a consumer products business to support it."

The test of whether the specific businesses should stay or go was whether the company could derive more value by selling it or keeping it. On that basis, Warner-Lambert decided to sell the Pro Toothbrush business to Gillette and to keep the Tetra Fish Pond business. Bids for Tetra were around $600 million, which was very attractive from a profit standpoint, but management believed the business was worth more like $800. The company decided to keep it and fix it.

The company also launched an initiative, called "Warner-Lambert Works," to improve operations. This effort included process reengineering for productivity improvement, a move toward global purchasing, and changes in procurement. As far as Goodes was concerned, cutting R&D was not an option. In his view, "Cutting R&D is admitting defeat. When you have a long-term focus in R&D and a planned investment of $450 million, you *could* cut $75 million a year for three years and call it productivity improvement. Some CEOs do that, and some short-term investors applaud that, but I know it's not good for the company in the long run."

Where the Board Comes In

At Warner-Lambert, the CEO takes the lead in communicating with investors. This, Goodes believes, is as it should be. The CEO bridges the gap between the company and its shareholders. The CEO also keeps the board informed about the company's efforts in the investor relations area. The board makes sure the CEO makes the effort.

The board receives all comments and investment recommendations from sell-side analysts. These are mailed out to the board in advance of each meeting. When there are problems with the external analyst view of the company, the CEO needs to be very open about the reasons for this and explain how the internal policy remains valid in the face of these external comments.

If the board isn't well informed about management's relationship with shareholders, directors should put the topic on the table. Goodes says: "Boards should insist that investor relations be discussed in the boardroom. What's the plan? How adequate is it? Especially if you have CEOs on the board, directors will know a good shareholder relationship when they see one."

Key Points

- The board is the best mechanism for balancing long-term and short-term goals and for making trade-offs between shareholders and other constituencies who eventually impact shareholder value anyway.

- Make sure management is listening to shareholders but not being coerced by them. The board should help CEOs stand up to maverick investors who try to force actions, particularly in the area of divestitures and restructuring, for their own short-term gain.

- Insist that the CEO has a comprehensive plan for communicating with shareholders and building credibility in the market.

- Let investors know that the board is working well. Good governance enhances market value.

CHAPTER SEVEN

CEO EVALUATION THAT ADDS VALUE

Most boards interpret their responsibility for monitoring the CEO far too narrowly. Their efforts to make CEO evaluations more meaningful have focused on questions of executive compensation: How much should we pay the CEO, and how can we justify that decision to shareholders and meet SEC requirements? They emphasize the mechanics of the CEO review process.

Boards at work use the CEO feedback process to create competitive advantage. Indeed, a well-designed CEO feedback process is the single best way for a board to add value to the corporation. It is absolutely essential to understand this point and get the CEO review process right.

A CEO feedback process should explicitly address the important question: Can this CEO take the company forward? It should help the board make a collective judgment about whether the CEO is matched to the job and make that collective judgment available to the CEO. Such feedback helps good CEOs perform better. It can even be career saving. Dick Brown, CEO of Cable & Wireless and board chairman of Pharmacia-Upjohn, says, "That kind of feedback is a gift."

A good CEO feedback process cements a critical link between the board's two most important roles. Joe Gorman, chairman and CEO of TRW, explains: "The board's first role is to select the right chief executive officer. Obviously, the nature of your chief executive depends on the company's strategic needs, which leads to the board's second role—strategy review and approval, and bringing different perspectives to that process."

Too often, boards merely go through the motions of a formal CEO review process and do not touch on the real issues. If directors feel compelled to discuss sensitive issues, they talk to the CEO in private. Although there is nothing wrong with one-on-one discussions between a director and the CEO, the lack of open communication within the board means the collective wisdom cannot emerge. The board cannot reach a collective judgment, let alone take collective action. Also, without open communication, a "caste system" often develops, leaving some directors to feel disenfranchised. Those who counsel the CEO in private miss the opportunity to test their opinions, and the CEO misses other directors' perspectives.

That is not how a board is designed to function. That will not turn the board into a competitive advantage. That is not a board at work.

Be Critical, Not Adversarial

Many CEOs continue to resist the notion of a formal performance review by the board and resent the idea of the board putting them under a microscope. Many boards sense the CEO's discomfort and back away from conducting a rigorous evaluation. As one director says, "I have yet to run across a board that really is willing to lay out its expectations for the CEO on a short- and long-term basis and evaluate the CEO on that basis. Many boards don't dare do it."

But the fact is, directors have opinions. Those opinions must come out in the open. This same director adds, "Evaluating the CEO is no different from assessing any other aspect of the business or its people. It must be done with the same rigor. And it must be done on two bases: the actual results of the company and the individual's behaviors. How is the company doing, and how is the CEO doing as a role model and the leader of a whole organization? Boards stay away from this area." Venture capitalist Marshall Turner says, "Unfortunately, the clearest feedback I have seen has been when a board member is pressed by a fired CEO to answer the question, 'Why?' Then it's too late to be helpful." In one case when a CEO asked the question, the directors declined to respond because they felt such discussion would be unproductive.

Some CEOs do welcome a rigorous, formalized review process that goes beyond mechanical formulas. Milt Honea of Houston-based NorAm, John Cleghorn of Royal Bank of Canada, Tom Loarie of Kera-Vision, and Ivan Seidenberg of NYNEX are among those who have encouraged their boards to make performance criteria explicit and subjective and to make the review process more formalized. As Honea's board discussed the idea of doing a formal CEO review, Honea said, "Whether the Compensation Committee does it or the full board, I welcome it. I might get killed, but we need it!"

Of course, boards do not kill companies. Lack of performance does. These progressive CEOs believe the board can keep them from being their own worst enemy.

CEO evaluation works at NorAm, NYNEX, and other companies in part because the boards have reconceptualized the evaluation process. The main thrust of the boards' oversight is vigilance and constructive input—a forward-looking "We'll help you" rather than a retrospective "We got you!" This fundamental shift in attitude is key to achieving the new vision of corporate governance.

Whereas independence of thought is necessary to preserve the integrity of the process, hostility is counterproductive. If the board focuses solely on its role as watchdog, it will have trouble achieving the kind of collegiality and cooperation that help the board understand the company and contribute to its success.

Look Forward, Not Just Back

Any board can make a mistake in choosing a CEO (the selection of a business leader is not a science), and external changes can make any CEO obsolete while still in the job. It is the board's job to recognize and remedy these problem situations promptly. Once a year, the board should consider:

1. *Where is the company headed?* Is the CEO building for the future? Is the strategic positioning likely to bring near-term and long-term success? This is an important way for the board to have input before an action is taken and to address weaknesses as they emerge.
2. *Does the CEO put reality on the table?* Does the company's strategic direction reflect reality, both opportunities and problems? Does he or she have a specific, realistic plan to deal with adversity? Has he or she considered a full range of options? What is Plan B? Directors can instinctively sense when they are getting only part of the story.
3. *Does the CEO have a handle on operations?* As one director puts it, "Is the steering connected to the wheel?"
4. *Is the CEO creating the management team of the future?* Is the CEO building and retaining the right kind of team of direct reports? The director of one large company wondered what was going on at the company when four key executives left within a few months.
5. *Is the CEO building positive relationships with external constituents?* For companies that depend heavily on constituencies beyond stockholders, how well is the CEO and the management team building those relationships? Is the CEO driven by ego or by shareholder interests?
6. *Does the CEO deliver results?* Are the commitments being met? Are patterns such as downward revisions four quarters in a row symptomatic of deeper problems?
7. *When the CEO is also board chairman, how well is he or she performing that role?* Does he or she invite the best and varied thinking of the board? Does he or she help judgment coalesce?

These questions are forward looking and subjective, but directors are generally quite skilled at deducing the answers through observation of the CEO's behavior, personality traits, and actions. This is not an inferior kind of information. On the contrary, it is the most relevant kind of information a board can derive. It is uncanny how quickly directors' individual judgments converge on such subjective matters.

William T. Solomon, chairman, president, and CEO of Austin Industries and director of A. H. Belo Corporation, underscores the need to look beyond mechanical formulas when evaluating a CEO: "Numbers are very important in terms of monitoring the CEO's goals, but the way he assesses the company's goals, the issues he thinks the company is facing, how he describes to the board how he's dealing with them, and how a year later he achieves what he set out to achieve—those are the kinds of things that cumulatively build a degree of confidence or lack of confidence in a leader. Evaluating a CEO along those lines is an intuitive process." Another director mentioned the need to view the CEO "holistically."

Discussions of CEO performance for the purposes of annual compensation tend to cut subjective issues short. Creating two separate processes can avoid that problem. The board can use one process to determine annual compensation and a separate process to evaluate the CEO's total leadership and to give the chief executive the benefit of that feedback. Separating the processes will help the board identify when a CEO who has been successful in the past is not the leader for the future and, more often, provide an opportunity for directors to give the CEO their thinking about what is going well and what he or she might improve. The NYNEX board held two discussions, one that looked forward and one that looked back.

Bring Directors' Instincts to the Surface

Most directors have their antennas up all the time and have an instinctive feel for the CEO's credibility and competence. Given performance data, contact with managers below the level of the CEO, and observation of the CEO interacting with direct reports and responding to questions, directors get an overall level of confidence in the CEO.

Directors should insist that the CEO periodically explain his or her major decisions, appointments of people, past performance, and the external environment. During these sessions, the watchword is *dialogue,* not monologue. Board members should not hesitate to ask their most incisive questions—and the CEO should encourage them to.

How well is the CEO dealing with problems that arise, and what is the overall momentum of the business? When things begin to deviate, does the CEO say it is an aberration, or is it seasonal, cyclical, structural, or permanent? (At Bausch & Lomb, the declining numbers in the contact lens business were caused by a structural change in the industry, triggered by Johnson & Johnson's disposable contact lens business.) Does the CEO's explanation coincide with what others are saying about the industry? Why is it different?

What opportunities are being missed, and why? Is the direction right but the implementation lousy? If earnings are declining after a major acquisition, ask if it was the wrong acquisition. What assumptions were made beforehand? Which of those were wrong? Or is the issue one of integrating the acquisition on a profitable basis? Are the problems being confronted there?

Many directors speak of the importance of getting insight into the CEO's mental process. Director Bill Adams says: "Discussing the company's major decisions does two things. First, it helps you understand the company's position in the world, how it plans to get where it's going. Second, it enables you to assess the thinking of management. You have the top guys there in the pit, so to speak, so you're able to get an idea of what their unprogrammed thinking is. From that, either I get a sense of confidence in the people, or I don't."

Some directors stress the importance of looking beyond the CEO to see whether the management is energized and aligned. Bill Solomon of Austin Industries says: "To evaluate the CEOs as a director of boards I've been on, I've found it necessary to have sufficient contact with the CEO in the context of running the business. Board members must have a chance to observe how effectively the CEO is leading the company toward the goals."

Boards should insist on getting the information and access they need and make it part of the CEO's evaluation. Then they must create an operating mechanism to bring the individual instincts to the surface into some kind of collective judgment. In designing a feedback process, accuracy, efficiency, and balance should be paramount. The group, not an individual, must be the focal point. As Dick Brown of Cable & Wireless says, "The board has to trust itself, individually and collectively, on the fundamental issue, 'Do we have the right CEO?' You can't decide whether the CEO is right or wrong on partial data or on the opinions of only some board members."

Some operating mechanisms are better than others. One option is for the chairman of the organization and compensation committee or the governance committee (or their equivalents) to solicit feedback from each director individually, synthesize the feedback, and present it to the CEO in a private meeting. This process, however, filters the information through one person without any cross-checks for accuracy and biases. Board members do not get to listen to and react to each others' comments, and a caste system can easily develop if directors feel their opinions have not been appropriately considered.

At some companies, the governance committee members divide up the task of getting feedback orally from individual board members. The committee then synthesizes the feedback. This process gets the whole board involved and allows the interviewer to clarify any ambiguities. This approach is time consuming, however. It does not ensure consistency, and the degree of distortion depends on the skill of the director who is conducting the interview.

Alternatively, the organization and compensation committee or the corporate governance committee can lead the board in designing a written questionnaire that each director completes. A board member, probably the committee chair, can collate the results. An *open-ended questionnaire* would ask one or a few simple questions about the CEO's performance and allow the director to write a page or so in response. Dayton-Hudson has used this format. The advantages of this approach are that it allows directors to discuss the CEO without having to pigeonhole their remarks and to be totally subjective, instinctive, and natural in how they express themselves. But it requires great analytic skill to find the center of gravity in the written comments. Third-parties are not always able to detect the nuances well enough to do a good analysis, and board members cannot always be objective in their interpretation of the data.

A *structured questionnaire* poses a series of questions that directors can answer on a numerical scale of 1 to 7 or by multiple choice. This approach ensures that all directors cover the same ground, is easy to analyze (a committee chairman can do it), and provides a road map for constructive thought. Disadvantages are that directors do not have the opportunity to explain or clarify their answers, and they may want to raise something that falls outside the range of questions. The nuances of judgment and instinct do not normally fall neatly into the designated categories.

The best and most popular alternative is to create a *hybrid* of the first two kinds of questionnaires—use structured questions but also include open-ended questions. This format combines the advantages of the first two. It makes it relatively easy to find the center of gravity and allows directors to express their instincts naturally. This type of format has been used successfully by at least three companies. The CEO and Chairman of Feedback Instruments at the end of this chapter are similar to questionnaires in actual use at those companies. One company uses the questionnaire as a guideline for discussion only; it does not require directors to complete the form in writing.

For practical reasons, a small group of people (ideally, three or four people rather than the full board) should work on the initial design of the evaluation process. At some companies, the governance committee has taken the lead in designing the process for evaluating the CEO's total leadership, while the organization and compensation committee leads design of the process of determining CEO pay.

Throughout the feedback process, confidentiality and professionalism are important. One outside director and former CEO says: "On one board I'm on, some board members are reluctant to put down what they really think about the chairman. They fear that if they do, they won't be on that board much longer. Any kind of survey has to be confidential and must go to somebody other than the CEO or chairman."

Deliver the Feedback in Two Steps

Getting the board's feedback can be a highly emotional experience for the CEO, especially the first time. Emotions can run the full spectrum from delight to despair. A good feedback process should take that reality into account. Some boards have found a two-step feedback process to be highly effective.

Step one: Once the board has thoroughly discussed the CEO's performance, two board members present the feedback to the CEO in private. The CEO can then think about the feedback and respond. This first step makes the process less threatening to the CEO and more conducive to dialogue and adjustment. The presence of a second director adds clarity and makes this step less personality-dependent.

Step two: The full board and the CEO discuss the feedback and the CEO's response to it at a board meeting. This second step forces a certain discipline in the first step. It ensures that the feedback was communicated accurately, and that it was received the way it was meant.

CEO Doug Olesen describes the feedback process at Battelle Memorial Institute: "The board typically meets with me for a while in an informal way to discuss how they feel about my performance against the goals, and so on. After that, the directors go into executive session and make an evaluation about me. The chairman of the compensation committee gives me the feedback in private."

Doug Olesen's further remarks indicate that the feedback process can take on a different cast depending on who is delivering the news: "The effectiveness of having one person talk to me is obviously very dependent on who it is and how aggressive and frank they are. Two different directors have done it in the past. One was far kinder and gentler, the other was much more blunt." Having two board members involved can make the feedback process less dependent on an individual's personality and also provides a check on the accuracy of the feedback and the CEO's response.

The CEO of a large North American manufacturing company, the largest in its field, experienced a lot of psychological stress when the board, having given him superficial feedback at the July meeting, postponed the full discussion of his performance review not once but twice. As the next board meeting approached, the compensation committee chairman failed to return the CEO's phone calls, and the CEO began to believe that his job was in jeopardy. When the board finally discussed the feedback in full, the CEO learned that while the board wanted him to move faster on the agreed-upon initiatives, it was generally supportive of him. The long silence had caused the CEO undue concern.

The effectiveness of the feedback process depends in large part on the degree of candor. A formal evaluation and feedback process does not mean that the atmosphere must be stiff. In fact, the board should strive for informality in the dialogue among board members and between the board and CEO. But the feedback also must be direct. Reprocessing of the feedback—that is, listening and restating it—can help ensure accuracy.

Directors may have to work at expressing their true feelings without reservation. Don't hide behind politeness. In designing ways to form collective judgment, boards should be keenly aware of directors' deep-seated desire to be nice. That is, many board members tend to go easy on the CEO out of a notion of politeness and protocol. Choose venues—both formal and informal—that foster candor and discussion leaders who are sensitive to board dynamics. Ability to lead a group discussion might, for instance, become a criterion for the chairman of the governance committee. It also helps to lay the groundwork when times are good rather than waiting until the CEO's leadership is in serious question.

The CEO can encourage candor by asking directors what they think and by suppressing any defensive reactions. One incoming CEO worked hard to change the board's polite restraint. A few months be-fore he took over, he visited with every director to get their thoughts about what the company needed. In the course of his conversations, he found that the directors discussed only the positives. They seemed to want to show their support for the CEO by avoiding the hard realities. The CEO persevered and eventually convinced directors that they could behave differently with the newcomer, and the dynamics inside and outside the boardroom began to change.

Give Directors Time Alone

Directors should pull their instincts together formally once a year, but boards that work well exchange opinions about the company and the CEO informally throughout the year. The "huddle," or meeting-after-the-meeting without the CEO, is a simple, effective way to do that. It gives outside directors a low-key opportunity to raise sensitive issues and learn what others are thinking without having to create a special event.

When the CEO returns after a "huddle," a board member should describe to the CEO everything that came out during those discussions, very specifically but without using people's names. Closing the com-munication loop in this way keeps the CEO aware of the board's thoughts and feelings, eliminates distrust, and avoids misinformation and misunderstanding. The huddle thereby becomes a tool for ongoing coaching and communication between management and the board.

The last hour of Tektronix board meetings are reserved for open discussion, during which time Chairman-CEO Jerry Meyer always of-fers to leave the room. He explains: "The outside directors usually say that isn't necessary. But I always give them the opportunity instead of making them ask me for it. At least twice a year, I leave anyway."

Meyer continues: "Some people argue that you should never leave the board alone because a lot of venom could come out. My response is that they're going to talk among themselves anyway if they're really upset. I would much prefer to have them talk among themselves in the protocol and discipline of a board meeting. But I also encourage the board to say whatever they want to about me and the company in the normal course of things."

Sam Eichenfield, chairman and CEO of The FINOVA Group, has a similar outlook: "I always give the outside directors the opportunity to meet alone. I've told them to feel free to plan their own meetings or to let us know and we'll take care of the arrangements. I think it is important for a CEO to encourage that. It gives directors a chance to come to common positions or to bring up certain things they might not feel appropriate to discuss in front of me during the board meeting."

Some CEOs leave the room for a mere ten minutes at the end of every board meeting. Of course, directors can take more time if they need it. When John Cleghorn used this mechanism at his first board meeting as chairman of Royal Bank of Canada in early 1995, the board members exchanged their views on how good the meeting had been. The positive feedback was very encouraging. The second time, the board made suggestions about how to improve the presentations by management.

As candor develops inside the boardroom, there is less need for directors to meet without the CEO, except for performance evaluation. Still, many boards see the value in making the huddle a routine mechanism as a safeguard and as another way to encourage new patterns of behavior.

Joe Gorman, CEO of TRW and director of P&G and other boards, says: "The lack of infrastructure can kill a chairman. If the infrastructure isn't there, directors won't meet without the chairman until they sense a crisis. Then when they start meeting in executive session, the chairman will be shaken, with good reason. But if the board is having executive sessions regularly, they might catch a gray area earlier and make it much less of a problem. The chairman would thank his lucky stars."

Creating a routine mechanism that allows directors to express their thoughts openly without the CEO eliminates one of the arguments for appointing a "lead director." The common rationale for the lead director concept is that directors can express their feelings to the lead director, and the board can gel in position more quickly. The huddle achieves the same benefits without the drawbacks of a lead director.

Turn Judgment into Action

Once the board has made a collective judgment, it has to decide whether to counsel, coach, probe, investigate, or cut the CEO loose. Coaching and counseling can go a long way in helping the CEO address weaknesses or differences of opinion. At one industrial company, the board was very satisfied with the CEO's performance overall but recognized one fundamental shortcoming: The CEO did not have a superior manager of information technology, and the company was at risk of falling behind technologically. The board advised the CEO to hire a technology expert from the outside to improve the company's information systems. The CEO accepted the recommendation.

In good times, CEOs benefit greatly from this kind of regular feedback. When things are not going well, the CEO is not surprised by the board's reaction, nor is the board surprised by the financial or market results the CEO generates. On rare occasion, the board will discover that it made a mistake in hiring the CEO (very unusual, but always a risk). Then it must move to replace the CEO. But that realization will not occur instantly, and given a well designed CEO review process, it will come as a surprise to no one.

Most often, the board's early attention to problems can help turn things around. Says Richard Koppes of Calpers in *Fortune* magazine in February 1995, "If you can get boards overseeing and challenging management early on, then you shouldn't have disruptive firings."

The challenge for boards is to gauge their actions appropriately. Sometimes success and failure are clear-cut, and the consequences then are straightforward, but there is much gray area. CEOs do not fail or succeed overnight. How should a board proceed when clouds begin to gather on the horizon or opportunities seem to be slipping by? When should a board ride it out with the CEO? When should it cut its losses?

Begin with Coaching

If the board has concern about the CEO's abilities, it should do all it can to help the CEO. Give advice and make expectations clear. This can be done by the board as a whole or by one or two individual board members who take the CEO aside and provide confidential, one-on-one advice. For the second approach to work, the board must be sure that its delegate is not seeking personal power over the CEO or vying for the job. At GM, John Smale, for instance, has proven to be sincerely interested in helping Jack Smith succeed by lending his marketing expertise.

When one company's compensation committee gathered directors' feedback on the CEO, a serious criticism came to the surface: the CEO, who had been brought in from the outside, was not learning the industry fast enough. As the committee chairman prepared to give the CEO the feedback, other directors were concerned about how it would be presented. The committee chairman explains, "Everybody tended to want to make her a success rather than fire her. We decided that the CEO needed some fundamental coaching around the major issues in the industry and we linked her with a retired senior executive from the industry for specific coaching."

Back the CEO You Trust

If the CEO continues not to meet expectations, the board should insist that he or she make the fixes concrete. Establish more frequent milestones to measure progress, and most important, listen to the CEO's rationale. As the CEO explains the problems and plans for getting through them, directors will get a gut feel for whether the person understands the real issues and is willing to tackle them. The instincts of seasoned business people, tested among their peers, are a reliable indicator of the CEO's ability to pull the company through.

If the board collectively believes the CEO is on the right track, it should present a unified front and stand firmly behind the CEO, even if things are likely to get worse before they get better. This is what the Citicorp board did in 1991, as mentioned in the previous chapter. Dealing with shareholders in such a situation may pose a challenge, but the decision actively to support a CEO through a transition is another way boards can add value. (For further discussion of such situations, see Chapter Six).

Use a Methodical Process to Replace the CEO

If problems persist and directors are not convinced that the CEO is dealing with them, the board can take incremental steps to limit the CEO's sphere of influence and find a replacement. When outsiders forced the Kodak board to focus on Kay Whitmore's performance, the board moved in steps. First it got more deeply involved in strategy, human resources, and finance, and only as the board continued to have concerns did it take the ultimate step to replace the CEO.

If the CEO has proven that he or she is unable to change, the board must face the tough decision and cut its losses. Bill Solomon of Austin Industries says: "For the individual director to reach the point of saying that the CEO has to go, it's an accumulation of judgment. You look at performance against stated objectives, you form an intuition about what is this person's accountability for these problems, the circumstances beyond his or her control. We all have a tendency to wait too long. I've waited too long instead of acting. As I've gotten older, I've relied more on my gut feelings for an issue. My gut says this person's got to go—and again, I want input from other people. But generally, we all wait a little too long."

One board, in its discussion of the CEO's performance, decided that the board would give the chief executive a year to improve in an area of fundamental weakness. If the CEO had failed to show improvement in that time, the board would strongly consider removing him. A director notes, "The review process put the issue on the radar screen." When the board's expectations and concerns are clear, the consequences are often self-evident. The CEO knows the board will not continue to back him or her if the targets are missed and will sometimes offer to resign.

The Soft Side of CEO Compensation

Much has been written elsewhere on the mechanics of CEO compensation. Boards have an important role in setting goals, a topic not fully explored. Goals should not be strictly formulaic and quantitative. They should establish what the CEO has to do in terms of management development, customer satisfaction, changing the organization's culture or "genetic code," or building competence for the future. At NYNEX, for instance, the CEO had to meet very specific goals in terms of strategic performance and management development.

The board must help establish the goals through professional dialogue and negotiation with the CEO. Directors do not have the depth of knowledge to know what areas are crucial. It is the CEO's job to identify them and to help ensure that the standards are realistic and relevant. CEOs should not abdicate their responsibility in this area.

If senior management is present during any part of the negotiations, the board should be careful not to come on so strong that it appears to challenge the CEO's leadership. At one company, following management's presentation of the strategic plan, several directors insisted on a much more aggressive financial goal using a tone that conveyed serious dissatisfaction. Although the directors were justified in raising the bar, doing so in the presence of ten senior executives undermined the CEO's authority.

Tektronix CEO Jerry Meyer describes how he and his board find agreement on his yearly objectives:

> I recall a board meeting a number of years ago where I said, "Let me tell you on four slides what the top management objectives are, going forward, because this is the day when we change from cut and slash to grow." I explained that we would not use the term *lay-off* for twelve months and that my letters to them would talk about customer calls and customer alliances, not excess property and excess assets. I established in the board's mind the fact that we are now in the second stage of our transformation and outlined our objectives.

I explained that the person who last year had been responsible for implementing the restructure program is now responsible for convincing the board that we have a strategy and an underlying business. That's his objective for next year; if he doesn't accomplish it, he doesn't get paid a bonus. The chief operating officer is going to accomplish several specific, measurable things: fix one of our units and get inventories down. The chief financial officer had four things to do, one of which was to fix our financial analysis and modeling capability so we would never again come out of the fiscal year complaining about our journal systems.

I went over these things on four slides in fifteen minutes, and the board really liked it. So we got buy-in from the board. From that, it was very easy to determine my own goals. Those four slides represented the CEO's objectives. The board and I were in complete agreement that those were the things I had to accomplish.

Creating CEO Review from Scratch at "Temple Ward Technology"

How the board brought its instincts to the surface and addressed the leadership problem in time.[1]

The board of Temple Ward Technology, formed when California-based Temple Technology merged with London-based Ward, plc, was just a year and a half old when it faced one of the toughest situations any board could contend with: lack of confidence in the CEO. The merger had created an $8 billion player, large and diverse enough to be viable in its competitive industry. Kurt Lanzet, CEO and chairman of Temple, became CEO of the newly created company, and Neville Pratt, CEO of Ward, became chairman (splitting the chairman and CEO jobs is common practice in the United Kingdom).

[1]This case describes a real situation. Names and some details have been disguised.

Boards on both sides of the Atlantic had entered the merger enthusiastically. The ten directors who remained on the newly combined board had no regrets about the decision and credited Lanzet with masterminding the merger. But directors did have some concerns going forward. As CEO of the newly created company, Lanzet seemed unprepared to integrate the two businesses. Throughout the first year, key people were leaving, and commitments were not being met.

Long before investors complained about financial performance, a few directors sensed dissatisfaction with the CEO's leadership among their board colleagues. They quickly created a process to ascertain how deep and widespread that dissatisfaction was and to help the board make a collective judgment.

By heeding the early warning signs, the board addressed the leadership problem in time to prevent a major market decline and a serious loss of talent. As one director put it, "When that process was over, the board knew and trusted itself very well."

The Instinct to Act

As with any merger, Temple Ward's success required fast work in the first year or two to make the necessary reductions in cost and head-count and realign loyalties and strategic focus. Otherwise, the P/E would quickly suffer. The newly created Temple Ward board had discussed the performance issues with CEO Kurt Lanzet at the time of the merger, and everyone agreed on the need to decentralize control and hit earnings goals. The CEO had gone one step beyond by setting stretch goals.

The CEO set out confidently and with the board's full support, but as that first year progressed, a few things happened that made directors somewhat uncomfortable. For one thing, the CEO seemed to distance himself from the board. He communicated with the board less and less often, and there were indications that the CEO had told his direct reports not to speak directly with any board members. Board Chairman Pratt heard rumblings from some people inside the company who complained that Lanzet's brand of leadership was alienating some of the company's top performers and was not likely to accomplish the integration that was necessary. Also, the CEO harshly criticized his direct reports in the board's presence, yet he gave them generous salary increases and bonuses.

Board members, meanwhile, were still getting to know each other. Despite the conscious effort to mix in (directors from Ward were intentionally interspersed with directors from Temple at meetings and dinners) and the common goal of making the new company successful, the board had not yet coalesced as a group, nor had it established all of its processes.

When the first set of annual financial results came in, they went directly to Ryland Miller, chairman of the compensation committee. The results were not good. CEO Lanzet was far below the original goals, let alone the stretch goals. The disappointing financial results raised doubts in Miller's mind. He wanted to know how other directors felt about Lanzet.

This was to be Temple Ward's first serious evaluation of the CEO, and the board discussed the details of the process in executive session. Some members wanted to discuss the results in an open forum immediately. Others wanted time to think about it. The compromise was to have Miller talk to each director confidentially and then for the board to discuss the results in an open forum. In making the rounds, all agreed, Miller should be as objective as possible.

Miller did as his colleagues suggested. He spoke with every director, assuming a neutral position, spending an hour to an hour and a half with each, writing down their comments verbatim, and reading them back to check for accuracy. Nearly every director expressed grave concern about Lanzet. By the time Miller had completed his task, he knew he was sitting on a powder keg. He was not sure whether to wait until the board met again or to do something in the interim. He ultimately decided to enlist the help of two of the more influential board members—Board Chairman Pratt and Nominating Committee Chairman Jean Estler.

When Miller told Pratt and Estler what he found, they were quite concerned. They quickly arranged a private three-way meeting among themselves in Bermuda to discuss the data and decide what to do next. They invited three outside experts to advise them: one on corporate governance, one on legal matters, and one on public relations in the event of a termination.

The Bermuda Meeting

In preparation for the meeting with Pratt and Estler, Miller organized the interview data into two categories: areas of CEO strength and areas of concern. The areas of concern were then broken down into five sub-categories: the business, the board relationship, the executive leadership team, external constituencies, and personal traits.

Many directors had commented that the CEO had much to recommend him. He was hardworking, intelligent, articulate. He was a bold, visionary thinker. He had set clear stretch goals and had superior knowledge of the industry.

But the areas of concern were more telling. Directors' verbatim comments included the following:

- The Business:

    Results are short of expectations.

    Makes unrealistic forecasts and has not lived up to them.

    Personnel reduction targets have not been met.

    The merger was right; the execution is not.

    More needs to be done in executing the merger and meeting the original objectives.

- The Board Relationship:

    CEO looks at the board as a challenge to his plans rather than a sounding board.

    Board is surprised too often.

    There is lack of time for meaningful discussion in board meetings.

    CEO needs to have two-way communication with the board.

    Problem areas are not discussed in the boardroom.

    Some directors will not continue if this CEO's tenure continues.

    A majority of directors question the CEO's ability to lead.

- The Executive Leadership Team:
    Support for the CEO is questionable. No team spirit at the top.
    Virtually every executive has serious problems with the CEO's
        leadership.
    Too much affinity for detail; checking every detail every week.
    Executives are afraid; they dare not tell the truth.
    The company will continue to lose senior talent if the CEO
        continues.
- The Externals:
    Communications/investor relations are not good.
    Analyst reports indicate morale inside is not good.
- Personal Traits:
    The CEO lacks sensitivity in non-numeric areas.
    He is insecure.
    He is listening but not reacting.

It was clear from the data that the CEO's credibility had been nicked both internally and externally and that his relationship with the board had been weakening. The board had essentially two options for action: have the CEO prepare a development plan and hope that he could change, or initiate appropriate separation discussions. The CEO seemed to have lost the board's confidence, and directors seemed to hold little hope that he could change.

Directors' comments were so heavily biased toward the negative that the board seemed to be leaning toward the second course of action—asking the CEO to leave. If that were to happen, there was much that needed to be done. Bringing the decision to a vote by the full board had certain legal and practical implications. For that reason, Miller, Pratt, and Estler concluded that it was best to keep the process informal and confidential a while longer to give the board a chance to find true consensus and prepare for the worst.

Yet time was of the essence. Information had begun to leak, making some directors better informed than others. It would not be long before rumors reached the CEO and worse, the press.

When and How to Act

Miller, Pratt, and Estler decided to relay the interview data to all the directors so everyone had the same information base and could think about it before the upcoming board meeting. Within a matter of days, two of the three (Miller and Pratt, Miller and Estler, or Pratt and Estler) contacted each and every director to discuss the interview results. They suggested that the board authorize two of them to discuss the feedback with the CEO and begin negotiating a smooth exit if, after a full board discussion, that was the chosen course of action. They also asked for the board's consent to begin advance consultations on law, compensation, and investor and media relations. The directors agreed to the plan.

The board decided not to discuss the feedback with the CEO in this particular situation, as is usual best practice in reviewing CEO performance, because it did not want to send mixed signals. That is, once it was clear that the board had lost confidence in the CEO, the board did not want to set off any internal or external politicking as the CEO tried to save himself.

The afternoon before the regularly scheduled board meeting, the full board met without the CEO. It had a brief discussion of the CEO's performance before taking a vote on whether in fact to ask him to resign. The vote was nearly unanimous: the CEO had to go. Once the decision was made, the board had to move fast. The board had already arranged for the CEO to arrive that evening and meet with the board chairman and the chairman of the compensation committee. Directors speculated that CEO Lanzet would be picking up signals that something was wrong.

Before adjourning, the board discussed how the two chairmen should present the decision to the CEO. The board wanted Lanzet to know that although the consensus was against him now, the directors were appreciative of his past efforts, and there were no ill feelings. The board determined who should be interim CEO, who should be on the search committee, and who in the company should contact key investors. The legal issues had been fully researched, and the board had prepared its message for investors and the press.

Miller and Pratt met with the CEO that evening. They explained that while the board recognized his contributions to date, it did not think he was the right person to contend with the current circumstances. The CEO was disappointed but not angry. Negotiations on a departure date and severance package began. Later, other directors stopped by and gave the CEO their best wishes.

The Work of the Board

The Temple-Ward board did what a board is supposed to do. It combined directors' subjective perceptions with quantitative performance data to make the difficult call about a CEO's suitability for the job. One conscientious director trusted his instincts and did not hesitate to raise the performance issue with his peers. Many of the directors had been through mergers of large organizations and had a deep understanding of the issues inherent in a post-merger situation—the need to shift power allegiances and adjust to new management, for example. They had a frame of reference for judging this CEO's progress in integrating the organizations.

The process at Temple Ward had all the elements of a good CEO review: It was fair, objective, constructive, forward looking; it was not based solely on financial results but considered the CEO's overall leadership; it allowed directors to express their "instincts"; and it kept individual directors' comments confidential. Only the collective judgment was conveyed to the CEO and external constituents. The collective judgment drove the board's decision to ask the CEO to leave with no further ado.

This board was able to separate the CEO's past achievements from his ability to take the company forward. Also, the board decoupled the question of who would replace the CEO from the question of whether the current CEO was fully capable. Perhaps most important, the three board members who held influential positions—Miller, Pratt, and Estler—did not use their positions to factionalize the board but rather to help the board reach collective judgment through an objective, fair process.

Key Points

- Timely, constructive feedback from the board is the single best way to make a good CEO better and create competitive advantage. Make the feedback process ongoing, not a special event.

- Separate past performance from the fundamental question: Can this CEO take the company forward?

- Establish routine operating mechanisms—time at the end of meetings and written questionnaires—to bring each director's instincts to the surface and make a collective judgment about the CEO.

- Give formal and informal feedback in the spirit of constructive criticism and coaching. Say, "We want to help you," not "We got you."

CHAIRMAN-CEO FEEDBACK INSTRUMENT

This instrument is designed to draw out each individual board member's judgment on the issues that are key to the chairman-CEO's and the company's success. It is one of several versions in use at real companies.

Such an instrument can be used in a variety of ways. One option is for each director to complete the instrument and then to discuss the results in executive session. The CEO can later join the group to hear the consensual feedback. Another approach is for the chairman of the corporate governance committee to collect and analyze the instruments. The committee chairman, with a second director present, can discuss the collective feedback with the chairman-CEO. Then at a subsequent board meeting, the committee chairman can present the board's collective feedback to the full board, along with a summary of the chairman-CEO's response. The process should not become rigid and mechanical. Constructive dialogue is what makes the process value-adding.

Confidentiality and intellectual honesty are key. Such an instrument can be quite damaging, when, for instance, the comments become loose talk in CEO circles or when a few directors try to use the process to undermine the CEO. The intent must be positive, and the results must remain confidential even years later.

CEO FEEDBACK INSTRUMENT

On a scale from 1 to 7, what is your best intuition about the following?
Avoid the 4's. Take a position.

	Definitely not					**Definitely yes**	

Company Performance

1. Did the company perform well
   financially and competitively
   over the past twelve months?   1   2   3   **4**   5   6   7

2. What are the two or three things
   the company is doing to support
   your evaluation?   _____
   _____
   _____

3. Do you expect the company to perform
   well in the next twelve months?   1   2   3   **4**   5   6   7
   the next three to five years?   1   2   3   **4**   5   6   7
   Why or why not?
   _____
   _____
   _____

4. Are the short-term and long-term
   moves of the CEO appropriately
   balanced?   1   2   3   **4**   5   6   7

5. Is the company's competitive
   advantage current?   1   2   3   **4**   5   6   7

Leadership of the Organization

6. Is the strategy robust?   1   2   3   **4**   5   6   7

7. Is the CEO confronting reality?   1   2   3   **4**   5   6   7
   Why or why not?
   _____
   _____
   _____

8. Is the CEO transforming the
   organization appropriately?   1   2   3   **4**   5   6   7

9. Is the CEO focusing on the right
   issues?   1   2   3   **4**   5   6   7

10. Does the CEO have an edge in
    execution?   1   2   3   **4**   5   6   7

CEO FEEDBACK INSTRUMENT, cont'd.

	Definitely not				Definitely yes	

11. What one piece of advice would you
    give the CEO regarding leadership
    of the organization?
    _____
    _____
    _____

Team Building and Management Succession

	1	2	3	4	5	6	7
12. Is the CEO's team collectively of high quality?	1	2	3	4	5	6	7
13. Does the pipeline of leaders ensure continuity for the future?	1	2	3	4	5	6	7
14. Is the team's energy well focused?	1	2	3	4	5	6	7

15. What one piece of advice would you
    give the CEO regarding team building
    and management succession?
    _____
    _____
    _____

Leadership of External Constituencies

	1	2	3	4	5	6	7
16. Is the CEO a good leader regarding external constituencies?	1	2	3	4	5	6	7

17. What one piece of advice would you
    give the CEO regarding external
    constituencies?
    _____
    _____
    _____

CHAIRMAN FEEDBACK INSTRUMENT

This instrument focuses on the CEO-chairman's role as leader of the board.
On a scale of 1 to 7, what is your best intuition about the following?
Avoid the 4's. Take a position.

	Definitely not				Definitely yes		
1. Is the CEO-chairman having the board focus on the right issues?	1	2	3	4	5	6	7
2. Regarding his or her leadership of the board, is the CEO-chairman providing useful information to the board?	1	2	3	4	5	6	7
3. Are board meetings							
a. constructive?	1	2	3	4	5	6	7
b. effective?	1	2	3	4	5	6	7
c. focused?	1	2	3	4	5	6	7
d. value adding?	1	2	3	4	5	6	7
4. Is the CEO-chairman drawing the best out of the board							
a. in meetings?	1	2	3	4	5	6	7
b. outside of meetings?	1	2	3	4	5	6	7

5. What one piece of advice would you give the CEO-chairman regarding leadership of the board?

_____

_____

_____

CHAPTER EIGHT

SUCCESSION PLANNING
AS A WAY OF LIFE

S ome of America's largest companies have fumbled succession planning in recent years. In the early 1990s, the board of American Express was bitterly divided about who should succeed James D. Robinson III, while Robinson insisted on choosing his own successor. When the IBM board tried to replace John F. Akers, it could not find an internal candidate with the necessary range of business skills. The GM board missed the mark in selecting Robert Stempel to succeed Roger Smith and then removed Stempel in a way that made sensational headlines. AT&T and Apple both bungled the succession planning process to the embarrassment of the entire business community.

Make no mistake about it: The responsibility for a smooth leadership transition rests squarely with the board. Boards at work can act confidently and fast, even when the CEO's exit is not planned. They have a foundation of knowledge about various leaders throughout the organization, and they are practiced at discussing individuals' strengths and weaknesses and reaching a collective judgment on the person. They do not view the choice of the CEO's successor as an isolated, eleventh-hour event. Rather, it is part of an ongoing effort to ensure the longevity of the corporation through the continual development of leadership talent at all organizational levels, not just at the very top.

Not long ago people wondered who would succeed GE's CEO Jack Welch. It is now well known that GE has six to eight candidates who have been nurtured internally—and whom headhunters regularly court to fill some of the nation's top leadership slots. In succession planning, GE is the benchmark to beat.

A well thought-out succession planning process, like GE's, adds value to the company in numerous ways. It matches the selection criteria to the organization's needs and ensures a wide range of options from which to choose the next CEO. It minimizes foot dragging by the incumbent CEO and prevents potentially debilitating "horse race" scenarios. At the same time, good succession planning removes the organizational impediments that block the progress of high-potential individuals, thereby releasing energy throughout the company and building a strong bench of capable managers. The board, the CEO, the organization and personnel committee (or its equivalent), and the head of human resources all have clear roles to play.

Conrail, TRW, GE, and Coca-Cola are among the large companies with strong succession planning processes. While the business press has speculated that Jack Welch, GE's well-known and influential CEO, has no obvious successor, GE in fact has an extremely robust process of identifying, attracting, and developing leaders, with heavy input from its board. It is a net supplier of CEOs to the world.

Clarify the Roles in Succession Planning

Succession planning works best when the roles of the board, the CEO, the human resources executive, and the organization and personnel committee are clear. The board must choose the CEO, but not in isolation. Rather, that decision is part of an organizationwide effort to identify and develop talent. The CEO, the top human resources executive, and the board's organization and personnel committee play important roles in that effort. Clarifying the roles ensures that the job gets done smoothly and professionally.

The Board's Role: Participation and Oversight

The board has several responsibilities related to succession planning. It must insist that the company has a process in place for identifying and growing talent now and for the future. It must continually challenge the criteria for promotion and recognition. It must give management its *collective judgment* on key insiders and take ownership of the final decision. And finally, it must clear the way for the new CEO to do the job, unhampered by the disgruntled "also-rans" or the former CEO.

Though the CEO and the human resources executive should take the lead in creating the process to evaluate people inside the company, it is the board's job to insist that they do. The board should require frequent contact with the company's top people and essential information on people a few levels below the CEO. Such exposure can assure the board that the company is in fact filling the leadership pipeline and that the criteria are right. At GE, for instance, the board gets updates twice a year (once via the Management Development and Compensation Committee, or MDCC) on the company's progress in developing and retaining promising leaders and pulling new talent into the leadership development system.

When discussions are highly intimate and interactive and take place over time, directors can form independent perceptions of people and make their judgments available to the CEO. These observations are highly valuable. Judgment on people is, in fact, one of the board's greatest opportunities to add value. When a group of experienced and proven leaders of leaders discuss their most honest impressions of a human being, convergence of judgment occurs rather quickly and clearly. Reaching this collective insight is the finest of fine arts. The board's collective judgment can be a competitive advantage, if the CEO is willing to listen to it.

At one manufacturing company, board members were quick to pick up on the number two person's inability to execute the strategy. A few directors had informally conferred among themselves and were in agreement in their perception. The CEO had a close relationship with the company president and could not see his shortcomings. When a few directors took the CEO aside and expressed their concerns, the CEO finally listened. When he replaced his direct report, the company was able to move forward. The CEO felt relieved, and in due time, the stock price began to recover.

In a discussion at GE, Jack Welch was singing the praises of an executive who had been successful in a series of positions at GE and was being considered for a key promotion. A seasoned board member asked, "But has this individual ever had a bad year?" When Welch questioned what he meant, the director continued, "Jack, have you ever had a bad year?" Of course he had. "Did you learn a lot?" Welch said that he probably learned more from the bad times than the good times. The discussion then turned to individuals who had demonstrated their ability to handle adversity as well as success. The director's question helped keep things in balance.

When Welch called the board's attention to a tremendous operational leader whom they thought should be identified as a potential successor to the CEO, a director asked, "But how good is the individual at making deals? You can't run the business without a good feel for how to run a GE Capital." Management began to think more about how to strengthen that area of leadership. William J. Conaty, senior vice president human resources, picked up on the director's question and adjusted the matrix used to evaluate insiders. "From that," Conaty explains, "it became readily apparent that deal-making skills are essential, so we constantly look for deal-making and business development opportunities to cultivate them in all of our businesses."

Allowing a CEO to stall the succession planning process is a dereliction of duty. Given the tremendous importance of selecting the organization's leader, a board that allows the process to be anything short of robust is not doing its job. Such a board is simply not working. It is a competitive disadvantage in the context of the capital markets.

CEOs, like everyone else, suffer from human shortcomings. They may occasionally drag their feet or keep their plans to themselves. Readers may know of times when a CEO dragged his feet or kept succession plans to himself. Former Conrail CEO-Chairman Jim Hagen points out, "Sometimes a CEO is reluctant to say anything about who he has in mind to succeed him because he might change his mind later. He's afraid he'll lose credibility."

According to Paul Ingrassia and Joseph B. White in *Comeback: The Fall and Rise of the American Automobile Industry* (Simon & Schuster, 1994), in 1991, Chrysler's board faced pressure from shareholders to replace CEO Lee Iacocca, who showed no obvious signs that he was planning to leave. With no succession plan in place, the board members leaned on Iacocca to find a strong candidate or risk being shut out of the process altogether. They also informed him that they were planning to meet in small groups with Chrysler's senior executives. In 1992, when the board decided to hire Bob Eaton as vice chairman—with plans to make him CEO and chairman in nine months—Iacocca protested. The board, however, prevailed.

Some CEOs, dreading retirement, subconsciously try to postpone it by convincing the board that "nobody is ready yet." Directors should beware of that alibi. One former CEO wanted to stay on beyond age 65 and, without saying anything to his board, put off developing a successor. Under pressure from the board, the CEO eventually brought in an outsider to run the company, but the foot-dragging simply took another form. The CEO continually implied that the successor was not quite up to the job and offered to stay on to coach him. Finally, several directors met with the CEO and told him in no uncertain terms that they expected him to retire on time.

One CEO of a $5 billion company and a director of numerous boards described this situation: "I know of a CEO who called his board members together and told them that he had just taken his heir apparent off the succession path. Actually, he had asked the person to leave the company. He had been telling the board for years that this was the person who would succeed him. Now he was saying that he would have to go outside for somebody else. Some of the directors were outraged, and the CEO didn't understand why. This was a good CEO who had done a good job by all measures, but nobody knew what was okay or not okay in this area."

Another director witnessed a similar turn of events: "The CEO had been telling the board that the president was the heir apparent. Then all of a sudden the president was removed from the company. No explanation was ever given." Such situations demonstrate the CEO's weakness and the failure of the board.

A board must be prepared to step in when a CEO's personal desires begin to drive the succession process. Board members can empathize with the CEO's psychological struggle, but they cannot let the succession process bog down. A formal discussion of the topic at least once a year will prevent the CEO from inadvertently derailing the process.

The chairman of the organization and personnel committee can put the topic on the agenda if the CEO fails to. The board should insist that the dialogue include discussion of the entire pool of candidates. Even when the CEO has an heir apparent, the board should insist on comparisons with others in the company and with outsiders who are potential competitors in the industry. If the board thinks the CEO's list is too short, it should insist that it be expanded. The large technology company described in the case at the end of this chapter did precisely that.

Including succession planning in the CEO's performance evaluation creates another opportunity for the board to address the issue. If the CEO resists pressure to take the lead, the board can gradually assert more control. Reluctance to force the issue is a serious indictment of the board. Given that the choice of a CEO and the pipeline of leaders can determine the competitive advantage of the company, the board simply cannot shirk its responsibility to take succession seriously, get involved, and exercise judgment.

The CEO's Role: Evaluating, Informing, Recommending

In companies with strong succession planning processes, CEOs are leaders rather than impediments. These outgoing CEOs can separate personal desires from the task of choosing a successor and creating the process to evaluate others inside the company. Their legacy is the robust process and strong successor they leave behind. They take the lead in establishing the internal processes for identifying and developing leaders and for keeping the board informed and involved. They do not hesitate to seek counsel from the board on such important issues as developing talent or choosing the right criteria to promote and reward people. They do not try to be the sole decision maker.

In these companies, the CEO works with the board and the human resources executive to design the company's leadership development processes. He or she also gives the board periodic updates on all the mechanisms that build leadership talent at the company, including management development training and job changes.

Some CEOs also create opportunities for the board to meet a number of top company leaders. Board meetings, for instance, should be designed to expose the board to a number of executives. The CEO should also arrange various informal mechanisms, like golf outings and dinners.

The informal mechanisms should encourage real dialogue, not just polite "hello's." Seating people at tables of four, for instance, makes it easy for everyone to participate in the conversation. At GE, Chairman-CEO Welch often arranges the foursomes in golf outings. As GE's Bill Conaty says, "Very little is left to happenstance."

If the board determines that the company needs a whole new leadership approach, it should further limit the CEO's role in succession planning. An uncooperative or nonperforming incumbent CEO forfeits the right to participate except at the board's request.

The Senior HR Executive's Role: Designing the Process

When boards insist on clear leadership development processes, the role of the senior HR executive expands. The HR executive can help by working with the board and the CEO to design the processes and criteria by which people will be hired, promoted, transferred, and rewarded. An experienced HR executive can be a critical resource in developing the structures that will grow talent. His or her judgments about key people can also be valuable. At GE, Jack Welch always gives his own candid opinions of individuals in the top executive ranks, and for the sake of intellectual honesty, he often encourages Bill Conaty to express his opinions as well—especially when they differ from Welch's.

The HR executive is a major player in the boardrooms of GE, AMP, Ingersoll-Rand, Praxair, and a thin handful of other companies. Bill Conaty of GE, Leonard Hill of AMP, Don Rice of Ingersoll-Rand, Barbara Harris of Praxair, Howard Knicely of TRW, and Larry Phillips of Citicorp are deeply involved in determining the criteria for the next CEO and for promotions at lower levels of the organization.

These HR executives communicate with the board frequently, sometimes through the organization and personnel committee and sometimes with the full board, to add their perspective and to keep directors informed about the company's leadership and management talent. James Perrella, CEO of Ingersoll-Rand, describes Don Rice's relationship with the board as a business partnership, to which Rice brings a great deal of "soft" information not otherwise available.

Howard Knicely, executive vice president of human resources at TRW, is not a member of the board, but he sits in on all board meetings, contributing his expertise regularly in give-and-take with the board: "When an issue arises around organization or compensation or management succession, I can respond. When we were discussing a $600 million acquisition we made about six months ago, for example, I was able to answer questions about an elaborate study we had done of how the cost of employee benefits would affect the bottom line. Also during discussion of the acquisition, board members asked a number of questions about organizational integration and the merging of two cultures. It was useful for me to be there to listen and respond."

Knicely participates in board discussions not just as a specialist but as a full-fledged member of the management team. "I of course interact heavily with the board on executive compensation, management succession, and organizational capability. But my HR expertise is always secondary to my expertise and knowledge about the business."

The prospect of board-level involvement will be exciting to many HR executives and threatening to many others. To be successful in this role, the HR executive must have a broad business perspective as well as functional expertise and a heavy dose of confidence. The CEO and the board must trust his or her judgment.

If the HR executive cannot be objective, the board must take hold of the process. It's okay for committee members to interview people below the CEO to sense how candidates are perceived. If he or she is not trusted, the person should not be in the job. At one company that was planning a major globalization effort, the HR director began to attend board meetings to discuss implementation issues associated with the company's growth plans. During those sessions, the board sensed that the HR director lacked the skills and sense of urgency to build the necessary cadre of global leaders. Eventually, the board urged the CEO to take a hard look at the HR director's performance. The CEO hired a new HR executive with a broader perspective, who now reports to the board regularly on his plans and progress for growing the talent needed for the company's expansion.

A surprisingly small percentage of human resources executives are involved at the board level. Either the HR executive has been coopted, is not up to the task, or has not won the board's confidence. Boards should address this issue to make sure they are not missing out on valuable expertise.

The Organization and Personnel Committee's Role: Doing the Legwork

While the entire board must participate in the most important aspects of succession planning, such as getting to know key insiders and choosing the next CEO, an organization and personnel committee can do a lot of the background and detail work. This system works well at GE, where Jack Welch and Bill Conaty give the MDCC (Management Development and Compensation Committee) a thorough overview of the company's leadership each June and the board an abbreviated version every December.

The meeting in June is an "executive organization and staffing review." The agenda usually includes profiles of every individual in the top ranks and some fast-trackers below them, a "report card" for new officers appointed over the previous year, and a progress report in areas such as cultural diversity and global management. Welch and Conaty discuss the progress of the most talented individuals at or below the senior executive level and what GE is doing with compensation and promotion to retain them.

Since the GE board is interested in whether talented people stay with the company, Conaty summarizes the defections. "We spell out how many officers we lost and break it down by category—resignations, retirements, and what we call 'our initiative.' In 1995–1996 our turnover among officers was 12 to 15 percent. That might sound high, but when we broke it down we saw that less than 2 percent were people we really didn't want to lose."

Perhaps the most highly anticipated segment of GE's MDCC meeting is Welch's views on each of the dozen or so senior business leaders and four senior staff leaders (as of September 1997). At each meeting, he tells the board about their progress, career paths, and possible successors to their positions. These personal assessments are candid, short, and informal. Welch typically reads from handwritten notes and then talks about each person in a conversational way. In discussing the person, Welch is not afraid to change his mind. The high level of trust and openness allows Welch to express his thoughts unfiltered without concern that he may be contradicting previous observations.

While GE's MDCC explores the issues in depth, the board is also well informed through annual updates and ongoing communication with committee members. Directors have commented that the sessions with the board are "extremely useful" and "really give us a feel." One outside director said, "I'm on the boards of several other major companies, and no other board gets such a thorough session."

Avoid "Horse Races" and "Crown Princes"

Proper timing of the succession decision can help ease organizational tensions, prevent the entire organization from becoming factionalized, and help stem the loss of talented individuals. The new world of succession planning keeps political maneuvering at a minimum by avoiding two-person horse races (where two individuals are put in direct competition with each other) and the "crown prince syndrome" (where the heir apparent is identified far in advance of the CEO's retirement).

Boards should insist that the succession planning process gather intelligence on some twelve to twenty up-and-coming managers and narrow the field only when the CEO's departure is a year or two away. Two- and three-way races, however common, can be destructive. People in the organization feel compelled to place bets on one of the individuals, causing factions that must later be unified.

In the 1950s, incumbent CEO Gaylord Freeman of First National Bank of Chicago set up a competition among the top three people. All three eventually left, and the experience destroyed the bank. The three-way race Walter Wriston set up at Citicorp in the 1980s caused the entire organization to take sides. John Reed, his successor, had to deal with the ensuing situation.

One can argue that identifying the successor early on allows the board to evaluate him or her along the way. At one large technology company, the CEO brought in an outsider to be his successor in three or four years. The incumbent CEO changed his mind about the candidate and broached the subject with the board: "I paid a lot of money to bring this person in, but if you were to ask me today whether I would choose him to succeed me, I would tell you no." The board members felt the same way, and the CEO started looking for alternatives.

But announcing an heir apparent too soon has several disadvantages. The competitive drive of others in the organization is such that even a small misstep can render the person ineffective internally and take the would-be CEO who deserves the job out of the running. The whole organization can go into turmoil as the search begins anew.

Also, the heir apparent can become impatient and take a "number one" position somewhere else, wasting the effort to retain the person. If the heir apparent becomes effective earlier than planned, he or she will instinctively seek more authority. As NorAm chairman and CEO Milt Honea points out: "As the younger person being groomed for the top job, I would naturally want the most authority and responsibility I could have, the fastest I could have it." In that case, the incumbent CEO must come to terms with the situation and get the person in the saddle quickly. Otherwise, the incumbent risks losing the successor or having his or her own authority undermined. One CEO says, "Within a year or two of publicly identifying a successor, the CEO becomes a lame duck."

Cast a Wide Net

Good succession planning processes are linked to leadership development and evaluation processes at levels below the top executives. They ensure a broad, diverse base of skills not only at the top but also at the lower ranks. They continuously refine the criteria for the top jobs, based on the changing needs of the company. (See the accompanying checklist of criteria for a CEO.) Casting a wide net helps the board see all the possibilities and minimizes the chance of a two- or three-way race far in advance of the time to choose a new CEO.

In general, the board should be well-informed about at least a dozen company executives and know who is coming into the pipeline several levels below the CEO. Looking deeper into the organization, not incidentally, can help the board track the progress of women and minorities and identify potential roadblocks.

At GE, as mentioned above, CEO Jack Welch talks to the board about the top twenty or so people in very specific terms. The GE board gets less detailed information on another 130 individuals below the level of the CEO's direct reports. Board members make their own notes, which they can compare from year to year. The process therefore has continuity, even as board members turn over, and is independent from the CEO.

Once a year, the GE board's MDCC reviews the company's progress in recruiting and developing women, minorities, and people from other countries and with different skills. At the June 1996 committee meeting, for instance, HR executive Bill Conaty reviewed with the MDCC several charts comparing overseas revenue growth with growth in the number of overseas employees and officers. Conaty also showed the MDCC what GE was doing to develop relationships with executive schools around the world and which functional areas people were going into. "We explained how our latest hiring initiatives are giving us a more diverse genetic code," Conaty remarks.

At least once a year, the board should discuss whether the company is producing the right kind of leaders and whether the criteria for selection are appropriate. One large technology company thought it had several viable candidates to take over when its CEO retired, but as external conditions took a dramatic unforeseen change, global experience became paramount, a criterion on which all the insiders fell short. The CEO and the board have since worked closely with the personnel committee to identify and track three outsiders—none of them a CEO—who might be able to take over. The board has decided to revisit the question every six months and has suggested hiring outsiders for positions that would test their ability.

IBM's meticulous succession planning failed to produce an internal candidate to replace CEO John Akers in 1993 because it missed the criteria. Until then, business acumen was not considered to be a central criterion, and the up-and-coming leaders did not cultivate broad business skills. When it came time to replace John Akers, the board tried to change that genetic code by seeking a sitting CEO who had demonstrated business acumen and had successfully implemented change in a large organization. The search ultimately focused on three people— Jack Welch of GE, Larry Bossidy of Allied Signal, and Louis Gerstner of RJR Nabisco. Industry experience, once considered essential, was not required.

With the criteria for advancement in sharp focus, the board can help the CEO and the senior HR executive make structural adjustments to allow high potential candidates to progress. Sometimes a position must be created to allow a candidate to be tested. Du Pont, for instance, appointed two vice chairmen for that purpose. Then when Jack Krol became Du Pont's new CEO, he did not use that structure. "I wasn't ready to have two vice chairmen," he explains. "When it comes to organizational structure, you have to be flexible to take the best advantage of the people and the dynamics at the time." In the late 1970s, GE created a vice chairman level. Although that particular structural change does create a horse race, it allows the board to see the candidates under fire, an advantage that sometimes outweighs the disadvantages.

Multi-industry companies have special reason to consider making a change in organizational structure for testing and organizational development. As Jim Perrella of Ingersoll-Rand says, "A person who is successful in running a single-industry business unit may not be able to make the leap to running multiple business units in a range of industries. The latter requires the ability to 'lead the leaders' by striking the delicate balance between encouraging initiative and abdicating control. Creating an organization of several business units can put a serious CEO candidate to the test."

Sometimes individuals have to be removed from positions to make room for high-potential people below them. When one person plateaus, he or she tends to block the progress of everyone in positions below him. When the board forces the company to do a thorough search for leadership talent, the "blockers" will also come to light. The organizational challenge then is to move the blockers to other assignments to free up the organizational talent.

Moving the blockers may seem like common sense, but it is rarely done. Of course, any organizational changes should be handled humanely and with the "blocker's" past contribution and continued value in mind, but the board should ensure that the changes are made. They are key to retaining, developing, and energizing those in the organization with the most promise.

Get to Know the Candidates

Good succession planning gives the board frequent opportunities to mingle with executives and observe their capabilities. Seeing managers in board meetings and social situations helps directors build a complete picture of individual managers. As Bill Adams points out: "Nobody would have picked Churchill to be Churchill. He was an opinionated, garrulous drunk—and just the right man. I think the best you can do is try to take potential candidates and see them in as many situations as you can, particularly where they own something and they've got to make it work."

Directors should be aware that social situations alone might not give them a well-rounded picture of the individuals. Lois Juliber, director of Du Pont and executive vice president of Colgate-Palmolive, warns, "When directors are exposed to people briefly, they make snap judgments. They might react more to cosmetics—how the person looks, how articulate he or she is—than to content. Boards need consistent exposure to potential successors to make the most fact-based assessments."

Alex Mandl of Teligent describes a range of vantage points that can give directors a fuller picture of the individuals: "The first data point is business results. Does the person consistently deliver good results, mixed results, or does he or she do a lot of explaining? Then there are the presentations, which do give you a sense of how the managers respond. A third data point is from informal networks. Directors usually see or hear about managers in other forums and environments. Is the person loud and obnoxious at industry conferences? And then there are the social occasions—dinners, cocktail parties, golf or tennis. Does the person drink too much during the cocktail hour or lose her temper when she misses the ball?"

Specific mechanisms that help the board get familiar with CEO succession candidates include one-on-one meetings between directors and managers; presentations to the board with lots of time for questions; and meals before and after board meetings.

Bank of America and The FINOVA Group invite managers to dinner the night before the board meeting. Conrail and KeraVision, the California venture capital–funded company, include their officers at almost all board events. KeraVision directors got to know the officers well, and thought so highly of them that they offered to coach them to help them adjust to their expanding roles.

Howard Knicely, executive vice president of human resources at TRW, describes the process by which the board stays informed about his organization's managerial talent: "At least once a year we present to our board the results of what we call the management review process, whereby we go through an assessment of our management strength and depth. We assess our critical competencies, look at the gaps, and then the operating heads develop specific action plans. That process bubbles up and is ultimately reviewed by the board. The CEO and the board also have a private discussion about individual members of the management committee. I sometimes sit in on that, and often the board will ask for my independent opinion."

Knicely says, "We have a responsibility to assure the board that we have in place the depth and breadth of management to run our business not just now but in the future."

When board members and the CEO share their insights on top managers' capabilities, the board can provide valuable advice on how to round out a CEO candidate. Bill Adams recalls how his board helped him develop candidates when he was chairman and president of Armstrong: "I remember one time when we were ready to move a line manager into a key staff job because he would be excellent at it. One of the board members said, 'Wait a minute, if this person is one of the four you said had the capability of becoming the CEO of this company, you should have him on a track that moves him up in line responsibility, not sideways in staff.' That was an excellent point."

One CEO notes that while coaching from the board can help develop senior officers, some executives are resistant, for the same reasons some CEOs resist input from the board. The CEO's continued encouragement can help executives overcome their concerns about losing autonomy or appearing to be indecisive.

Hire from Outside When Necessary

If a good management development plan is in place, it should not be necessary to hire a CEO from the outside. On the other hand, the board must have the courage to go outside when the internal candidates fall short for whatever reason. The common tendency is to look in the rearview mirror at improvement over past performance rather than deciding what it will take to perform in relation to the present and future uncharted outside world environment, and then asking: Who is the best person to take us there?

Finding an outside candidate requires extraordinary diligence, even when the board uses a headhunter. The criteria must be clear, prioritized, and specific. Although the total set of criteria is likely to be similar across companies, and headhunters tend to have a list of people who meet them, the board must tell the headhunters which criteria are dominant. Business acumen was the dominant criterion when IBM found Lou Gerstner. Prioritizing immediately rules out many possible candidates headhunters would otherwise bring forward.

The board also must be diligent in evaluating the individuals' personal strengths and weaknesses. Headhunters know that the candidates have performed, but they have a harder time evaluating the individual's psychological bent and his or her chemistry with the board. The board should not delegate that task but perform its own due diligence on the candidates. Reference checking must go beyond the confines of a checklist to include personal traits that determine true leadership ability. Directors should use their informal networks to glean as much information about the person as they can and take time to get to know the candidates as well as possible.

Listen to what the outside candidate says, and scrutinize his or her track record to judge what the person really has in mind for the company. Once the decision is made, carefully monitor the new CEO's performance. Discuss it explicitly every six months for the first year or two.

The board of one New England company was unhappy with the company's mediocre performance and decided it needed a change agent to take a whole new look at the company. That meant going outside for a new CEO for the first time in the company's long history. Although the board used a search firm, it did not delegate the important work of determining the criteria and getting to know the candidates.

The board formed a search committee, which was a subset of the compensation and organization committee, and in a somewhat unusual move, chose one director who was not on that committee to lead the search. This one person, everyone agreed, was the most experienced person for the job. He had participated in an enormous number of acquisitions, which required assessing numerous CEOs in multiple industries over time.

The board's "search expert" worked with a search firm to generate a list of candidates, continually kept the committee members informed about the individuals, and at the appropriate points, involved the whole board. Although the incumbent CEO made himself available to give his opinion on whether the individual would fit within the company and to explain the company to the candidates, the board owned the process.

As the search focused in on one promising candidate, committee members had lengthy discussions with the individual. Before any offer was made, the full board met with the candidate for a long dinner, during which directors asked questions like, "Having seen the company, what would you do differently? How would you globalize this company? What is your philosophy on cultural diversity?" The candidate, who ultimately got the job, says, "It wasn't 'Tell us about your family and your golf game.' It was clearly a business interview."

By the end of the dinner, board members had assured themselves that they had a person who would drive the kind of change they felt was needed. If the chemistry had not been right, the decision could easily have gone the other way.

Hiring a new CEO from outside the company may require a whole new approach to compensation, as it did at the New England company. The existing compensation system rewarded everyone at a middle level. The board realized that it had to break the framework to attract the new CEO by offering compensation tied more closely to performance. In the first six months with the new CEO, the board gained confidence in its decisions as the company's stock price rose 50 percent.

Have an Emergency Plan

How does the board address the uncomfortable thought of a CEO's death or another crisis that suddenly leaves the company without a leader? When Conrail's board chose Richard Sanborn to replace outgoing CEO L. Stanley Crane in 1989, the appointment was hailed by the railroad industry and by Conrail's own managers. Sanborn had an impressive performance as President of CSXT, the railroad business unit of CSX, and Conrail was looking forward to a prosperous future under its new leader. This exuberance, sadly, was short-lived. Sanborn died from a heart attack within months of taking office. At KeraVision, founder John Petricianni was diagnosed with terminal cancer just a few years after starting the company, and the board was forced to find a successor on short notice.

A thorough, frequently updated review of the company's leadership, like GE's, prepares the board to act quickly when an unexpected crisis hits, but other interim solutions also make sense. One is to identify a senior person, 55 to 58 years old, whose ego has subsided and is willing to provide leadership for a period of a year or so. Another is to identify a board member who can become a substitute interim chairman, as happened at Conrail.

A third approach is for the CEO to make a recommendation that is held confidentially with a few directors. This practice, generally known as the "field envelope," is becoming widespread. The CEO's recommendation is usually put in writing and kept in a safe. Every year Jim Broadhead, Chairman and CEO of the FPL Group (which owns Florida Power & Light), reviews with his board the three or four people in sight to be CEO. At the end of that discussion, he always says, "And if I were hit by a bread truck tomorrow, here's who I think my successor should be."

At smaller companies, which seldom have the capacity to grow their own CEO candidates, agreement on a process is critical. For example, the board of a phase-two-development-stage company discussed the succession planning issue and agreed that no internal candidate could succeed the CEO. Then it developed a process for finding a successor from the outside. Many of the directors could draw on their vast network of industry contacts and were confident that they could move quickly if they had to.

Give the New CEO a Clean Slate

There comes a time when the board must move from the question of "Whom do we choose as the CEO?" to "How do we make this person successful?" Once the board has selected the new person, it must help the chief executive assert his or her leadership quickly. Directors must not let their ties to the outgoing CEO get in the way. They can help the new CEO in two ways: (1) not intervening when good people who were passed up decide to leave the corporation and (2) making sure that the outgoing CEO makes a clean break.

The announcement of a new CEO will be a letdown for some talented insiders. Particularly when the board chooses a young CEO, two issues arise: retaining and motivating older managers, and keeping younger managers who will not want to wait for their shot. The board can try to help the CEO come up with creative solutions, like creating the Office of the Chairman, but ultimately the board must face the possibility that the company will lose a few good people. A new CEO must consolidate power and eliminate energy drains quickly; the board should support those efforts.

If the board has created an Office of the Chairman as a way to bolster the CEO, it has not done its job in choosing the right leader. Such structural solutions cannot compensate for a CEO who is not up to the job.

The succession-planning process is not complete until the outgoing CEO completely relinquishes his or her influence on the business. No board should allow the outgoing CEO to stay on the board. The practice postpones the leadership transition and weakens the organization.

Behind-the-scenes research conducted over twenty years confirms that no new CEO wants his or her predecessor on the board, although he or she cannot say so. Incoming CEOs tolerate the practice because they want to appear to be nice to the outgoing CEO whose past contribution is appreciated, who may have powerful allies on the board, and who may have recommended them to the CEO position. Boards should recognize the awkwardness of the new CEO's situation.

When the outgoing CEO remains on the board, his or her sacred cows—acquisitions, investments, joint ventures, favorite people, or even the incentive system—can inhibit the new CEO from making necessary major shifts in strategy and organizational structure. In one large medical technology company, for example, the former CEO, who stayed on the board, had shepherded the development of a product without following the company's usual protocol. The product failed to make it through the regulatory processes in Washington, leaving the successor with a very expensive failure that no one wanted to talk about.

The new CEO said: "Nothing slows down operations more than having your ex-chairman on the board. Our ex-chairman asks twenty questions, thinking he's being helpful, but other board members have had to tell him to please be quiet. And there's no question that you alter your language and in some cases, alter your proposals to cater to consideration of his poor policies. I think the SEC or shareholder activists should come down hard on the practice."

When the new CEO and the predecessor disagree, the former CEO sometimes calls the new CEO's competence or new direction into question. This was true at Alcoa in the 1980s and at Philip Morris in recent years. Boards cannot rely on the former CEO to make a judgment on the current leader. That responsibility rests squarely with the board.

Former CEOs can use their influence to indirectly attack their successor. When the performance of one large company began to flag largely because of unexpected moves by competitors, the former CEO put the blame solely on his successor. He made offhand comments to some outside directors and talked with people inside the company. Boardroom discussions became highly charged. The other directors eventually concluded that the former CEO had to go, and the agenda has since progressed.

Former CEOs tend to act like they are still in charge and are often perceived as still in charge. At one highly respected company, the former CEO continually asked questions of his successor in a tone that put the new CEO on the defensive. The constant focus on operational details left little time to discuss external changes and the big picture. Finally, the new CEO approached several directors individually to ask for their help in dealing with the situation. The other directors asked the former CEO to quiet down or resign.

Arguments in favor of keeping the outgoing CEO on the board simply do not hold up. Experience? True, outgoing CEOs know the business and industry well, but they are convinced that their judgments, their assessment of trends, their identification of key strategies are correct. Attachment to the retiring CEO may be attachment to an outdated strategy. Besides, in today's fast-changing world, a former CEO's knowledge quickly becomes obsolete and irrelevant. If help is needed, the former CEO is just a phone call away.

Contacts and relationships? Former CEOs can do great things for their companies. After his retirement, Don Kendall helped Pepsi develop the Russian and Eastern European markets through contacts he had made in the 1950s. David Rockefeller used his connections in China to help Chase Manhattan open a branch there after the revolution. But new CEOs must build their own contacts. The outgoing CEO should make any transfers of contacts or relationships while he or she is still in the job or as a consultant who does not sit on the board. Board members and other members of the management team can provide the institutional memory.

Even defending the new CEO against certain board members can be more hindrance than help. The new CEO must build his or her own relationship with the board. At one $3 billion company, when the new CEO was challenged by another director, the former CEO took the director on. That quieted the meetings, but it also delayed the new leader from asserting his leadership and developing his own support within the group.

Board members can help the new CEO take hold by building relationships with him or her. When Dick Brown was chosen as CEO of UK-based Cable & Wireless, directors arranged two two-hour luncheons at which he could talk informally with some of the directors. Brown, who had come from outside the company (he was formerly vice chairman of Ameritech and later CEO of H&R Block), says, "The directors opened up and gave me a lot of information. I remember it to this day because it helped me get to know the board members and the company."

Each director of Cable & Wireless also made a point of doing something socially with Brown and his wife. "Those occasions made it easy for me to ask the directors what they wanted to see happen in the company and the board, and I was able to assert my leadership very quickly." In his first six months as CEO, Brown set Cable & Wireless on a new strategic course, laying the foundation for future growth. The market price rose over 50 percent within a year, making British Telecom's offer to acquire Cable & Wireless in 1996 appear too small in retrospect.

Although every rule has its exceptions, in this instance, exceptions are few and far between. Even when the board is convinced that the outgoing CEO's presence is necessary, his or her board term should be no more than a year. It is up to the board to ensure that the new CEO is in no one's shadow.

Putting Succession in High Gear at "Bedford Industries"

This board led the charge to build a wide and diverse range of succession candidates on short notice.[1]

In 1994, the board of Bedford Industries thought it had succession planning well in hand. With five years to go before the CEO's scheduled retirement, the board of the $10 billion manufacturer recommended that the CEO hire two high-level executives from the outside

---

[1]This case describes a real situation. Names and some details have been disguised.

who had CEO potential. The incumbent CEO and the board would carefully track the progress of the two new hires and a third internal CEO candidate.

In 1996, however, when all three top candidates had begun to show serious weaknesses, the board had to rethink its succession plans—and fast. Working closely with the CEO and the top human resources executive, the board designed a process to accelerate the identification and development of high-potential individuals.

False Security

Bedford had a long history of growing its own CEOs and passing the baton smoothly. But in 1994, when the board had begun to discuss who would succeed the CEO when he retired in five years, the board grew concerned. Frank Booth, the only internal candidate who seemed viable, had serious shortcomings. Although he had seeded several new businesses, he lacked maturity and seemed to lack certain operating skills. He had to be considered a long shot.

In 1994, Bedford needed more options, and the board had some suggestions. The chief financial officer was about to retire, so the board recommended that the CEO hire someone into the job who had CEO potential. That would give them a second candidate. The board also recommended an organizational restructuring that would create an opportunity to bring in and test another outsider at a high level. They got the CEO to create North America as a stand-alone division. The new head of the North America division would be a third succession candidate.

Because of the company's long history of promoting from within, the CEO had no experience hiring people at such a high level. He asked for the board's help. Some directors interviewed the job candidates, and the chairman of the compensation committee actually ended up participating in negotiations of the compensation package for the North America candidate. The board's involvement was unusual but useful under the circumstances. The new hires knew they were being considered as the possible successor, and the board prepared to watch them closely. The CEO also assigned someone to help Frank Booth, the new business development executive, broaden his skills.

Although the board needed time to get to know and observe the new hires, succession planning seemed to be on track. Then three years before the CEO's planned retirement, the process began to unravel.

Succession Planning Derailed

At the July 1996 board retreat, succession was not on the agenda, but performance was. In the normal course of events, the CEO began to discuss the poor performance of the North America division. The CEO warned that the 1996 numbers probably would not be met, and from there, began to cast doubt on whether Trent Paterson, the head of North America, was up to the job. "I'm doing the best I can to coach him," the CEO told the board, "but I don't think he's going to make it." EPS, projected at around $5.10, was going to come in at around $4.60.

This was alarming news because the board had come to consider Paterson as the top succession candidate. Frank Booth had shown that he was not mature enough yet, and a majority of directors had concluded that while Rich Blair, the CFO hired from outside, was doing well in the finance area, he did not seem to have the broad perspective required of a CEO. Sure, the board was concerned about the EPS shortfall and its effect on the stock price, but it was equally concerned that the strongest candidate for succession now seemed to be floundering.

Two directors who had just joined the board immediately began to scrutinize the performance issue. Both were CEOs—the only active chief executives on the board. They understood the need for companies in fast-changing environments like Bedford's to stay ahead of the pack, and they did not hold back their questions and comments. They began to ask pointed though tactful questions about the industry, the company, and the succession candidates. When they spoke up, the rest of the board listened, and soon other directors were equally engaged.

Several directors who were knowledgeable about the industry began to question why the North America numbers were coming in so low, and management partly attributed the problems to the economy. Based on what the directors were seeing in their own industries, that did not sound right. The directors called an executive session without the CEO.

"We need to find out what's happening here and what the plan is going to be," one director said. The board members agreed that management had not done a good job of spelling out the reasons for the lack of performance. Maybe the North America division was failing because its leader could not do the job—or maybe because he was not getting the backing he needed from the CEO.

Before the retreat, Trent Paterson had begun to complain to some directors that he was not getting any help from the CEO. The CEO, meanwhile, had spoken negatively about Paterson, and some directors were sympathetic. They had begun to think that Paterson was superficial—great with customers, great at making presentations, but unwilling to dig into problems.

The board concluded that it had to take a stronger stand. It sharpened its focus on the two outstanding issues: getting to the root of the business problem and expanding the search for a successor. The clock was ticking. With the CEO's retirement just three years away and the top candidates showing serious weakness, there was no time to lose.

Forcing the Issue

The board had to act fast. The directors did not want to undermine the CEO's operational authority in any way, but they insisted that succession planning be a top priority. The board made it perfectly clear that it would not extend the CEO's term in office and then imposed discipline on the succession planning process by setting a tight time limit: By mid-1997, the board would decide whether the current succession candidates were viable. In the meantime, the board would prepare for the possibility that they were not.

Driven by the two newest members, the board of Bedford Industries set out to ensure that the company created a more objective, clear-cut process for analyzing and comparing the internal candidates. Working closely with the senior HR executive, it helped design a template for evaluating them.

The board was very comfortable with Bedford's strategy, having been through it thoroughly at the 1995 board retreat. The template captured on one page the criteria that were absolutely essential to implementing that strategy. The criteria were grouped into four sections. Along the righthand margin was space to rate the individual on each criterion on a scale from 1 to 7.

The first section focused on the "givens." This section was the "toll gate" that every candidate had to get through. It included qualities such as decisiveness, the ability to conceive of and implement change, and the commitment to excellence. The second section was labeled "business acumen." It considered whether the person knew how to make money and had a "feel" for the business. Section three looked at leadership of people. Could the person identify and develop other leaders and match their skills with the business requirements? Section four was perhaps the least tangible. Did the candidate have intellectual curiosity, and was he or she comfortable with different cultures, change, and technology? A second page gave the evaluator space to summarize the person's deficiencies and to lay out a plan for development.

Meanwhile, the board was intent on finding out what was going on with the North America division. Was it the economy, market share, or something else? Was the CEO doing a poor job of coaching the division head or was the person truly over his head? It explicitly instructed the CEO to help the North America person to try to improve his or her performance. It also designed a process whereby the board would get quarterly progress reports. That way, the board would be able to tell which way things were going.

Finding the Movers and Shakers

In the following months, as the CEO evaluated the succession candidates and the board tracked their progress, it became clear that none was up to the job. But surely a company as large and successful as Bedford had loads of leadership talent in its ranks. The board was determined to find it and fill the leadership pipeline. It gave the HR director an ambitious goal: to identify within the next three months some fifteen to twenty movers and shakers who, with the right experience, might be the future CEO of Bedford. The template used to evaluate the three current CEO candidates formed the basis for identifying these other high-potential leaders throughout the company.

Once identified, the board would track the progress of these fast-trackers and help management identify the kinds of assignments that would develop them further, such as international experience or managing a higher level of complexity. After the initial round, HR would expand the search to include some 150 individuals who might be considered for the job ten years down the road. The board did not intend to monitor all of these individuals; that was management's job. Its purpose was to ensure that management had a process for identifying and nurturing leadership talent.

The vice president of HR executed the plan to a tee. Almost immediately he began to bring forward names of high-powered, high-potential managers. By April 1997, the company had evaluated forty-seven individuals worldwide, about three of whom had the potential to become CEO within five years.

Removing the Blockage to Leadership Growth

The process of identifying movers and shakers brought a stark reality into focus: Many high-potential individuals were in dead-end positions. Of the twenty-nine individuals with high or "back-up" succession value, fourteen were subordinate to individuals who were not on a growth track by virtue of age, experience, or ability. The progress of fourteen high potentials was blocked and, in fact, Bedford was at risk of losing them.

When the high potentials were held up against a final set of criteria, other important information came to light. This last set of criteria was based on the particular demands on the CEO by the global and external environment in the year 2000 and beyond. By articulating these demands, it became clear that the organization as a whole was not emphasizing some important skills, namely, marketing and business skills. This, too, needed fixing.

The board, the CEO, and the HR executive discussed the results of the process and how Bedford should proceed. Management had to weed out the nonperformers, but dealing with the "blockers" posed a different dilemma. They were still valued. Everyone agreed that management had to treat them fairly and humanely while clearing the path for the future leaders.

The organization had to give the high potentials opportunities to grow and develop. That meant designing career tracks based on the areas each person had to strengthen. Meanwhile, the organization had to build into its genetic code the ability to meet a tough standard of accountability and delivering on commitments. The CEO set out to make the appropriate transfers and reassignments.

Removing the blockers was painful for some, but applying the same template companywide gave people the sense that the process was fair. Those who were suddenly unblocked had a surge of energy. Many more people are building the business and marketing skills the company will need in years to come.

Still two and a half years away from the CEO's retirement, the board has not made a final choice of a successor but continues to get updates on the candidates. Through the board's determination and professionalism, as well as the cooperation and skill of the CEO and the senior HR executive, Bedford now has the foundation for a smooth leadership transition in two years and for many years thereafter.

Key Points

- Succession planning, a fundamental responsibility of the board, can be a competitive advantage. The board must take the lead and discuss succession at least once a year. Boards cannot let the CEO stall the process.

- Developing good leaders must be a conscious and constant effort. When the criteria for the CEO are linked to leadership development throughout the organization, boards do not have to scramble to find a successor. Boards must ensure that "blockers" are removed and the pipeline is filled with talent.

- Directors have good instincts about people. When they get to know the candidates far in advance and in a variety of circumstances, their collective judgment about people is value-adding.

- Do not let the outgoing CEO remain on the board. New CEOs cannot take hold when their predecessors continue on the board, and necessary changes are delayed.

CRITERIA FOR A CEO

How to Use This Instrument

Choosing a CEO is inherently a judgment call, but the process can be rigorous nonetheless. The board should use this instrument (based on interactions with some fifty CEOs and directors) as a guide for articulating the relevant criteria. Bearing in mind that no CEO candidate is perfect, be explicit about which criteria are absolutely critical to the business and which are less important. Here directors' judgment is key.

With the criteria in hand and a clear understanding of how they should be weighted, each director should lay out his or her thoughts about how the candidates measure up. Through open, honest discussion, directors' individual instincts will quickly converge, and the board will improve the quality of its collective decision.

The CEO criteria can also be used as the basis of 360-degree review throughout the organization. Doing so embeds those leadership qualities into the organization's genetic code and fills the pipeline with leaders.

The Criteria

1. Managing the Externals
   - Intellectual capacity for dealing with complexity.
   - A leader in the race for global change.
   - Influences and communicates well with external constituencies.
   - Identifies opportunities.

2. Business Acumen and Business Positioning (Strategic Direction)
   - Business instincts.
   - Intellectual edge.
   - Incisive.
   - Change agent.
   - Demonstrated business judgment.
   - Decisive.

3. Selection of Key People
   - Superb at selecting individuals, especially at top levels.
   - Aligns energy.
   - Eliminates energy drains.
   - Creates leadership depth and pipeline of future leaders.
   - Natural coach and motivator.

4. Organization's Social Architecture
   - Energizes the organization.
   - Builds organizational capacity and capability.
   - Champion of global diversity.
   - Communicates openly, directly, superbly.
   - Agent of social change.

CRITERIA FOR A CEO, cont'd.

5. Edge in Execution
   - Confronts reality.
   - Delivers measurable results.
   - Establishes priorities and develops actionable critical tasks.
   - A mover and shaker.
   - Follows through.

6. Leader in Corporate Governance
   - Makes the board a competitive advantage.
   - Builds positive working relationship with the board.
   - Taps the board's knowledge and wisdom.
   - Totally honest in keeping the board informed of positives *and* negatives.

7. Personal Leadership Traits
   - Demonstrated will and capacity to learn.
   - Integrity and intellectual honesty.
   - Tenacity and confidence in dealing with adversity.
   - A natural high-energy leader.

Note: "Industry knowledge" is intentionally excluded. Many organizations overstate its importance and overlook otherwise strong candidates. The boards of IBM, AT&T, and a growing list of other companies are finding that leadership traits more broadly defined are far more important to the success of the business.

PART THREE

BEGINNING AND CONTINUING CHANGE

CHAPTER NINE

INITIATING CHANGE:
EASIER THAN YOU THINK

The move to reinvent corporate governance has begun. The vision of a board that is fresh, alive, full of constructive controversy and debate, and in which directors are not only individually strong but also able to pool their experience and perspectives to help the CEO and the company compete is now becoming a reality.

Boards that have not yet begun to improve their practices will soon find themselves far behind the times and targeted for "solutions" imposed from the outside. It is time for boards to take control of their destiny and begin the change process.

Many critics of corporate boards and many directors themselves sense the overwhelming power of the ingrained "culture" of the boardroom. They share a kind of despair that change will come painstakingly slowly and at great risk. There is good news for them: change is easier to accomplish than many people think. The real risk lies in preserving the status quo. When the CEO or even just a handful of directors turn their motivation into action, change happens quickly. Boards are relatively small groups of people. The openness and candor of one or two people can be infectious and have an immediate effect on the rest of the group. Momentum builds quickly, because most directors really want to understand and help.

Any board member, including the CEO-chairman, can be the ice-breaker or catalyst who gets the change process started. All of the successful practices described in earlier chapters were adopted when one or two individuals took the first step toward creating an active, value-adding board. They themselves started behaving differently, or they advocated simple changes in board practice that made behavioral change easy.

CEOs: Lead the Change

CEO-chairmen are in the best position to lead a change in corporate governance because they typically control the meeting schedule (frequency and duration of meetings), the agenda, and most important, the atmosphere in and around the boardroom. They are the ones who "tell" directors not to get involved by reminding them that time is limited ("We have a lot to cover in the next two hours"), discouraging questions ("This is just for your information"), or showing disapproval in their facial expression or tone of voice.

While a growing number of CEO-chairmen want to tap the board's business wisdom, many are held back by their own fears and insecurities. Even those who have performed well in the past and have good relations with their boards can feel uneasy about forging a new relationship with the board. CEOs cannot leverage the board's experience unless they overcome the psychological issues.

A CEO's deepest fear is the loss of power, if not his or her job. Many chief executives assume that soliciting the board's ideas and opinions will be viewed as an invitation to micromanage. Or they fear that an individual director or small group will misuse the more open communication channels against them in a power struggle. Perhaps the board is factionalized, or the CEO has a personality clash with a particular director.

Open dialogue might go in unpredictable directions. The CEO of a $5 billion consumer goods company hotly resisted the practice of outside directors meeting without him for ten minutes at the end of every board meeting. Despite clear signals that the board was satisfied with his overall leadership, he feared that the discussions would go off track and erode his authority.

Another CEO was highly skeptical of board retreats to discuss corporate strategy. He says, "I've always had a fear that the board would try to create the strategy rather than assess the strategy developed by management."

There is no denying that these risks are real. When one CEO-chairman set out to improve the functioning of the board, a few directors led a move to replace him. This CEO-chairman clearly paid a penalty. But chances are that the directors would have found a way to remove him eventually. The CEO is respected for having acted on his own beliefs and for leaving behind a board intent on improving its own and the company's performance.

CEOs must simply face these possibilities. If the board is in fact factionalized or the chemistry is bad, it is better to take the leadership now, when things are not in crisis, and try to make change constructive. The pressures on boards will not subside soon. As shareholders press directors to become more active, a CEO who insists on an arm's-length relationship with the board will only increase the board's dissatisfaction. The 1990s has shown us that boards, particularly when external pressure mounts, can get through a CEO's toughest defenses.

The vast majority of CEOs are not chronic underperformers and do not have "bad blood" with directors. They will find that an active, participative board is more helpful than threatening. Even when directors have areas of concern, they are often a long way off from wanting to remove the CEO altogether. A wise CEO will try to find out where the board sees weaknesses and solicit directors' help in addressing them. One director said of the CEO whose board he serves on, "I wish the CEO and his team would understand that the company hasn't really made the changes they think they have. Whatever they achieved yesterday will not be sufficient for tomorrow. I also wish the CEO would realize that the board can help him a lot more than he's allowing us to. If not . . ."

Remember the experiences of Ivan Seidenberg, Bob Weissman, and Milt Honea, all of whom found that empowering the board did not mean losing the ability to lead the board or the company. Rather, the board increased the CEO's authority and helped him succeed. Seidenberg was the youngest member of the board when he took the initiative to reshape his relationship with the board.

It does not take a new CEO to be an agent of change. CEOs who have been in the job a while and have established relationships with the board may find confidence in part from making a sharp distinction in their minds between the roles of CEO and chairman. It is, after all, the chairman's responsibility to lead the board. Another part of that confidence can come from honing their skills in managing the board dynamics.

Directors: Be the Catalyst

External pressure has forced some directors to rethink their behavior on the board. Conscientious directors can in fact create change in a positive, professional manner by doing two things: speaking up and reaching out. Do not be quiet, and do not try to go it alone. Trust your instincts, muster the courage to speak your mind, and quickly find others who can help you institutionalize the change process.

Many directors are reluctant to suggest that the board do things differently or to question the CEO's leadership. They hold back simply because they do not want to damage their reputation in the eyes of their peers. A corporate board is one of the few situations in which a director's judgment and thinking is exposed to others who are equally successful and powerful. Many directors do not want to be thought of as a troublemaker.

One director commented, "On boards, as in most situations, people behave differently one-on-one than when they are in a group. They express certain feelings or beliefs more freely one-on-one, but in a group of ten of their peers, they hold back." Also, directors do not want their comments or questions automatically to trigger a coup.

Some highly confident directors are comfortable speaking up without knowing how others will react. Ivan Seidenberg says he never tries to sell NYNEX's board practices to other boards he serves on, but he adds, "As a director, I just behave the way I want to behave and say what I want to say. I try to make my interactions with those other boards as open and spontaneous as possible. Situations vary, but openness is always necessary." Such candor can be contagious.

Another director who is trying to initiate change on a board he recently joined says he constantly asks questions about strategy. Where are we trying to take the corporation? What should the portfolio look like? How does a particular activity add value to the strategy? How does it help us implement the strategy? He has asked the CEO to give the board a complete strategy review and a more in-depth analysis of people. The CEO, initially defensive, is now trying to be responsive. The director says, "It's not always a comfortable feeling to be pushing against the status quo and questioning a lot of history and culture. But I don't know how to operate any other way."

Du Pont's Chad Holliday says, "Sometimes groups can't come together because they're working from a question that's only on the surface. Putting the real question on the table can bring people together. If, for instance, you're discussing an acquisition and there are different views on whether it's too much money and whether we should buy it with stocks, the real issue can get buried. A director who asks, 'Is this the key competitive move we need to make?' can really get the others engaged."

There are times when a director has great difficulty participating in the dialogue during regular board meetings. When it seems impossible to introduce a new topic, a concerned director should consider several alternatives. He or she can talk to the CEO directly, raise issues in executive session or committee meetings, or talk with the head of the compensation or governance committee.

CEO John Cleghorn describes how Royal Bank of Canada's Governance Committee provides an outlet for directors: "Our Governance Committee, which comprises outside directors only, was created with the mandate to monitor, evaluate, and continuously improve corporate governance. It leads a formal process to evaluate the board's performance and is receptive to issues directors want to raise informally with committee members. Also, non-executive directors meet after every full board meeting. There, directors have the opportunity to express any concerns they may be reluctant to raise in front of management."

Put Change in an Institutional Framework

The director who puts a sensitive issue on the table is making an important change in how the board functions. That change may not last, however, unless he or she quickly finds allies to institutionalize mechanisms that support new ways of interacting and carrying out board responsibilities. The director needs the help of others—whether a core group of peers, the board chairman, or the heads of key committees.

When the CEO is doing fine but the director thinks the board should function better, he or she should try to persuade the CEO, who is usually also board chairman, to lead the effort to improve corporate governance. Any approach should include specific suggestions for how to begin, such as conducting a board self-evaluation or holding a breakthrough session to discuss the board and/or corporate strategy. Another viable option is to talk with the chairman of the governance committee. Since every committee should lay out an agenda for the next twelve months, it is legitimate to ask the committee chairman what issues the committee will tackle and to suggest that board improvement be included.

If the board does not have a governance committee, the director-as-change-agent should initiate a discussion of the board's committee structure. In this day and age of large institutional investors tracking board performance, every company should have the equivalent of a governance committee. The board improvement efforts at Royal Bank of Canada accelerated with the creation of such a committee.

Many change agents are surprised at how easy it is to find allies. On the other hand, some do meet resistance. Longtime board members can be defensive about their practices. The board described at the end of Chapter Three staunchly defended its practices until several directors and the CEO attended a program on corporate governance at a leading business school. The program allowed them to compare themselves with their peers. When they returned, the change process began in earnest.

In the presence of powerful board members who defend the status quo, building support behind the scenes is essential. When one outside director of a large industrial company questioned the board's effectiveness during a regular board meeting, another powerful director shut him down immediately. The first director had failed to solicit support behind the scenes, and other board members lacked the courage to take on the outspoken and very senior director.

In this case, however, the well-meaning director was not dissuaded. After the meeting, he began to talk among his colleagues informally and at committee meetings. He soon had a core of people who agreed that the board should discuss its own performance and improve its dynamics. When he raised the issue again during a board meeting, several board members spoke up to reinforce his point.

The director who is initiating change by continually asking about strategy says of that board: "Some members have been on the board a long time and have special relationships with the CEO. Frankly, they don't see the need to change." He has found support from several other directors who talk informally outside board meetings about how to keep the change process moving.

Sometimes a key committee chairman blocks any effort to change. Reassigning committee responsibilities, creating an ad hoc committee, or disbanding a committee (for instance, the executive committee) are ways around that problem. At one board, the chairman of the nominating committee had no interest in finding director candidates outside the traditional network. The CEO-chairman, intent on shaking the board's complacency, worked to revise the charter to give another committee responsibility for making the board more effective. The new mandate was broad enough to allow the de facto governance committee to touch on the issue of who should be on the board.

Breaking the taboos and protocols to question the CEO's leadership and/or the board's effectiveness takes a certain amount of courage. Directors can muster that courage by, first of all, reminding themselves that as Calpers and other institutional investors gain strength, boards cannot be immune to change. Pension-fund owners are getting bigger and more sophisticated. As they make the connection between board effectiveness and company performance, every board will have to demonstrate its contribution. Directors who ignore the trend risk public embarrassment, if not legal action.

When it comes to raising issues about the CEO's performance, remember that asking questions is not by definition a dilution of the CEO's power. A director's instincts are highly valuable (in the words of Cable & Wireless CEO Dick Brown, "a gift"). In today's environment, failure to make those instincts and experiences available to the CEO is a serious neglect of duty. If a director has concerns about the CEO, the sooner those thoughts and feelings are expressed, the more time there is to help him or her and to stem damage to the business.

Boards often can come up with ways to help the CEO, say, by laying out an agenda for the CEO to show value creation. Jack Krol, Du Pont CEO and director of Mead and J. P. Morgan, says, "What you don't want to do is overwhelm the CEO. What you do want to do is speak up in a positive, constructive way. Try to get the CEO to feel comfortable with the dialogue by letting him or her know off-line that you're trying to help and that your suggestions should always be taken in that spirit."

Dick Brown adds, "Package any criticism in a constructive way. How does it contribute to the betterment of the business? Other directors are more likely to rally around an issue presented that way than if it were lobbed out there as a naked criticism."

When a director has strong feelings that the CEO is the wrong person for the job, he or she should act on those feelings but focus on board processes. That is, the director should help the board institutionalize a CEO review process, however informal to start, that will do more than issue a one-time edict on the incumbent. At Temple Ward (the fictional name of the company described in Chapter Seven), the compensation committee chairman expressed his concerns about the CEO as soon as they surfaced but without assuming the outcome. As the directors began to discuss the performance issues, people had a chance to confirm each other's opinions. Ultimately, the board concluded that there was no way to save the CEO. In the meantime, it had created a process that made CEO review ongoing.

Transform the Board Dynamics

Institutionalizing open, critical dialogue is the greatest challenge of all for a board leader intent on change. Meeting formats and open exchange of information can contribute to openness in the boardroom, but poor leadership of the board dynamics can just as easily squelch it. Conversely, when board dynamics are positive, things like seating arrangements become less important. One new director who was from a small company and joined the prestigious board of a very large company was initially overwhelmed by the size and formality of the boardroom. But as soon as he realized that the board discussed the issues informally, he felt "very comfortable and willing to contribute right away."

A CEO can transform the board dynamics by sending subtle but clear signals that he or she is open to feedback and criticism, values the board's input, and believes that management and the board are working toward a common goal. Chuck Ames of Clayton Dubilier & Rice says of his experience as board chairman, "I really work at becoming the leader of the group as chairman. I let the conversations go forward, and I'm very happy when directors talk among themselves, to each other."

Jim Hagen of Conrail, Ivan Seidenberg of NYNEX, Tom Loarie of KeraVision, and the chairman-CEOs of many other effective boards have a knack for getting everyone in the room to participate and stay on point. They draw out directors who have tremendous insight but may be reluctant to speak out, and they manage those directors who tend to dominate or go off on tangents.

Some of the techniques for opening up the board dynamics may seem obvious. Part of it is making sure the directors feel that the CEO is interested in their comments. Former Conrail Chairman Jim Hagen says, "I would keep looking up and down the table to see who was sitting on the edge of their chair waiting their turn to talk. Once in a while I would point to someone who had nothing to say on the subject, but most of the time they did. I like meetings to run on time, but occasionally I sacrificed that so everyone was heard."

As chairman of NYNEX, Seidenberg was careful not to try to control everything that was said. "When I presented information," he says, "I tried to do it in a way that let them know I didn't have a certain expected response." To make people from outside the industry feel comfortable, he avoided speaking in "telephone-ese."

Another CEO said he often draws people in by saying to the individual, "You have some experience in this. How did you handle it at your company?" This technique is especially useful in helping a new director break the ice.

Some CEOs have other ways to get the discussion rolling. Some give a quick recap of the previous meeting and the topics at hand. At NYNEX, Seidenberg started every meeting by quickly laying out the externals—Washington, industry structural changes, acquisitions and mergers by others, what it means, how the landscape changes as other players make moves, and what is good and bad about NYNEX strategy in that context.

Chad Holliday, director and CEO designate of Du Pont, says, "A CEO needs to know each director really well and not run with the stereotype. At Du Pont, for example, Bill Reilly came out of the EPA, but he's not just an environmental expert. He has insight into lots of other issues. The same holds true for every director. If a CEO can uncover that other thing that people understand but may not be noted for, he or she can release a lot of energy."

Sometimes the old patterns of behavior are so entrenched that it takes a lot of coaxing to get the directors to open up. Some directors may, for instance, have a hard time moving away from a narrow focus on financial reports and the like. As one board member said, "Some directors think they are adding value by nit-picking on the numbers. They lose sight of the big picture." One director spent half an hour of the board's time arguing about whether an ROA goal should be adjusted up or down by a tenth of a percentage point. As the board dynamics gel and change gains momentum, these time drains are easily plugged.

A change of venue, such as an off-site board retreat, often helps transform the board dynamics. The board of the former Dun & Bradstreet was accustomed to one-way communication in the boardroom, but during a board retreat, the board dynamics changed dramatically. CEO Bob Weissman wanted to use the retreat to educate the board about some pressing issues the company faced and to gain support in choosing a strategy amidst tremendous industry flux. The retreat included presentations by management, but Weissman frequently stopped to ask directors to react and ask questions. At one point, management asked, "What two questions are we not asking that we should be asking?"

At first, directors seemed reluctant to speak. But the questions got their interest, and by the end of the first day, everyone was actively participating in open discussion. The next morning, the directors raised questions they had thought of overnight. Every single person had thought of something new. After two days of intense discussion, directors were energized, not drained. One director's comment was typical: "This meeting has been very exciting. We have never participated in this way. I get a sense that the board and management are being knit together, yet the thinking is independent. We should do this again."

Conrail's board dynamics had begun to open up in the years leading up to the 1994 retreat. Directors had developed open communication among themselves beginning in 1989 with the unexpected death of Chairman-CEO Dick Sanborn just six weeks into the job. With no succession process in place, the board had to act quickly, and formality fell by the wayside.

The search for a permanent successor ended with the selection of Jim Hagen as Chairman and CEO, who from the start viewed the board as a partner in a difficult situation. He gave directors more information than they had ever had and encouraged them to express their opinions freely. "The directors never tried to tell us our job or anything," Hagen says, "but they really started working hard to say what they think."

The 1994 retreat pushed Conrail's good board dynamics to a whole new level. As former Conrail general counsel Bruce Wilson notes, "Before the retreat, communication between management and the board was better at Conrail than at many companies. The directors had told Jim Hagen, who was then chairman, that they wanted more exposure to people at the operational level, and Jim quickly agreed to have them at the next meeting.

"But directors sensed that some senior managers still felt the board was something to be feared rather than being there to be helpful," Bruce Wilson continues. "We had to look for ways to break the barriers down further to reduce the apprehension about telling the board the bad news as well as the good." Everyone on or close to the Conrail board agrees that the two-day meeting in September 1994 is the event that really got the board dynamics to gel. "After that," Wilson says, " we evolved very quickly."

Once the suppressive atmosphere has been broken, the board can use simple techniques to jump-start the board dynamics at subsequent meetings. One technique is to invite a guest speaker to dinner before the board meeting. The speaker can be an expert in an area of particular concern to the business or simply provide a novel perspective on a topic that is intellectually stimulating. Du Pont discovered the benefit of this technique by accident when one of its board members, Percy Barnevik, arrived late due to a flight delay.

When Barnevik arrived, he explained to the group that he had just come from Russia. In response to directors' questions, he gave the group an on-the-spot overview of the situation there. The board was so engaged that the level of energy and excitement continued throughout dinner and into the meeting the following day. The free flow of questions and answers had set the tone. Du Pont has since decided to invite guest speakers to other dinner sessions to enhance the board's learning and to get directors thinking and talking.

KeraVision, the California-based medical technology company, also has used this technique. The CEO of a publicly held ophthalmology physician practice center discussed the future of ophthalmic care delivery, and the chairman of marketing at UCLA discussed consumer marketing—both issues of current interest to the company.

Seize the Opportunities for Change

Some situations are natural invitations for change. Mergers, acquisitions, spin-offs, IPOs, a new CEO—each of these situations is a perfect occasion to do things differently. Ivan Seidenberg says that when his predecessor and the general counsel at NYNEX retired at the same time, "it gave us the opportunity to go further and use the events to do a whole review of our board practices. Whenever the environment is right, do it."

As new chairman and CEO of Stanley Works, John Trani met one-on-one with each board member to hear their concerns about the company, to learn the kinds and frequency of information they wanted, and to solicit advice. He says, "New CEOs who may not have dealt with boards before must be very conscious of what they're doing with the board. They should lay out their objectives and keep the board updated, and in that way, begin the dialogue."

Start-up boards have the opportunity to establish good group norms at the beginning. Venture capitalist Marshall Turner notes, "The good ones do." When CEO Bill Lichtenberger was creating a board from scratch after Praxair was spun off from Union Carbide in 1991, he considered the kind of board he wanted: "Did I want a board that would basically salute me every time I said something, or did I want a board that was going to argue with me and be interactive? I made the decision that I wanted board members who would speak their mind."

Starting with the premise that the board could be value adding, Lichtenberger recruited members who had a broad range of expertise and worked well as a group. As he asked each member to join, he explained what he was looking for: people who would become interested in the company and were willing to help. Have he and the company benefited? "Absolutely," Lichtenberger says. "I don't get direction from my board, but I do get valuable and useful input."

Sometimes an event creates a change in behavior. The board of a large food company thought it had total access to the company because senior managers made detailed presentations during board meetings. Directors didn't realize that the chairman was controlling every comment, every slide, and every answer. Then in 1996, an unexpected event in the external environment broke the company's steady stream of earnings. The seriousness of the business situation spurred the board to start asking questions and demanding more candid information. As one insider notes, "Now the directors spend time in executive session discussing the real issues, as they should. That behavior did not exist four years ago."

Directors should not wait for a negative turn of events. They should act before the company suffers a severe blow or finds itself in crisis.

As Alex Mandl, CEO of Teligent, says, "One or two board members can make a huge difference. If a board member sees early trends that are pointing toward decline and weak performance, the person should raise those issues at the board level right away. If management does not get engaged on those issues, then there have to be direct conversations with the CEO. If those don't work, then the board member should suggest that management be reviewed and introduce the possibility that changes need to be made. Obviously, all of this must be done with the right balance and in the right sequence. But it *can* be done. That's what board members must remember."

Don't Quit Without a Fight

Some directors have expressed their serious disapproval of the current CEO and/or the board by resigning. In 1994, Zbigniew Brzezinski and Peter V. Uebberoth, directors of Morrison-Knudsen, abruptly resigned as the company's financial troubles worsened. In early 1997, Jesse L. Upchurch resigned from the Tandy board when he and other board members had an apparent disagreement over the performance of CEO John V. Roach.

Dick Brown of Cable & Wireless notes, "You can't have great directors of a bad company over time. Really effective directors don't stay on rubber-stamp boards." But Brown sees resignation as a last resort. "Directors owe it to the chief executive to say what they think. If they keep trying and the CEO makes it clear that the directors cannot be fully engaged and contributing, then they better get out or they'll get splashed."

Resigning from a board because of dissatisfaction with the status quo can save a director embarrassment, and, as one board member states, "It can give the CEO a wake-up call, particularly if the investment community takes notice." But resignation is an ineffective tool for creating lasting change. As one director remarked, "To me, resigning from a board when it's in trouble tells the shareholders you're there for the retainer as opposed to taking on the problem. It's not right." Changing the practices of one of the boards he served on was an arduous process, but he adds, "Now the company is starting to do better, and I have the satisfaction of knowing I had something to do with that."

Venture capitalists of course have little choice but to try to influence management. Their resignation would put their entire investment at risk. Their frame of mind and pattern of involvement may be useful to other boards that want to change.

Taken by Surprise: The Case of "Richard Tomkin"

*This CEO made his "good" relationship with
the board even better—because he had to.*[1]

Richard Tomkin, chairman and CEO of Gage Medical Development, had every reason to believe that he had the board's full support. He had positioned the company well in a turbulent industry, developed a strong management team, and had friendly relationships with all the directors. But on Thursday, May 12, 1994, Tomkin was forced to question his standing with the board. That morning, just before he left for Chicago to attend a trustees meeting for the United Way, he got a startling telephone call from Ron Warner, 73 years old, a friend and board member.

"I just got a call from Tag and two of your other senior officers," Warner explained. "It caught me by surprise. He said they have some real concerns about you as CEO and about the direction you're taking the company, particularly the proposed merger. . . . Look, why don't I give you a chance to digest this. Then call me back."

Tomkin was stunned. He had always been open and honest with his three top executives—chief financial officer Tag Foster, chief operating officer Frank O'Keefe, and general counsel Michael Hogan. He had even recommended Foster to the board. Now he felt shocked and betrayed. "It was like someone saying my kid was on drugs and robbing grocery stores," he said. "I went through all the emotions a person can go through, from disbelief to disappointment to anger."

Tomkin had to overcome the emotions. "When Ron called me, I didn't know what the board was going to do—or what I should do. I just knew I had to act fast."

Tension and Dissension in the Ranks

Tomkin had become the head of Gage Medical Development, a developer and tester of medical devices, in 1988, when it was spun off from a large pharmaceuticals and medical research company. Under

[1]This case describes a real situation. Names and some details have been disguised.

Tomkin's leadership, Gage grew to be very profitable and went public. As the health care industry began a major transformation, the challenges intensified. Consolidation and intense price competition forced companies to become ever more efficient. Speed to market was vital. Most pharmaceutical and medical research companies began major restructuring efforts to cut spending and fight for market share.

Tomkin, like every other CEO in the industry, had to make tough decisions about how to position the company. Recognizing the limitations of Gage's marketing and administrative resources, he developed a strategy to form alliances with other medical device and testing companies. He believed Gage could create shareholder value by remaining independent but acknowledged the need to continually revisit the possibility of merging. Gage had to pick the right product areas and the right partners—and perhaps the right time to merge. The prospect of a merger made Tomkin's top managers anxious.

In May of 1993, Tomkin unwittingly gave his managers another reason to be anxious. He agreed to be a part-time government advisor on health care reform. The board wanted Tomkin to run Gage Research at the same time. If after one year he was spending too much time in Washington, he would leave the company, and one of his top managers would succeed him.

While his work schedule was reduced, Tomkin gave his direct reports more exposure and accountability. Foster and O'Keefe, for instance, became more involved with the Wall Street investment community. At first the arrangement worked well, but as the health reform movement gained momentum, word got out that Tomkin might be leaving the company, and Gage began to hear from friendly and unfriendly suitors. In February of 1994, the board concurred that they wanted Tomkin at the helm full time, and Tomkin agreed.

Gage's top managers were not happy. They expected Tomkin to resign and were disappointed that they would not be considered to succeed him. Tomkin brought in an industrial psychologist to help reduce the stress and get things back to normal.

Meanwhile, market forces were encroaching. In March, DC Medical, the second largest manufacturer of medical devices, expressed an

interest in merging with Gage. Tomkin felt obliged to consider the proposal. He had Foster and Hogan sit in on some of the discussions, and
he kept O'Keefe informed.

On a Wednesday afternoon, Tomkin asked Foster to prepare a confidentiality of exchange information. He explained that he would be
calling a special meeting of the executive committee of the board to tell
them that Gage had been approached and to seek advice. He needed
his key managers to help prepare the presentation materials.

Action Amid Self-Doubt

When Tomkin got the phone call from Warner early Thursday morning, he did not know which way the board would go: "There were these
three bright, young managers I had bragged so much about, and I was
an old guy. Maybe they thought it was time for a change. Doing something rash—like terminating the managers, which I really thought
about—wouldn't help and definitely would have hurt the company on
Wall Street."

Tomkin flew back from his trustees meeting Thursday evening and
spent Friday at home making phone calls to the directors. He explained
the situation and urged them to attend an emergency board meeting on
Saturday. The first phone calls were the hardest because Tomkin was
not sure what to expect. The directors were as surprised as Tomkin.
One director read a copy of a note he had sent Tomkin the previous
week: "Just a note to tell you how impressed I was last week with the
caliber of your team. You have put together a terrific group of people
who show a remarkable combination of intelligence and initiative. You
deserve high marks for bringing that about." The director remarked, "I
just can't believe this is the same group of people."

By noon Saturday, the entire board was assembled, along with the
three senior managers who had made the complaints. The managers
told the board that they were opposed to the merger and then restated
their complaints about Tomkin. As the board sifted through the complaints, the managers did not provide any convincing evidence. When
two of the managers complained that Tomkin had forced them to
communicate to the investment community, for instance, one director

countered that such exposure could be considered useful and flattering. The managers conceded that it had been a positive experience.

Then the board wanted to talk with the managers alone, and Tomkin excused himself. As he waited, he began to realize that he had not done a very good job of keeping the board informed. He regretted the fact that the board was not fully informed about the dynamics of the industry, the company's strategy, or the internal tensions.

Less than two hours later, the board called Tomkin back in. The board was united in feeling that the managers had not used good judgment in presenting their complaints, and a few directors chastised Tomkin for not creating avenues for such dissatisfaction to be communicated directly.

But the board was divided about the proposed merger. Some directors said the company should stay independent at all costs; others wanted to consider the proposal. The board asked Tomkin not to have any further discussion about a merger. A week later, at another full board meeting, the board changed its mind and designated a committee, including Tomkin, to talk with the interested parties. In the meantime, one senior manager was changing his story. He said he had been under a lot of pressure from his associates. His flip-flop created credibility problems with the board.

The Wake-up Call

In the days and weeks following, Tomkin continued to have one-on-one conversations with the board members. He learned that they were pleased that he had kept a cool head through what he called the "palace revolt" but they did not want any more surprises. Tomkin wondered whether keeping the board better informed would mean losing his autonomy.

"I'm sort of from the old school with boards," he said. "I've always thought that the more you got them involved, the more you had to defend yourself and the more they'd try to second-guess your decisions. But after the palace revolt, I was forced to do things differently. So I started informing them better, and they started participating more. They went from being passive reviewers of material the staff puts on the table to active challengers of management's direction."

Tomkin started feeding directors a lot of information between meetings. Management started sending out "care packages" every two or three weeks with updates on health care reform and the grass roots efforts Gage was making to influence reform.

The information packages created a mechanism for more one-on-one communication. They gave Tomkin the opportunity to call individual directors to say, "Did you get my package? What do you think about that last proposal?" Or directors could call him, "Is Congress really going to cut Medicare to that extent?"

Board meetings became more interesting as a result. Directors began to give more useful input and ask better questions. Tomkin explains: "The directors became more in tune with our business. We got into a lot more depth about what our future would be like under different alternatives. What if we stayed independent, or merged with this company or that company?

"We were talking about acquiring certain capabilities over the next two or three years. If the board didn't understand where the industry was going, how products were going to be developed and marketed, and the importance of alliances, it surely wasn't going to sign off on making certain capital decisions. Boards are more likely to defeat an agenda item if they don't understand it."

Tomkin soon realized that his fears about micro-management were not warranted: "To my surprise, the board really doesn't micro-manage. Some board members have a tendency to get involved in areas where they have expertise, but most of them intentionally avoid getting involved in the day-to-day stuff. It seems to me that micro-managing goes on when board members don't know what's going on and they have to start asking. Or it's an indication that the directors have lost a little confidence in the CEO and the CEO's lost some credibility."

Tomkin has become a true advocate of keeping boards well informed. "I truly believe a CEO has a tremendous responsibility for providing information and overviews and developing good reviews of the strengths and weaknesses of the key resources of the organization, including the people. When the board is informed, they can be tremendously helpful. When we transformed from a private company to a public company, I think I did a good job with the road show, but if I had had my board properly educated, I could have gotten a lot more mileage from them. Some of my board members have been through those trials and tribulations more than I have."

While Tomkin tried to strengthen his own relationship with the board, he also contemplated the relationship between the board and his senior management. He concluded that the board should have more—not less—exposure to management. He encouraged informal exchanges outside the boardroom and created opportunities for the board to meet managers below the level of his direct reports. "I wanted the board to know that the company wasn't run by four or five people, so we started inviting the top twenty to thirty managers for lunch following the board meetings, just to talk informally. I suppose some CEOs might be afraid that the board will find out something they don't want them to know. My feeling is that the board will discover those things anyway. If I'm doing something inappropriate, the board *should* have a means to find out, and there's always a back door."

Tomkin's palace revolt was a wake-up call. "My relationship with the board became stronger than ever, and one or two directors even said I became a better CEO."

The deal with DC Medical was taken off the table because they could not reach agreement about price. Then six months later, DC Medical made a new bid and the companies were merged. Tomkin said he was determined to apply his learning to the new board, of which he became chairman.

A Lone Voice: The Case of "Glen Michaels"

This outside director won the struggle to get an indifferent board to address the company's slack performance.[2]

In 1993, Glen Michaels, chairman and CEO of $1 billion Castle Electronics, was honored to join the board of Supertech, a $2.2 billion electronics company. Supertech had on its board some of the country's most

[2]This case describes a real situation. Names and some details have been disguised.

illustrious business leaders, including six CEOs of major U.S. corporations. Michaels welcomed the chance to network with the other directors and to pick up good ideas to apply at Castle.

Michaels also believed that his wide range of experience in the electronics industry could be of use to Supertech. "The company was positioning itself to grow through acquisition of electronic companies in the $30 to $40 million range," he explained. "Having been in various parts of the industry, I was in a good position to help management identify and select good candidates. Plus the company was doing some work in the area of long-term compensation, which I had just been through."

But Michaels soon learned that the CEO of Supertech did not want any input from the board—or any serious challenge. Michaels had to take some big risks to break the silence.

The Newcomer's Concerns

At the first few board meetings, Michaels had his eyes and ears wide open. The company had not been growing, was not generating any exciting new products, and shareholders were not getting the return they expected. Although Michaels sensed that other directors were concerned, no one said much at board meetings.

Then after several meetings, management came through with a plan to get costs under control. The whole board was elated. It was what everyone had been waiting for. Management's plan included writing down a big chunk of shareholders' equity. The board asked a few superficial questions and approved the plan. Michaels did not think the financial restructuring alone would help the company grow, but he thought it was a reasonable starting point and supported the move.

As the months passed, Michaels noticed that the CEO was not coming forward to say where he was taking the company next. Michaels explains, "There was no creativity, no structure, no strategy. I wouldn't have minded if the CEO said he was having trouble and needed to hire some consultants to help him figure things out. Instead, the CEO simply failed to deal with what he didn't understand."

Michaels concluded that the CEO was avoiding the problems and taking the company nowhere. Supertech had done the restructuring, but as the second quarter of the new fiscal year approached, nothing was different. The growth still was not there, products still were not flowing, and shareholders were not doing any better.

The Brick-Wall Protocol

Michaels had some tough questions to ask the CEO, but he was not at all sure how to ask them. The atmosphere of the boardroom was not conducive to open discussion. "In meetings, we had all these 'givens,'" Michaels recalls:

The first given was time. The meeting started at 8 and was over at noon. Since everyone had planes to catch, we had to break up before lunch. The second given was the agenda. There was always a long list of things that had to be done—scheduling the annual meeting, selecting the auditors, approving the agenda—and we obediently marched through them, one after the other.

The third given was respect for your peers. It's like what we were taught in fifth grade: you listen when I speak, and I listen when you speak. It was a sort of "be nice" rule that made it almost impossible to say, "Hey, I noticed things aren't going very well. What's the problem?"

Then there were these psychological contracts. People came together as a board from various parts of the country just in time for the meeting. We didn't know each other well or talk very often. So no one was ever sure whether they were the odd man out. Maybe the other nine members felt confident, and you're concerned because you don't know the business well enough. You don't want to be embarrassed in front of these big shots. Just about the time things warm up and people start talking, it's time to go, and you don't see those people again for two months.

At one point, Michaels suggested to the CEO-chairman that he leave some time in the board meetings for open discussion. The CEO responded, "When the directors are together without an agenda, it's sort of a feeding frenzy." Michaels thought to himself, "You can't tell me that the vice chairman of one of the world's biggest defense companies lives on feeding frenzies! The CEO clearly doesn't understand."

The CEO's attitude notwithstanding, open discussions did begin—in the committees. The audit committee meetings, which were supposed to be an hour long, started lasting for three hours because people were talking about the company's situation. The personnel committee was not approving stock options because they were troubled by the situation. Yet board meetings continued to be non-events.

Michaels's concerns and frustration deepened.

I figured one of two things was going to happen—the company would hit a major disaster like running out of cash or a bunch of shareholders were going to do our job for us. So I started convincing myself that I had to do something. I didn't care if I upset management. But frankly, I didn't want to make a fool of myself in front of the vice chairman of one of the country's largest industrial companies and the top executive of a major transportation company. I know how quickly reputations get around.

I also felt it was wrong to express my feelings strongly to the other directors outside the board meeting. If that happened, it was like sowing the seeds for a management coup. This was less than a year after the coups at GM, Westinghouse, and American Express. I didn't want anyone to get the idea that I was triggering an overthrow.

The Opportune Moment

While Michaels was trying to figure out how and when to speak up, it was time for the annual meeting. Annual meetings at this company had always been the kind where you wondered why you even had them, but this time was different. Shareholders and analysts started standing up and asking, "Why is the average age of your board so old? How can an electronics company have such an old board?" and "When are we going to start seeing improvement in shareholder return?" At the next board meeting, Michaels decided it was time:

> I couldn't let things go on. So when management began its presentation, I stopped them and said, "We're talking about the wrong things. This company is on the road to failure." Management got very uptight, and the other board members got very uncomfortable. I had broken the protocol.
>
> The CEO immediately said, "I don't understand your question." I responded, "What are your plans to get this company to a 12 percent return on equity, or another measure you choose to use that delivers return to the shareholder?" And then I kept asking questions totally off the agenda. Within minutes the CEO said coolly, "Look, we're running out of time. We've got an agenda to approve," and he marched us through it. The other directors didn't say anything, so management got out of the hot seat pretty quickly.

Michaels did not get his questions answered, but he had created a stir that no one could ignore. After the meeting, he wrote to the CEO-chairman to explain why he had taken the position he did. The CEO responded by calling him on the phone, Michaels says, to try to calm him down.

But Michaels got other phone calls as well. "After the meeting, several directors called me. One longstanding director said he agreed with me. But he was choosing a different approach—if he didn't see some progress soon he would resign from the board.

"Then another director, a very senior guy who was also on the board of one of the big auto companies, called to say he supported me completely. He went on to say, 'You're what this company needs, someone who will be candid.' He said he didn't have the guts. He had kind of settled into some longstanding relationships with people. I was a newcomer, so I guess it was logical that I would be the one to disrupt things."

American Business Macho

Signs of support from other directors eased Michaels's discomfort, but to his great disappointment, the board did nothing to address the issue. He raised the subject in an audit committee meeting, but it went nowhere.

Meanwhile, the CEO continued with his brick-wall defense as he set out on an ambitious acquisition strategy. "We were trying to help the CEO, but he didn't want to accept the value added. Like a lot of others in his position, he had a big ego. People don't want to ask for help until they're almost beyond the point where they can use it. It's the macho of American business."

The CEO's response convinced Michaels that the company needed a new leader. "I knew in my gut it was time for a younger, more aggressive CEO," Michaels says. "He had been the perfect CEO for getting rid of excess people, selling off the businesses that were a drag, and so on. He could run the place really lean. But he had no idea how to invest, where to invest, or how to evaluate the markets that have the highest probability of success. And he didn't want to learn. He was absolutely the wrong person to build the company for the future."

It took a year and a half, but Michaels finally found the mechanism to create change. One day he shared a cab with another director, who confided in Michaels that he, too, was very concerned about the CEO's leadership. The two men worked together to solicit support from other directors. Through their phone calls, Michaels and his ally learned that many directors did not like the long-term incentive plan—but had voted for it—and did not like the acquisition theory—though they did not say so.

As directors found their points of agreement, they started speaking up in meetings. They told the CEO they would not approve any acquisitions unless the CEO laid out a full plan. The newly engaged board kept returning to the growth strategy, and the CEO could see which way things were going. He retired within a year.

Key Points

- The unwritten rules of corporate governance are changing. Most existing board practices do not meet today's demands. Standing still makes boards obsolete quickly.

- The change process takes root quickly when a CEO or director puts a substantive issue on the table and people begin to talk. The right operating mechanisms can encourage open dialogue.

- Changes in leadership or ownership are golden opportunities to do things differently. But directors and CEOs should not wait. Take the lead when times are good.

CHAPTER TEN

CONTINUOUS IMPROVEMENT AT THE TOP

Many boards have begun to do some kind of review of their practices. A select few have become very good at it and have benefited from it. Most, however, do not overcome the real barriers to improvement. One CEO and director remarked, "The only thing boards do less well than review CEO performance is review their own performance in a meaningful way."

Often in the name of politeness, accurate descriptions of reality do not get put on the table. These may include board behavior or the relationship between the CEO and the board. When board self-assessment is well designed, it brings the issues people instinctively dodge into an open forum for discussion and debate. It can help make board deliberations intellectually honest.

Survey instruments and questionnaires should not be used mechanically. Their value comes from the discussion that ensues, not from numerical tabulations of the results. As John Trani, chairman and CEO of Stanley Works, says, "An honest board periodically asks itself whether it collectively can take the company to the next level." Discussion of the answer leads to many points of action. More important, as the discussion takes place, the behavior patterns begin to change, and new board dynamics begin to emerge. The process can be transforming.

Ultimately, efforts to help the board function at its peak should get down to the level of each individual's performance. But boards should proceed cautiously when venturing into the murky waters of director peer review. Although evaluation of individuals can help a well-functioning board become world class, it tends to exacerbate existing tensions. When the board is already factionalized, peer review can become a witch hunt.

Board Self-Evaluation: A Bare Essential

Boards at work continually try to improve their ability to function as a collective body. They understand that unless the board is functioning well as a group, it cannot provide the appropriate oversight, let alone add value. As one GM director said of the company's troubles in the early 1990s, the issue was not only with the evaluation of the CEO but also with the board. The board itself had to improve.

Continuous improvement of the board is a simple extension of continuous improvement principles applied elsewhere in the organization. It is typically driven by some form of board self-evaluation. One corporate chairman says, "We do 360-degree reviews all the way down through the whole organization. Why should it stop at the top? We're talking about the same rules for everyone up and down the line. The board should set the pace." Lois Juliber, executive vice president of Colgate-Palmolive and director of Du Pont, says simply, "The height of a good board is its willingness to evaluate itself."

While self-evaluation is becoming more commonplace, particularly as Calpers and other activists push boards to adopt it, some boards still resist. One new CEO struggled with how to motivate the board: "The board kept saying, 'What's wrong with us? We think we've done a good job.' They didn't know how many calls I'd been getting from shareholders asking why we should keep the same board that stood by when the stock price went from $32 to $9."

Some directors believe that if the nominating committee picks good people, the board has no need for self-evaluation. Choosing good directors is important, but it has been shown that capable individuals are often ineffective as a group. Boards must assess their performance as a collective body. Besides, the principles of continuous improvement apply to people; there is always room to improve.

Resistance to self-evaluation often comes from one or two directors who tend to speak first when board self-evaluation is proposed. Other directors often defer to them in the name of politeness or deference to their seniority. Those who are in favor of creating such a process should be aware of this dynamic, however, and not let the reactions of a few forceful individuals prevent further discussion. Each and every director must take responsibility for creating a robust self-improvement process.

Boards should customize the self-evaluation process. Each board must determine the degree of formality it is comfortable with, whether or not to use a written survey instrument, and who should analyze the results. The important thing is that the process has rigor. Does the process get the board engaged in honest dialogue on the board's ability to function well? Does it help directors speak the unspeakable?

Although a nominating or governance committee can work out the details of the process and/or design the self-evaluation instrument, the whole board must be deeply involved. TRW CEO Joe Gorman explains: "These issues are so overriding and so important that the whole board should be focusing on them, not just a group of three or four people."

Some boards have been able to improve by discussing their practices informally. One director describes his board's ongoing, low-key efforts to improve its own performance: "From time to time we look at how often we're meeting, how often we want to meet, and how we're using our meeting time. Recently our Planning Committee gave management some guidance on how we'd like to spend more time on strategy and less on financial reports."

Similarly, the Citicorp board discusses the functioning of the board informally at the end of its annual two-day July meeting. CEO-Chairman John Reed asks questions like, Is the committee structure okay?

and Are we covering the right agenda items? "We usually get about an hour's worth of conversation," Reed explains. "Much of how we operate is a by-product of things that have come up during those sessions."

Soon after George Davidson became CEO of Consolidated Natural Gas, he asked individual board members what they liked and did not like about the board. As the process has evolved, it has become more formalized. Once a year, the corporate secretary gathers feedback from directors, and the CEO discusses the suggestions and concerns with the full board. As a result of directors' comments, CNG has reduced the number of board meetings, lengthened them to allow for more discussion, and started holding informal dinners the night before. One active, experienced director said CNG is the best board he has served on.

One-on-one discussions with directors can complement a board self-evaluation. At TRW, CEO-Chairman Joe Gorman meets with individual directors periodically to get their thoughts about the board. He uses a list of topics to structure those discussions. In July 1997, the list included the following items: company relationship with the directors, number and location of meetings, information given (at meetings, written, strategic, operational), number and mix of directors, retirement age, committees (make-up, meetings, mission/duties), compensation, management visibility, succession planning, approvals, the experience of boards of other companies, the management structure, and other requests or advice. Gorman says those discussions help him sense the board's social architecture. Not checking in with individual directors is, in his words, an opportunity missed.

When a written survey instrument is used, questions should cover the basics: Do you feel this board is as effective as it could be? Is there sufficient initiative to improve it? How well is the board ensuring that the CEO and top management have the right skills, talents, energy, and determination, that the company has the right strategy, and that the team is executing in such a way that will allow the objectives to be achieved? How can the board do better? Further detail is a matter of choice. (The Corporate Board Self-Evaluation Instrument at the end of this chapter is a detailed version from which boards may want to draw.)

A thorough self-evaluation looks at board dynamics as well as specific practices and structures. At Royal Bank of Canada, the board does a rigorous self-assessment that elicits responses on items including the need for additional—or modifications to existing—corporate governance principles, structure and processes; the group dynamics of the board; best practices in other companies; any emerging corporate governance requirements; and progress in developing a corporate governance culture.

Forcing directors to articulate their own, usually unspoken, assumptions about the role and behavior of the board usually sparks a lively debate. What do directors think an ideal board should do? Is it enough for the board to meet fiduciary responsibilities or should the board be expected to contribute to the strategic wisdom of the company? Should board members feel free to request information and express their opinions candidly? Should board meetings be a forum for intellectual give-and-take? What is the common vision of the board's ideal board dynamics?

Questions about the board's performance will follow: Does the board have the right processes to help management deliberate on strategy, succession planning, and major decisions? Is the board finding the right balance between governing and micromanaging?

The CEO should participate in these discussions and have a chance to articulate his or her expectations of the board. In a 1995 speech to the National Association of Corporate Directors entitled "What the CEO Should Expect from the Board: One Leader's Perspective," former Bell Atlantic director Bill Adams outlined a few such expectations that are, as he says, important and not commonly fulfilled. Directors should get to know the company, its markets and the general environment in which it operates and competes; bring the best they have to offer—and use it; help make the CEO the best he or she can be; do all they can to release the power in the relationship with the CEO; and accept responsibility for their own improvement—as individual directors and as a board.

Most directors want to do the right thing. In the process of designing the survey instrument and discussing the results, people tend to get involved and participate. The behavior begins to change.

What to Expect from Board Self-Evaluation

The process by which a formal board self-evaluation will be distributed, collated, and discussed must be carefully designed and have buy-in from all board members. When a written survey instrument is used, there are a variety of ways to execute and collate the results.

Written results can be collected by the chairman of the corporate governance committee or the corporate secretary. Alternatively, some boards have found it useful to send the completed survey instruments to a third party for analysis, especially when the process is new. The full board gets the aggregate results only. As the board becomes more comfortable with self-evaluation, the committee chairman can do the analysis.

Regardless of who does the analysis, the important thing is to focus on how the board actually functions and not get mired in statistical detail. Do not let the numbers drive the results. The point is to identify issues the board needs to discuss. Draw problem spots to the surface and let the board get involved.

Dispersement of responses can be telling, as can the tone of open-ended responses. Open-ended responses can be grouped into categories according to their overall thrust. Some comments might fall into the "enthusiastically positive" category; others might be "mildly critical," "harshly critical," or "downright damning." Another useful technique is to group the comments that ask for more of something or less of something.

When a board self-evaluation asks substantive questions and directors are assured their answers will be confidential, board members feel more free to lay the reality on the table. When one company asked a range of questions about the board's contribution to company strategy, its composition, the atmosphere and structure of board meetings, and whether adequate attention was given to shareholder interests, verbatim comments showed that directors pulled no punches:

"We need fewer reports and more time for candid discussion."

"The board should spend more time exploring the company's strategic options."

"Information packets arrive too late."

"Need more data on the competition."

"We need expertise in new product development—a qualification for a new director."

"Too many insiders."

Especially the first time around, board self-evaluation often touches on the relationship between management and the board. References to the CEO or a committee chairman can be very threatening to those individuals. For this reason, boards should tailor the presentation of the feedback to the particular situation. If, for instance, the feedback reflects poorly on the chairman-CEO, the board should be sure that the person gets the feedback in private from an individual he or she trusts before discussing the feedback with the full board. This two-step process gives the person a chance to digest the information and overcome defensiveness.

One large company faced precisely that problem. The board's first-ever self-evaluation showed that directors thought the CEO was defensive and tried to control meeting content too closely. These comments came in response to questions about the leadership of board meetings and the board's ability to discuss important business issues. When asked about the board's ability to discuss issues, for example, one director wrote, "Every time we debate, management goes on the defensive." In response to another question, directors wrote "Management should listen to the board more" and "Management is oversensitive to constructive criticism."

The board had not even the slightest intention of removing the CEO. On the contrary, it wanted to help him and saw room for improvement. But sensing that the feedback might affect the CEO's morale, the senior human resources executive and the corporate governance committee chairman decided that the HR executive should talk with the CEO in private first. When the results were later discussed among the full board, the CEO had maintained a constructive posture. The process of improving the board's relationship with the CEO had begun.

Those who question the usefulness of board self-evaluation should consider the specific action plans that come from intellectual honesty and involved discussion. One board converged on the following actions: give the board more time to discuss the company's strategic direction and management development; keep directors better informed; make discussions more candid, less rehearsed; reduce the insiders on the board and seek new members with relevant experience. Another board felt it needed more executive sessions of outside directors only to deliberate on certain issues. These are all clear steps toward positive change.

The specific action steps will vary from one board to another. Bill Hudson, CEO of AMP, says, "Because each board has its own personality and character, using one set of guidelines universally is not healthy. There must be a process for each board to deliberate on how it can work more effectively to ensure that the board is indeed governing and providing guidance to management, and that the company is performing to the benefit of its shareholders."

Director Peer Review: Walking on Eggshells

A few exceptional boards have undertaken director peer review, whereby directors evaluate each other. Most boards, however, fear the negative consequences of having board members "grade" each other and resist the notion, even when the CEO advocates it with evangelical zeal. This trepidation is understandable. Peer review is a difficult process to execute well, and as Bill Adams says, "Directors fear the criticism of their peers more than anything else." When there is distrust between directors and the CEO or among the board members, director peer review can damage rather than improve the board dynamics. It has happened.

When, however, a board is "mature" and the board dynamics are already quite good, peer review is a powerful tool for helping each director learn how to be a more effective member of the group. The point is to draw out each person's best, not to take a vote on whether someone should be retained or dismissed.

Executed properly, the effects of peer review are far more positive than negative. When the board of one large industrial company conducted a peer review, one director received feedback on how much his colleagues valued what he said. This encouraged him to participate more.

Even if the feedback is not entirely positive, if handled properly, it can be constructive. A director received feedback that his colleagues thought his questions were nitpicky and detracted from board discussions. The peer review process alerted the director to his behavior without the embarrassment of a personal confrontation.

Peer evaluation at another board had positive results. The CEO explains: "One board member who ranked very low on the performance criteria had all the right credentials but seemed to be sitting there just to earn his retainer. When I sat down with him, I told him how much we needed him and his experience. Then I actually made him chairman of a committee. This guy completely turned around. He turned out to be the best member we've got."

As for board self-evaluation, the governance committee can handle the details of a peer review process, but the board as a whole must agree on the characteristics of a good director. These might include the following:

- sees the total picture.
- remains current about externalities.
- has good judgment.
- is committed and dedicated.
- exercises independent judgment but is a team player.
- has the courage to ask incisive questions.
- has high integrity.
- is free of conflicts of interest.
- fits with composition of the whole board (represents a viewpoint that is missing, adds a certain kind of value that is missing, meets certain board dynamic requirements, has expertise a committee needs).
- makes a meaningful contribution.

The board must then translate the desired characteristics into questions about specific performance issues. Some issues, like attending meetings and coming to meetings prepared, are straightforward. Many others are not:

Does the person sidetrack the discussion, or deepen the discussion and help the group reach closure?

Does the person seem to grasp the depth and breadth of issues or get lost in minutiae?

Does the chemistry work, or does the person seem noncongenial? Be careful, though, that a person who tries to shake things up in a constructive way is not chastised for not being a team player.

Does the person live in the past or is she open to new ideas and perspectives?

Is the person passive? The board should expect everyone to contribute or make room for someone else. Be sure to distinguish between the quality and the volume of the contribution.

The specifics of the process should be carefully thought out and suited to each particular board. Directors must feel comfortable with it (and CEOs should not push it too rigorously for this reason). Some boards have distributed a written questionnaire and asked each director to evaluate every other director. This process works when there is already a high level of trust between the CEO and the board and among board members. If distrust is high, directors may use the process to fire salvos at each other. Trust in the person who is analyzing the results is also crucial. Without it, directors tend to hold back, and intellectual honesty is sacrificed.

Using a carefully chosen third party to tabulate the survey instruments can help. One director explains his board's decision to use an outsider: "We've had quite a bit of discussion about whether you could really evaluate performance of individual board members. There seemed to be a feeling among the participants that it should be done but that it was very ticklish. We decided we needed an outsider's help."

The third party should not, however, convey the results to individual board members. This is typically done by the board chairman, who reports the results, including the verbatim comments without attribution, to directors in one-on-one meetings. If the situation is emotionally charged, the chairman can enlist the help of the governance committee chairman to present the other directors' feedback. In any case, these meetings should be nonthreatening and invite dialogue. If the situation is really bad, as a last resort the CEO might ask the director, "What are your plans for the future?" If the director wonders why the question is being posed, the CEO can explain that other board members have some concerns.

An alternative—and for most boards, better—form of peer review is for the governance committee to discuss the performance of individual directors as they come up for renomination and for the committee chairman to discuss any sensitive issues with the individual director. This process has several points to recommend it. First, it is totally in keeping with the principles of intellectual honesty and dialogue. Second, it strikes a balance between openness and sensitivity to directors. Third, the thrust is constructive problem-solving and individual responsibility. Bill Hudson, CEO of AMP and director of Carpenter Technology, says that Carpenter uses this approach as an alternative to term limits.

The board of one large company, whose membership is staggered, has used this process very successfully. Each year the nine-member governance committee, along with the general counsel and the CEO, evaluates the three or four directors who are up for renomination. The evaluation consists of a discussion of how that person is doing against a set of six criteria: contribution to the board, interest in corporate matters, level of knowledge of the corporation, participation in committee activities, attendance, and conflict of interest.

If the director is commonly perceived to be top-notch, the discussion tends to be only a few minutes long. If there is a problem, the discussion runs longer. When, for instance, a director was missing a lot of meetings, the committee discussed the problem at length because the person possessed a valuable perspective the board had worked hard to find.

The outcome of such discussions has, for this board, always been clear. Most of the time, the evaluation is entirely positive and the committee chairman simply states to the full board that the candidate meets the criteria and is being renominated. On rare occasion when a problem comes up, the committee chairman meets with the director to discuss it. The chairman says, "Nobody wants to make anyone else feel bad. I'll say, 'We've noticed your attendance is poor. Is there a problem?' Or, 'We feel your participation is lacking. Is there a particular reason?'" The problems are addressed tactfully and resolved promptly.

Help Directors Exit Gracefully

Both peer review and board self-evaluation can bring individual directors' shortcomings to the surface—peer review quite directly, and both processes by making the expectations explicit. Directors often will recognize when they do not meet the criteria and offer to resign.

But what about those situations when a director's performance clearly falls short yet the person seems intent on staying? How can the board "dis-invite" one of its members? What to do about a director who has served long and well but is no longer a contributor? Or a young director who is years from retirement but seems to have lost his or her initial spark, or a venture capitalist who is there in name only? Companies always pay a price when a board retains a director who is not fully engaged. That price is enormous when the company reaches a strategic or organizational watershed.

Some boards have tried to keep themselves fresh and energized by creating more turnover—lowering the retirement age, for instance, setting term limits of, say, ten years, requiring retirement upon change of job status, or making renomination an annual event. These approaches are worth considering, if only as guidelines in principle. For instance, it is very important to recruit directors who meet the nomination criteria and are in their forties. The board might want to set the expectation up front that their term would last no more than ten years. Similarly, directors who retire from active duty or change jobs should expect to resign from their post on the board. Boards also should see mergers as an opportunity to reconsider their composition.

Beware of mechanical solutions, however. It is hard to make general rules that address the board member who meets the written requirements of directorship but is not really contributing much, or worse, is draining the group's energy and time. Such situations require care and common sense.

Either kind of review (peer or board self-evaluation) can provide the occasion for a CEO-chairman to talk to an individual director about his or her behavior. Most often, the problem is self-correcting. Unless the director has a self-interest in staying on the board because he or she owns a lot of stock or is so entrenched in the board dynamics, the person will try to save face by offering to resign. Few directors will fight to stay when they know the group does not support them.

One member of the board that reviews directors as they stand for re-election says, "We've never pushed anyone out, but some directors have decided not to stand for reelection because they could see they were not meeting the criteria. The process guides a better match of directors' capabilities to the board's needs. It's a win-win situation."

When feedback on a director is unmistakably negative and the person does not get the message and intends to stay, the CEO-chairman simply has to address that reality. Dodging the issue because it seems so unpleasant undermines the board's entire effort to contribute and improve. The CEO should move to the next phase: removing any doubt in the director's mind that the information is from multiple sources. If necessary, the CEO and the chairman of the nominating or governance committee can meet with the director. The dialogue can become more specific or comprehensive, and other board members can be included if the person resists.

One CEO-chairman describes the challenge of presenting the negative feedback: "The most difficult thing I've had to do was ask two board members to step down. You can't ask them to step down without saying why, and if you say why, you're telling them that they didn't perform, and if they didn't perform, you're kind of telling them that they also didn't have the courtesy and awareness to know that.

"In one case, I simply said, 'Look, I'm going to suggest you not stand for reelection,' and there was basically no discussion. In the other, I said, 'I know you're going to be mad at me, but it has to be said—you're not adding value to this board and you never have.'" The CEO had discussed the outcome of the survey with several key directors before making such strong comments to the director.

Some boards have directors who do not add value but are there because of ownership or family ties. Given feedback and a constructive atmosphere, some of them can learn to be better board members. But others will continue to drain the board's energy. Assigning the noncontributors to an advisory board is one way to keep them from interfering with the work of the board. If these board members continue to interfere, the chairman should address the subject directly using the power of the full board to suggest a clean break.

One board made it a rule that every voting board member had to take on a special assignment of some kind. One noncontributor who was on the board because of ownership opted not to vote. The other board members felt better about the work load and responsibility they bore.

CEOs and directors can raise issues about directors even when a formal review is not conducted. The same general approach can apply. CEO John Reed of Citicorp encourages other CEOs to do so. "Some directors have their own agendas and are destructive to the board's social dynamics," Reed explains. "As chairman and CEO, you've got to be willing to eyeball them." Twice Reed has gone to the nominating committee to share his feelings about a director he felt was detracting from the rest of the board. In both instances, the board agreed that the member was disruptive and should leave. With the board's backing, Reed met with the individuals to suggest they not stand for reelection.

It is important to note that the tenacious noncontributor is likely to be quite rare. As boards improve their recruiting practices, make expectations explicit, and undertake self-evaluation of some kind, directors will be chosen because of their ability to contribute. Less capable directors will bow out voluntarily, making room for those with the desire, skills, and vigor to contribute fully, and the board will continuously improve.

Key Points

- Board self-evaluation can identify areas to improve, but more important, it gets directors talking about real issues in an open forum. The board dynamics begin to change.

- Board self-evaluation should not be forced or mechanical. Trust is everything.

- Director peer review can help good boards become world class. But it is not a shortcut to good board dynamics. Unless conditions are right, it can damage board dynamics or worse, become a witch hunt.

CORPORATE BOARD SELF-EVALUATION INSTRUMENT

This instrument is designed to help the board identify specific areas for improvement. It is similar to instruments used at several companies. It can of course be abbreviated to include only a few questions in each section.

This instrument can be used in several ways. One option is to use it as a discussion guide only. Another is to ask each director to complete the instrument and have the results compiled by a third party. The board chairman or the corporate governance committee can then lead a discussion of the results. Alternatively, the chairman of the corporate governance committee can compile the results. Confidentiality will encourage candor.

The instrument should be used in the spirit of constructive criticism.

Directors should avoid choosing "4." The instrument is more useful when directors take a position.

CORPORATE BOARD SELF-EVALUATION INSTRUMENT, cont'd.

	Deteriorating				Improving		

Section I. The Company as a Whole

1. Is the company's health improving or declining

   a. compared to the last two years? 1 2 3 **4** 5 6 7

   b. compared to the competition? 1 2 3 **4** 5 6 7

   c. compared to the external environment? 1 2 3 **4** 5 6 7

	Definitely not				Definitely yes		

2. Is the company fully capturing potential opportunities? 1 2 3 **4** 5 6 7

3. In your assessment, does the board as a whole expect the company to perform well

   a. this year? 1 2 3 **4** 5 6 7

   b. over the next three years? 1 2 3 **4** 5 6 7

4. Do you yourself expect the company to perform well

   a. this year? 1 2 3 **4** 5 6 7

   b. over the next three years? 1 2 3 **4** 5 6 7

5. In your assessment, does the board as a whole concur with the company strategy? 1 2 3 **4** 5 6 7

6. Do you yourself concur with the company strategy? 1 2 3 **4** 5 6 7

7. In your assessment, does the board as a whole believe the company has the right balance between short-term and long-term goals? 1 2 3 **4** 5 6 7

8. Do you yourself believe the company has the right balance between short-term and long-term goals? 1 2 3 **4** 5 6 7

CORPORATE BOARD SELF-EVALUATION INSTRUMENT, cont'd.

	Definitely not				**Definitely yes**		
9. In your assessment, does the board as a whole feel that the company has the right CEO?	1	2	3	4	5	6	7
10. Do you yourself feel that the company has the right CEO?	1	2	3	4	5	6	7
11. Does the board as a whole believe the company is confronting the fundamental realities that, if not dealt with, are likely to cause a decline in long-term health and performance?	1	2	3	4	5	6	7
12. Do you yourself believe the company is confronting the fundamental realities that, if not dealt with, are likely to cause a decline in long-term health and performance?	1	2	3	4	5	6	7
13. Does the board as a whole believe the company has the right compensation strategy?	1	2	3	4	5	6	7
14. Do you yourself believe the company has the right compensation strategy?	1	2	3	4	5	6	7
15. Does the board as a whole think the top management succession process is effective?	1	2	3	4	5	6	7
16. Do you yourself think the top management succession process is effective?	1	2	3	4	5	6	7

Section II. The Board as a Whole

17. Does the board as a whole seem to have a clear understanding of its roles and responsibilities?	1	2	3	4	5	6	7
18. Does the board have a sufficient understanding of the company's philosophy and strategy?	1	2	3	4	5	6	7

CORPORATE BOARD SELF-EVALUATION INSTRUMENT, cont'd.

	Definitely not				**Definitely yes**		
19. Does the board confront the real issues?	1	2	3	4	5	6	7
20. Does the board have a full-year agenda?	1	2	3	4	5	6	7
21. Is the leadership of the board effective?	1	2	3	4	5	6	7
22. Do board meetings allow enough time for the exchange of ideas?	1	2	3	4	5	6	7
23. Is the information the board receives for board meetings							
a. useful?	1	2	3	4	5	6	7
b. adequate?	1	2	3	4	5	6	7
c. in an efficient format?	1	2	3	4	5	6	7
d. sufficiently related to the external environment?	1	2	3	4	5	6	7
24. Do board members come to board and committee meetings fully prepared?	1	2	3	4	5	6	7
25. Are presentations to the board. . .							
a. focused on the right issues?	1	2	3	4	5	6	7
b. clear and succinct?	1	2	3	4	5	6	7
c. helpful?	1	2	3	4	5	6	7
26. Is the board functioning to its full potential?	1	2	3	4	5	6	7

Why or why not? _____

_____

_____

Section III. The Board's Group Dynamics

	Definitely not				**Definitely yes**		
27. Is the board's dialogue of high quality?	1	2	3	4	5	6	7
28. Does the board have sufficient dialogue?	1	2	3	4	5	6	7

CORPORATE BOARD SELF-EVALUATION INSTRUMENT, cont'd.

		Definitely not				Definitely yes		
29.	Is participation in the dialogue sufficiently broad?	1	2	3	4	5	6	7
30.	Is the dialogue exciting and insight generating?	1	2	3	4	5	6	7
31.	Is the dialogue focused?	1	2	3	4	5	6	7
32.	Does dialogue take place among directors (not just between directors and the CEO)?	1	2	3	4	5	6	7
33.	Do board members take reasoned, independent positions?	1	2	3	4	5	6	7
34.	Do board members share their knowledge and experience to help the CEO and the company?	1	2	3	4	5	6	7
35.	Are board discussions open and candid?	1	2	3	4	5	6	7
36.	Do board members listen to and consider each others' comments?	1	2	3	4	5	6	7
37.	Does the atmosphere of the boardroom encourage critical thinking?	1	2	3	4	5	6	7
38.	Do board discussions reach closure?	1	2	3	4	5	6	7

Section IV. Committee Performance

Board members should complete this section for each committee they are on.

Committee: _____

		Definitely not				Definitely yes		
1.	Is this committee effective?	1	2	3	4	5	6	7
2.	Is the output of the committee supporting the full board?	1	2	3	4	5	6	7
3.	Does the committee confront the real issues?	1	2	3	4	5	6	7

CORPORATE BOARD SELF-EVALUATION INSTRUMENT, cont'd.

	Definitely not				**Definitely yes**		
4. Does the committee give the CEO candid, decisive feedback?	1	2	3	4	5	6	7
5. Does the committee's feedback accurately reflect the views of all committee members?	1	2	3	4	5	6	7
6. Is the committee able to make collective judgments about important matters?	1	2	3	4	5	6	7
7. Has the committee laid out a full-year agenda?	1	2	3	4	5	6	7
8. Is the committee's composition appropriate?	1	2	3	4	5	6	7
9. Is the leadership of the committee effective?	1	2	3	4	5	6	7
10. Does the committee chairperson elicit contributions from all members?	1	2	3	4	5	6	7

	Not enough			**Just right**	**Too much**		
11. Does the committee allocate the right amount of time for its work?	1	2	3	4	5	6	7

BOARD MEMBER PEER REVIEW INSTRUMENT

This instrument identifies specific areas for individual directors to improve. It is similar to an instrument in actual use. If the board chooses to use an abbreviated version of this instrument, be sure it covers a range of contributions. Directors add value in a variety of ways.

Note: Peer review is best suited for use by boards that are functioning well and have a high level of trust. If serious tensions exist among board members or between the CEO and certain directors, peer review is likely to exacerbate those tensions. Under no circumstance should it be used to remove targeted individuals. If the board indicates resistance to the process, it is best to find other means of improving board performance. Misuse, whether intentional or inadvertent, will breed distrust.

When board dynamics are healthy, peer review can strengthen individual performance. It can be exercised in several ways. One option is for each board member to complete a review instrument of each of his or her colleagues and have the results compiled by a third party. The board chairman or chairman of the corporate governance committee can discuss the composite results with individual directors one-on-one. Alternatively, the corporate governance committee can use the instrument as a guide for discussing the performance of individual directors as they come up for renomination. The fact that the process exists will begin to influence behavior.

Confidentiality is crucial.

BOARD MEMBER PEER REVIEW INSTRUMENT, cont'd.

Director's name: _____

A. Preparation and Participation

	Definitely not				Definitely yes		
1. Does this person come to board and committee meetings fully prepared?	1	2	3	4	5	6	7
2. Does this person seem to understand the company's philosophy and strategy?	1	2	3	4	5	6	7

B. Behavior

3. Does this person enhance group discussions in the following ways:

a. pushes the discussion forward	1	2	3	4	5	6	7
b. integrates various viewpoints	1	2	3	4	5	6	7
c. helps discussions reach closure	1	2	3	4	5	6	7
d. encourages openness and candor	1	2	3	4	5	6	7
e. pushes the group to confront reality	1	2	3	4	5	6	7
f. brings new thinking	1	2	3	4	5	6	7
g. challenges other directors who sidetrack discussions or dwell on minutiae	1	2	3	4	5	6	7
h. helps draw out contributions from others	1	2	3	4	5	6	7

4. Is this person a "good" board member in the following ways:

a. is a team player	1	2	3	4	5	6	7
b. listens to and considers others' comments	1	2	3	4	5	6	7
c. is willing to change his or her viewpoint	1	2	3	4	5	6	7

BOARD MEMBER PEER REVIEW INSTRUMENT, cont'd.

	Definitely not					Definitely yes	

d. accepts challenge from others without becoming defensive   1 2 3 4 5 6 7

e. has the courage to say what is on his or her mind   1 2 3 4 5 6 7

f. is free of conflicts of interest   1 2 3 4 5 6 7

g. exercises independent judgment   1 2 3 4 5 6 7

5. Does this person's behavior reflect an understanding of the difference between managing and governing a corporation?   1 2 3 4 5 6 7

C. Quality of Value Added

6. Does this person understand and focus on issues that are key to the business?   1 2 3 4 5 6 7

7. Does this person help colleagues understand and focus on issues that are key to the business?   1 2 3 4 5 6 7

8. Does this person cut through complex issues?   1 2 3 4 5 6 7

9. Does this person help colleagues cut through complex issues?   1 2 3 4 5 6 7

10. Do you consider this person's questions or comments to be:

a. incisive and penetrating?   1 2 3 4 5 6 7

b. appropriately timed?   1 2 3 4 5 6 7

c. value-adding?   1 2 3 4 5 6 7

11. Does this person keep discussions on track by avoiding talking too much, reminiscing, or engaging in philosophical arguments?   1 2 3 4 5 6 7

BOARD MEMBER PEER REVIEW INSTRUMENT, cont'd.

	Definitely not				**Definitely yes**		
12. Are this person's judgments genuinely independent of management?	1	2	3	4	5	6	7
13. Does this person apply his or her experience and business wisdom to matters that come before the board?	1	2	3	4	5	6	7
14. Does this person take into account the viewpoints of all stakeholders?	1	2	3	4	5	6	7
15. Does this person contribute to the CEO's perspective and wisdom in running the company by sharing his or her knowledge and experience:							
a. privately (in person or by phone)?	1	2	3	4	5	6	7
b. in board or committee meetings?	1	2	3	4	5	6	7
16. Does this person open doors to his or her network to help the CEO and the company?	1	2	3	4	5	6	7

CHAPTER ELEVEN

CONCLUSION: THIS IS THE DAY TO PUT YOUR BOARD TO WORK

There is no time to lose. In this day and age of continuous radical change and intense global competition, unlocking the board's intellectual power, wisdom, and insight is absolutely essential. Not doing so should be considered a failure of the CEO, of each and every board member, and of anyone outside the boardroom who does not insist that corporations tap this vital resource. Boards must learn to become effective.

Most directors are individually competent. Collectively, something falls short. Almost always, the problem is the board dynamics. Boards that address the problem will release the competitive power of the collective body. Boards that do not will remain passive, detached, and ineffective—and will put the company at risk. There is no middle ground.

The most revealing indicator of board effectiveness is the quality of the dialogue in committees and in the boardroom. If discussions are not on the "real" issues and do not cause spontaneous, value-adding conversations in sufficient depth and breadth among the directors (versus between individual directors and the CEO), something is missing. Every director, including the CEO-chairman, must take responsibility for creating the excitement and learning that come forth when a variety of insights and viewpoints are expressed and explored. Adopt practices that open the dialogue. Cultivate the trust and candor that allow the board to make a contribution.

From open, substantive dialogue comes learning. CEOs and their senior management team discover flaws in their assumptions, blind spots in their assessment of the business landscape, and unexplored opportunities. Judgments are reconsidered, and adjustments are made. Directors learn, too, and so increase their desire to be actively engaged. The enthusiasm is infectious; top-notch directors want to join.

Such dialogue requires longer meetings. Directors must have a chance to get immersed in the issues and dig below the surface. Two-day "breakthrough sessions" can kick start the dialogue for boards that are not accustomed to talking openly. These sessions can establish new norms of behavior that carry over into regular board meetings. They push the board dynamics to a whole new level.

Balanced participation follows when every director has something important to contribute and fits with the group's chemistry. Boards must continue their efforts to make the nominating process objective and criteria-driven. Be particular and specific. Good directors are out there. Find them, and assimilate them right away.

Information to the board is absolutely critical. Board members who have been successful business leaders know how to see the company as a whole in an external context. They also know how to select and motivate people. To bring these critical faculties to bear, they must insist that the CEO inform the board of external trends and internal capabilities in the normal course of storytelling. Lay out an agenda that creates a total picture of the business and its leadership.

CEOs today are paying tremendous attention to investors and security analysts. They must build credibility in the market through word and deed and balance the demands of multiple constituencies. The insight and judgment of their fellow board members can be of tremendous value to them in setting the right goals, pushing back against maverick investors, and delivering earnings in the face of structural changes and other major discontinuities. Learn from the directors, draw them out.

The board must make a collective judgment on whether the corporation has the right leader and whether that leader is setting a strategic course that is appropriate, clear, and specific. Boards must separate past performance from what is required to take the company forward. Make CEO review forward-looking and routine. Draw directors' instincts to the surface and make them available to the CEO. Let the feedback process make a good CEO perform even better. A ten-minute "huddle" at the end of a board meeting keeps communication flowing. It is a superb coaching tool.

Boards must take a stronger hand in succession planning. Make sure the company is filling the pipeline with leaders who meet the important criteria and get to know the candidates well ahead of time and in a variety of situations. Often, when directors have doubts about the CEO's direct reports, they are reluctant to express them. Do not hesitate. Make an input when there is time to round out the candidates or to identify more.

CEOs, do not wait for a crisis. Have the self-confidence to seek the board's input now. If you do not think your board is up to the task, reconstitute it. Directors, if you feel that your intellectual power is not being used, do not resign. Take the initiative to find your own point of entry. Put the issues on the table. You will soon have allies.

Typically, the behavior of one or two directors inhibits the board from being effective or value adding. These directors wield their influence by virtue of seniority, by virtue of an aura, or by virtue of having done something great some time ago. Maybe they talk too much, maybe they wander off the track. Board self-evaluation and peer review are delicate tools for confronting improper behavior and encouraging productive behavior. Use them carefully and only when the board is ready. Do not let overzealous directors sacrifice trust in the name of good governance. Without trust, boards cannot be a competitive advantage.

CEOs and directors now know enough to act. Boards must not only protect shareholder value but also help create it. Set the objective and move fast. Articulate the new norms of behavior and select the operating mechanisms that make sense for your board.

As we enter the new millenium, the business world will continue to be rich with challenge and opportunity. Errors in judgment will hit hard. Business leaders who can release the board's intellectual fire-power will have a distinct competitive advantage over those who cannot. Do not let your company, your CEO, your shareholders, your employees, and the economy as a whole be surpassed. Begin the process. Put the board to work.

Commandments of Good Governance

Those who are serious about tapping the board's competitive power should make the following commitments:

Management Will . . .

Lead the board in understanding the changing external environment (industry, competition, global factors) from different viewpoints.

Tell the board what it is trying to accomplish in the near and longer term.

Provide sufficient, efficient information to allow the board to assess whether the goals are being achieved.

Put good and bad news on the table.

Create an atmosphere conducive to critical discussion of key business issues.

Listen to and learn from the board.

Put intellectual honesty first.

The Board Will . . .

Take an independent view on the company's strategic direction, the CEO, and the senior management team.

Keep up-to-date on the company from an external viewpoint.

Ask all its questions and state all its concerns as they arise.

Make its perspectives, experience, and judgment available to management to improve the performance of the company.

Seek to improve its own performance and keep its composition evergreen.

INDEX

A

A. C. Nielsen, 23
A. H. Belo Corporation, 155
Accountability, mutual, 32–33
Adams, W., 29, 31, 41, 47, 54, 115, 121, 156, 193, 194, 244, 247
Agee, W., 17
Akers, J. F., 179, 191
Allied Signal, 42, 77, 138, 191
Aluminum Company of America (ALCOA), 80, 199
Amelia, G., 138
American Cyanamid, 143
American Express, 23, 31, 179
American Home Products, 143
American Hospital Supply, 90
American Telephone and Telegraph (AT&T), 7, 77, 78, 82, 136, 179
Ames, C., 221–222
AMP, 40, 73, 84, 186, 247, 250
Analog Devices, 83, 85
Anders, W., 105
Apple, 6, 81, 82, 138, 179
Armstrong World Industries, 29, 41, 121, 194

Ashland Oil, 141
Associated Communications, 7, 72
Austin Industries, 155, 156, 165
Avenor, 40, 56

B

Bank of America, 40, 58, 121, 141, 193
Barnes-Hind and Flow Pharmaceuticals, 90
Barnevik, P., 224–225
Battelle Memorial Institute, 41, 105, 159
Bauer, C., 89, 91
Bausch & Lomb, 156
Baxter International, 102
"Bedford Industries," 201–207
BEI Electronics, 33
Bell Atlantic, 8, 9, 29, 30, 45, 74, 115, 122, 123, 244
"Best and Worst Boards, The," (*Business Week*), 139
"Blair, R.," 203
Board effectiveness: and accountability, 32–33; and boardroom taboos, 21–23; dialogue test for,

36; and expectancy to add value, 28–29; focus and, 31–32; and informed trust, 26–27; and involvement in strategic issues, 30; and open dialogue and open information, 23–26; and power balance with CEO, 30–31; and shift from coach to fiduciary-at-risk, 27–28; synergy and, 33–35
Board member peer review instrument, 260–263
Board operating mechanisms: and Conrail's two-day breakthroughs, 60–62; and executive committees, 45–49; and lead directors, 49–50; and outside director as chairman, 50–52; and retreats or breakthrough sessions, 55–60; and segregation of formalities and substance, 52–55; and size of board, 40–41; and structural solutions, 39–40; and use of committees, 42–45; at "Wynnet, Inc," 62–68
Board self-evaluation. See Continuous improvement